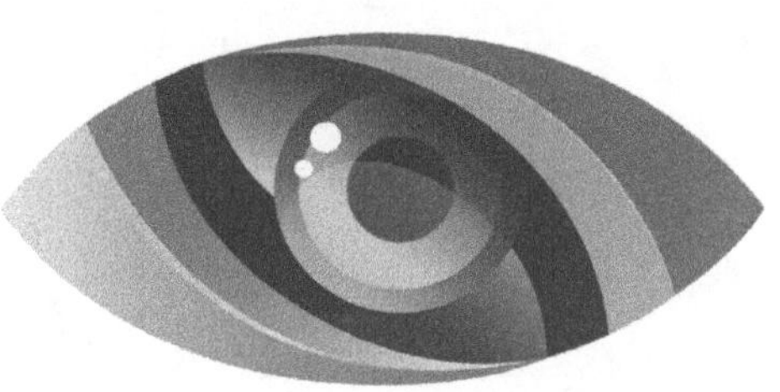

COLOUR

How We See It and How We Use It

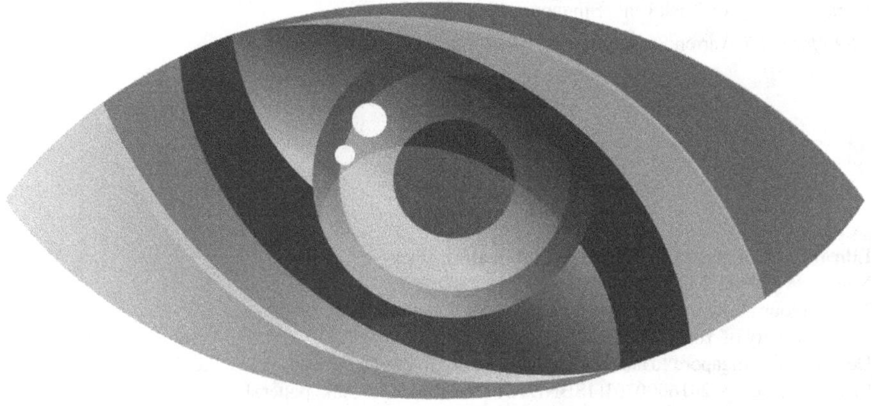

C O L O U R

How We See It and How We Use It

Michael Mark Woolfson

University of York, UK

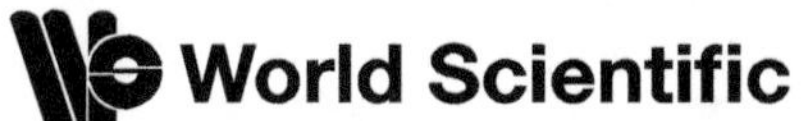

World Scientific

NEW JERSEY · LONDON · SINGAPORE · BEIJING · SHANGHAI · HONG KONG · TAIPEI · CHENNAI · TOKYO

Published by

World Scientific Publishing (UK) Ltd.

57 Shelton Street, Covent Garden, London WC2H 9HE

Head office: 5 Toh Tuck Link, Singapore 596224

USA office: 27 Warren Street, Suite 401-402, Hackensack, NJ 07601

Library of Congress Cataloging-in-Publication Data
Names: Woolfson, Michael M. (Michael Mark), author.
Title: Colour : how we see it and how we use it / Michael Mark Woolfson
    (University of York, UK).
Description: Singapore ; Hackensack, NJ : World Scientific Publishing Co. Pte. Ltd., [2016] | 2016
Identifiers: LCCN 2016000701| ISBN 9781786340849 (hc ; alk. paper) |
    ISBN 1786340844 (hc ; alk. paper) | ISBN 9781786340856 (pbk ; alk. paper) |
    ISBN 1786340852 (pbk ; alk. paper)
Subjects: LCSH: Color.
Classification: LCC QC495 .W56 2016 | DDC 535.6--dc23
LC record available at http://lccn.loc.gov/2016000701

British Library Cataloguing-in-Publication Data
A catalogue record for this book is available from the British Library.

Desk Editors: Dr. Sree Meenakshi Sajani/Mary Simpson

Typeset by Stallion Press
Email: enquiries@stallionpress.com

Contents

Introduction

I am looking out of the window of my apartment on an unusually bright autumn day. The sky is mostly blue with fluffy white clouds lazily drifting southward. The weather forecast is for strong northerly winds, perhaps bringing snow that will blanket the colourful scene I now see in more-or-less uniform white. However, for now the solid phalanx of trees that dominate my southern view, present me with a wide variety of shades of green, plus hues varying from red to yellow and brown, of the leaves that the coming strong winds will soon deposit on the ground. Now I transfer my gaze inwards towards the bookshelves that cover the walls behind my desk. Without my spectacles I cannot see most of the titles on the book spines but, nevertheless, I can recognize most of the books by their thicknesses and colour.

We live in a colourful world but it is not something that is in the forefront of our minds. We take it for granted, like most things that form part of our everyday lives. However, I have had colleagues who have suffered from a form of colour blindness in which they cannot distinguish red and green, and the colours between, in a spectrum. They too live in a colourful world, but one that is different and less colourful than mine. How is it that I see all the colours I do and why is it that they see less colour than I do? Anyway, what is this colour that we see differently? These are the questions addressed in the first part of this book. The basic mechanisms of the eye are described together with the processes that enable us to see colour, although it is only possible to say *what* happens and virtually impossible to say *how* it happens. The brain is the 'black box' that carries out processes that we do not fully understand. We can locate parts of it that are dedicated to processing sight, speech and other senses, but what is actually happening in those parts to create the sensations we experience is a complete mystery — at least for now.

The colour I see out of my window is nature's colour and the colour I see on my bookshelves is man-made. It is probably true to say that for urban dwellers the great majority of the colour they see is man-made. There is evidence that humankind has an innate tendency to produce artistic works and part of that artistic expression involves the use of colour. The evidence for this goes back more than 40,000 years to cave paintings, made by our forebears, in which coloured pigments were used, consisting of ground-up rocks suspended in water, saliva or grease, with colours mainly at the red-to-yellow end of the spectrum. As time progressed so the artistry has evolved in its style and to the present availability of pigments of every conceivable colour. The book describes the evolution of painting, in particular relating to the pigments available to the artists of different ages. Other aspects of man-made colour is artistry concerned with the decoration of useful objects such as pottery of various kinds and the dyeing of clothes, the histories of both of which activities are narrated.

There are three linked technologies that began their existence in black-and-white form but evolved to be in full colour — photography, cinematography and television. The first two of these are linked because they developed using similar materials and techniques — firstly glass plates, then film and finally digital methods — and the last two are linked because they produce moving pictures. The stories of the development of these technologies are related, which include the seminal contributions of many individuals whose names are largely unknown. How many know the names and contributions of the three Frenchmen, Joseph Nicéphore Niépce, Louis Ducos du Hauron and Louis Le Prince, who respectively produced the first permanent black-and-white image in the 1820s, the first coloured photograph in the 1870s and the first moving picture in 1888, or the name of the German inventor, Paul Nipkow, who designed the first television system?

The penultimate chapter of the book is dedicated to describing various forms of light displays, mostly designed for entertainment and spectacle — *son et lumière*, advertising and shop displays with fluorescent and neon light sources, and displays with fireworks and lasers. The final chapter describes the way that colour can be used in practical situations, for example, in providing safely for roads and railways, in hospitals, factories and homes Other practical uses of colour are for marking resistors used in electrical circuits, in making complex diagrams, such as the London Underground map, more comprehensible and in advertising.

Throughout the book the underlying technologies and science have been described and explained in a general broad-brush way without getting involved in the fine details that would only be of interest to professional engineers and scientists. Colour makes our lives more interesting — how dull it would be in a black-and-white world! Colour can please us aesthetically, it can entertain us and it can be useful.

Chapter 1

Eyes

When the word 'eye' is used it is usually taken to mean the human eye, or perhaps similar eyes in higher life forms such as other mammals, birds and fish. However, nature provides many types of eye, some of which are just light-detecting organs while others produce images, but with widely varying resolutions. Here we restrict our attention to two types of eye that produce images of moderate-to-high resolution. In the following chapter the evolution of the mammalian eye will be described; in the evolutionary process leading to eyes such as ours, other eye forms occurred, some of which are present in extant organisms, and the creatures with these eye forms will be identified.

1.1 The Compound Eye

The most abundant life form on earth is arthropods (insects and crustaceans) and the eyes of most of them — *compound eyes* — are based on a completely different principle from the human eye. An electron micrograph of a typical compound eye, that of the fruit fly *Drosophilidae*, is shown in Figure 1.1. Each of the tightly-packed units forming the surface of the eye is a separate lens, constituting the light receiving end of an *ommatidium*, a basic light-detecting structure (Figure 1.2).

Below the ommatidium lens is a crystalline cone that further concentrates the light in a downward direction. The arrangement of lens and crystalline cone ensures that the ommatidium is detecting light coming in

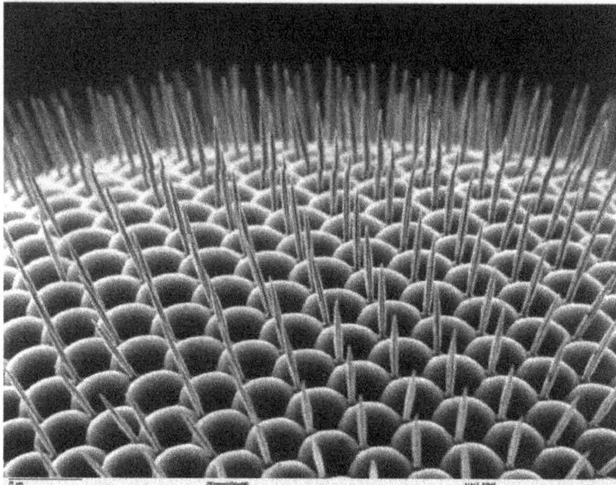

Figure 1.1   The surface of the eye of the fruit fly

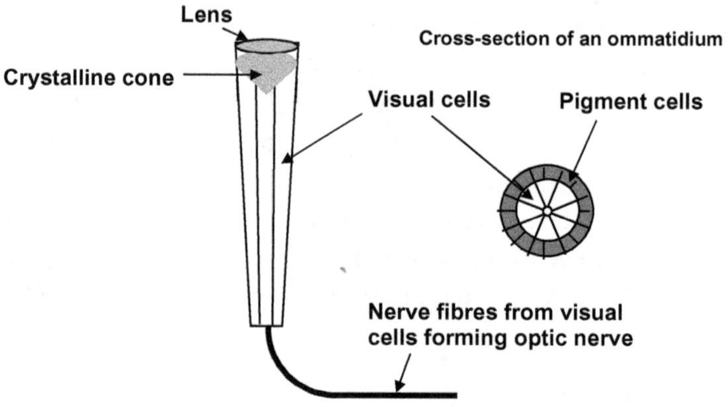

Figure 1.2   A schematic representation of an ommatidium of a compound eye

from only a very narrow angular range in one direction. This light then passes through a cluster of visual cells that convert it into an electrical signal of strength proportional to the intensity. At the end of each visual cell there are nerve fibres forming the optic nerve. Around each cluster of visual cells there are other cells containing an opaque pigment which prevents light passing from one ommatidium to its neighbours that, if it happened, would cause blurring of the image. Since each ommatidium receives light from only a small region of the field of view, the resultant from all the ommatidia is a halftone picture, formed as a grid of small

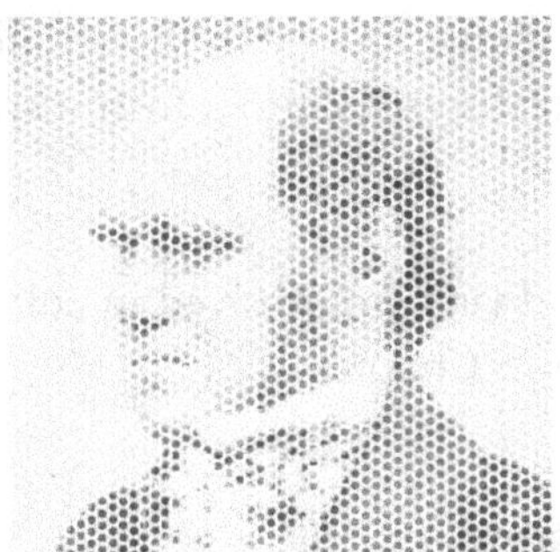

Figure 1.3   A fly's-eye image of Charles Darwin

dots of different intensities. An example of a low resolution image formed in this way is given in Figure 1.3. Some insects have eyes with very large numbers of ommatidia and hence produce images of reasonable resolution but at best they attain only one or two percent of the resolution of the human eye and at worst they see the world as rather indistinct patches of light.

The compound eye performs particularly well in the detection of motion — hence the difficulty of swatting a fly. As an object moves across the field of view, different ommatidia switch on and off, something that insects are programmed readily to detect. However, a slow approach with a transparent container, such as a drinking glass, is not detected and an insect can easily be trapped in this way.

1.2 The Human Eye

Although we are describing here a human eye it is, in fact, an eye form shared by other mammals, birds and other types of creature, such as the octopus. There are many variants of this form of eye and some creatures have eyes that, to meet their survival requirements, have evolved to be much more efficient than those of humans. However, all these variants are similar in their basic structure and there are three distinct components of the human visual system:

(i) An optical system that produces an image,
(ii) A neural network that converts the image into a stream of electrical impulses that are sent to the brain,

(iii) An interpretation system, located in the *visual cortex* of the brain that converts the electrical signals into a form through which the field of view is visualized.

Components (ii) and (iii) are involved in colour vision, the details of which will be dealt with in Chapter 4.

1.2.1 The optical system

The optical system is very simple and produces an image in the same way as by a convex lens, as illustrated in Figure 1.4 where the image of an arrow is projected onto a screen.

For an object at some specified distance from a particular lens a sharp image is produced at a particular distance from the lens and if the screen is closer to, or further from, the lens then the image would be blurred. For objects at different distances sharp images could only be formed by having screens at different distances. Alternatively, if the screen had to be at a fixed distance from the lens, sharp images could be formed only if there were a different lens, of different focal length, for each object distance.

A simplified diagram of the human eye is shown in Figure 1.5; the combination of *cornea* and *lens* produces a sharp image on the *retina*, acting as a screen. Since the distance of the retina from the lens is fixed and the objects being viewed can vary from being very close to very far (effectively at an infinite distance), there is a mechanism to vary the focal length of the lens. This is done by the *ciliary muscles* that, by squeezing the lens by varying amounts, change its shape and hence its focal length. The contribution of the cornea in the focusing process does not change but in a

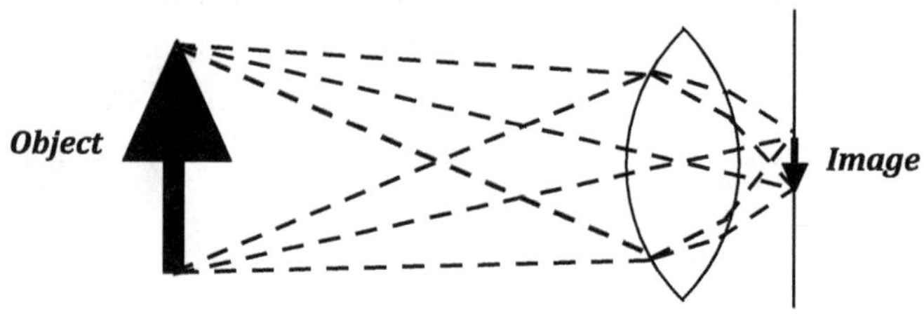

Figure 1.4   Producing an image on a screen with a simple convex lens

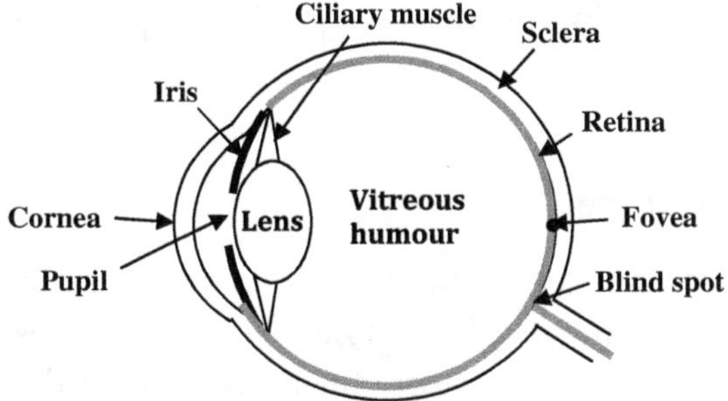

Figure 1.5 A schematic representation of a human eye

normal eye the total variation in the focal length of the lens is sufficient to allow clear images of both near and far objects. This variation is called *accommodation*. Some individuals are unable to cover the full range of distances and need spectacles to deal with the problem; those only able to bring close objects into focus suffer from short-sightedness, or *myopia*, while those only able to focus on far objects suffer from far-sightedness, or *hyperopia*. Another very common problem is *astigmatism* where the curvature of the cornea is different in different directions. This means that light rays coming from a point on the object do not focus at a point on the retina. However, this problem is normally so slight that it causes no difficulties to an individual. Where it is more severe then, once again, suitable spectacles can compensate for it.

The interior of the eye is occupied by a transparent colourless gel called the *vitreous humour*, all contained within the combination of the *sclera* (Figure 1.5) and cornea, forming the outer shell of the eye. The cornea is clear, because it has to admit light, but the sclera is a milky-white colour, giving what is known as the *white of the eye*. The eye operates best at moderate light levels. It is comparatively inefficient at very low light levels where there is too little light energy to give a strong visual signal, and at very high light levels, which saturate the visual system and give rise to glare and an indistinct, if bright, image. The *iris*, the coloured disk that gives eye-colour, controls a variable circular aperture that, by opening and closing, adjusts the amount of light falling on the retina. This aperture, known as the *pupil*, is seen as a black circle in the centre of the iris. In dim light the pupil opens wide to let through as much light as possible while in very bright conditions it closes up to reduce the amount of light entering the eye.

1.2.2 The photoreceptors

In order to interpret the image formed on the retina, the information contained within it must be transformed into electrical impulses that are then transmitted to the brain. To perform the initial stage of this task the retina consists of a tightly packed array of *photoreceptors*, each of which converts the light energy falling on it into electrical pulses. There are about 130 million photoreceptors, most closely packed in the *fovea* region of the retina (Figure 1.5) with the density falling off with distance from the fovea. This gives the greatest resolution of the visual image in the centre of the field of view; the field of view covers almost a complete hemisphere but peripheral vision gives only a vague impression of what is present.

There are two kinds of photoreceptors. The first is *rods*, on account of their long rod-like shape, and they are extremely sensitive and are capable of recording very low light levels. They give what is known as *scotopic vision* that would operate, for example, if a scene were being viewed by moonlight. The second kind, which are stubbier in form, are known as *cones* and they operate at high levels of illumination to give what is known as *photopic vision*. Apart from their sensitivity, rods and cones differ in another important respect — the way in which they discriminate colour. The rods do not differentiate coloured objects but represent them in shades of grey, although objects seen by moonlight seem to have a slightly bluish tinge. By contrast the cones give fully chromatic vision. This is obtained through the agency of three types of cone, containing different *visual pigments*, with different colour responses and the way that they give the perception of colour will be explained in Chapter 4.

1.2.3 The functioning of nerve cells

The way that nerve cells function is quite complex and involves physical mechanisms triggered by chemical agents. Here we just give a simple description of a typical *neuron* (nerve cell) which will indicate the general form of some processes that occur in the eye.

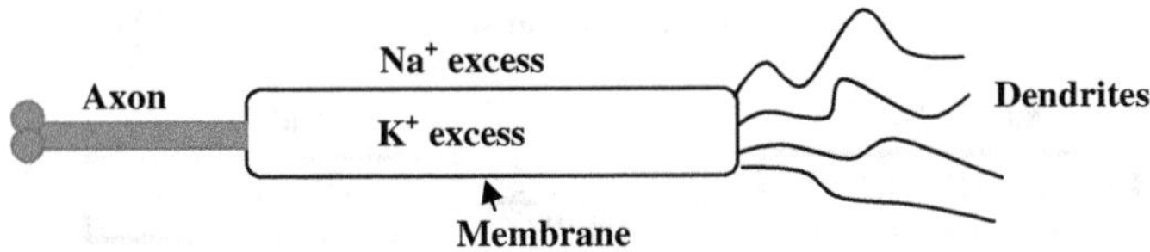

Figure 1.6   A schematic nerve cell

A schematic neuron is shown in Figure 1.6. At one end are the *dendrites* that receive information from other neurons. At the other end is the *axon*, a channel along which electric impulses from the neuron travel and the terminus of which connects with other neurons through their dendrites. The interior of the cell contains potassium ions, K$^+$ — potassium atoms with one electron removed — the positive electrical charges of which are only partly balanced by negatively charged molecules. Outside the cell there is an excess of sodium ions, Na$^+$, and when the neuron is in a resting state the electrical potential outside the cell is greater than that within. The ions can pass through the membrane, which acts as a sheath for the cell, but chemicals within the membrane act like ion pumps, a separate one for each ion, so maintaining the relative concentrations of the two kinds of ion. A cell in this situation is said to be *polarized.*

The axon-dendrites connection is called a *synapse* and for all cells, except those in the brain, the signal is transmitted across a synapse by chemicals known as *neurotransmitters*; in the brain signals are passed from one neuron to the next by an electric current, which gives a much faster response. The neurotransmitters cross the synaptic gap and pass along the dendrites into the main body of the neuron where they attach themselves to chemical receptors. Depending on the process that occurs, when the neurotransmitter arrives the activity of the cell can be either stimulated or inhibited. The action of a stimulated cell may be followed by reference to Figure 1.7.

Stimulation occurs when the neurotransmitter opens up sodium channels so that sodium ions enter the cell. Now the inside becomes more positive and the outside less positive so the potential difference between the outside and inside is reversed. The cell is then *depolarized* and when the depolarization potential difference reaches a certain level, known as the *threshold potential,* an electrical impulse passes along the neuron.

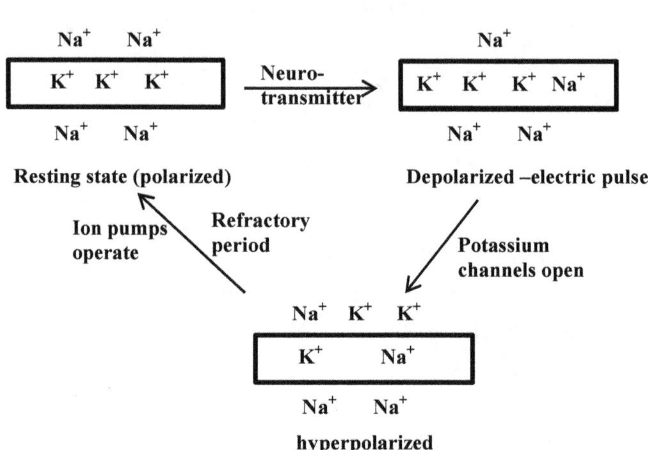

Figure 1.7   The cycle of producing a spike discharge from a stimulated neuron

As sodium channels open up in one part of the cell the potential difference reaches the critical value further on and, in this way, the impulse travels along the cell to reach the axon in a few milliseconds. Once the pulse reaches the end of the axon the membrane allows the passage of doubly-charged calcium ions, Ca^{++}, into the cell and this triggers the release of neurotransmitter towards the dendrites of the following cell. The form of the potential difference at each point of the cell with the passage of time, known as the *action potential,* is shown in Figure 1.8. The passage of sodium ions into the cell stimulates the potassium channels to open and potassium ions pass out of the cell so restoring the cell to the polarized state — actually with a slight overreaction so the cell becomes *hyperpolarized,* where the potential difference between the outside and inside is higher than in the resting state of the neuron. During the hyperpolarization state the sodium and potassium pumps return to their normal mode of action and restore the concentrations of sodium and potassium ions outside and inside the cell to the resting state. While this state is being restored the cell cannot be activated and is in its *refractory period.*

The rate of generation of action potential spikes depends on the strength of the stimulation but, at a certain level of stimulation, saturation is reached and no greater rate of spike discharge is then possible, no matter

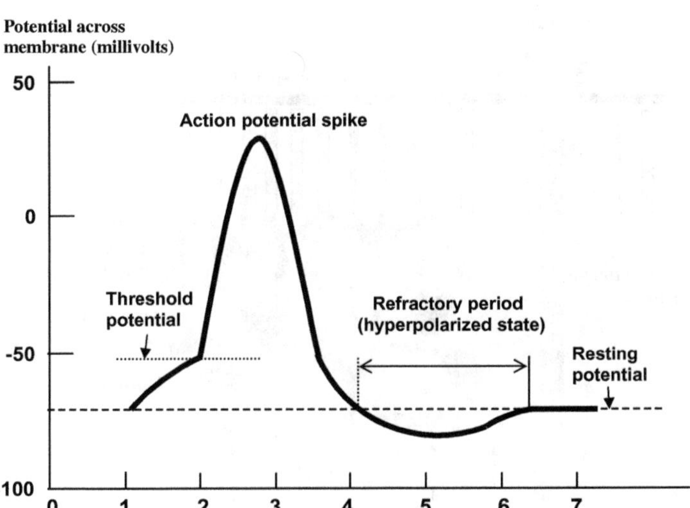

Figure 1.8 The action potential of a neuron. The potential across the membrane is the potential inside minus the potential outside and hence is negative in the resting state

how strong the stimulation. It will be seen in Figure 1.8 that a complete impulse cycle takes about 6 milliseconds so that the maximum rate of spike discharge is about 160 per second. The neuron reaction just described is when it is excited by the neurotransmitter.

Even in the absence of stimuli, neurons emit spontaneous bursts of spikes. However, there can be an inhibitory response of the cell, when the potassium rather than the sodium channels are stimulated to open. In this case potassium ions flood out of the cell, it becomes hyperpolarized and the spontaneous activity is stopped dead in its tracks. Both excitatory and inhibitory reactions are important in the functioning of the optical neural network system.

1.2.4 The neural network of the eye

There are four layers of different kinds of neuron between the photoreceptors and the optic nerve fibres that transmit the image information to the visual cortex. These four layers, in order from the photoreceptors, are — *horizontal cells, bipolar cells, amacrine cells* and *ganglion cells.* These are

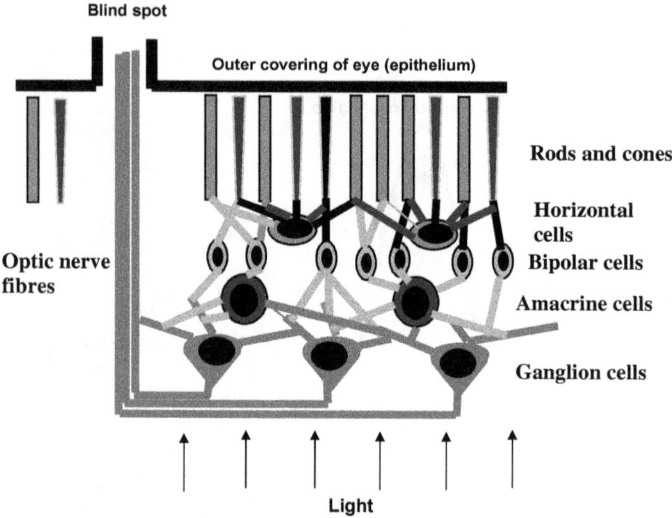

Figure 1.9   A schematic representation of the neural network structure of the eye

shown in schematic form in Figure 1.9. Actually for many of these cells —
horizontal cells, bipolar cells and some amacrine cells — the behaviour is
not as described in Section 1.2.3 since they do not give potential spikes, the
frequency of which indicate the strength of the signal, but rather generate
a steady potential that governs the rate of emission of neurotransmitter at
the end of the axon. However, some amacrine cells and all ganglion cells
give spike potentials, so this is the kind of information passed on to the
visual cortex.

There is one feature of the arrangement of neurons in the human eye
that can only be regarded as 'faulty design'. Before the light reaches the
photoreceptors it has to traverse all four layers of neurons. This has two
adverse effects. Firstly the light is slightly absorbed and scattered before it
reaches the photoreceptors and, secondly, in order for the signal to reach
the brain from the ganglion cells, the optic nerve has to pass back through
the layers of neurons and photoreceptors thus leading to a *blind spot* in the
visual field (Figure 1.9). Detecting this blind spot can be done by a very
simple experiment. Draw two dots on a sheet of plain paper about 10 cm
apart. Then, with the dots horizontal, just using the right eye, focus onto
the left hand dot. If you start with the paper about 40 cm away and slowly

bring it inwards then at a distance of about 30 cm the right hand dot will disappear — its image on the retina is at the position of the blind spot. The octopus, and similar creatures called *cephalopods*, has eyes similar to those of humans but with the advantage that the layers of neurons are reversed so that light falls on the photoreceptors directly. For this reason there is no blind spot since the axons of the ganglion cells, forming the optic nerve fibres, can link with the brain without traversing the layers of neurons and photoreceptors.

Many connections from rods and cones are made directly with bipolar cells and, indeed, this kind of direct link is dominant. There are several types of bipolar cell, all responding to stimulation by varying their internal steady potentials. Some are attached to numbers of rods and others to numbers of cones; no bipolar cell is attached to both rods and cones. The other division is between ON and OFF cells. When a photoreceptor is not illuminated it releases a neurotransmitter known as *glutamate* (glutamic acid), which inhibits the responses of ON bipolar cells and stimulates the responses of OFF cells. However, when the photoreceptors are illuminated they generate less glutamate and this polarizes the ON bipolar cells, hence activating them, and hyperpolarizes the OFF cells, so making them inactive. The effect of activating some bipolar cells and deactivating others by illuminating the photoreceptors means that the overall magnitude of the signal by neurotransmitters is little affected by the intensity of illumination of the photoreceptors, so preventing overloading the visual cortex with electrical signals, and information about the intensity is contained in the relative response of ON and OFF bipolar cells in any tiny region of the retina.

Some of the rods and cones link to horizontal cells, each of which has links with several photoreceptors. In addition horizontal cells have links with bipolar cells. This combination of the information from photoreceptors via the horizontal cells is a stage of a funnelling process by which the information from 130 million photoreceptors eventually gives spike potentials in just one million optic nerve fibres. Another important function of horizontal cells is to modify the response of photoreceptors to light. When horizontal cells receive glutamate from the photoreceptors they produce another neurotransmitter called *GABA* (gamma-aminobutyric acid) which is passed back to the photoreceptor and decreases its activity. This gives a negative feedback process. The greater the intensity of light on the photoreceptors the less is the production of glutamate that, in its turn, gives less production of GABA in the horizontal cell. However, GABA inhibits the activity of the photoreceptors so a reduction in GABA passing back to the photoreceptor leads to an increase in glutamate production. With no feedback mechanism at some level of illumination all glutamate production would cease and any increase in illumination would have no effect on the photoreceptors. With feedback the reduction of glutamate production with increasing light intensity is lessened, which increases the range of intensity of illumination that the photoreceptor can discriminate before glutamate production ceases.

From electron micrographs it is seen that rod bipolar cells never directly link to ganglion cells but only do so via amacrine cells. The function of amacrine cells is not well understood. They are part of the process of funnelling information from photoreceptors into many fewer optic nerve fibres but what else they do is obscure.

The overall effect of the neural network is that each ganglion cell is influenced by the illumination falling on a particular small circular patch of the retina. It is excited by a circular region at the centre of the patch and inhibited by the surrounding annular region. The greatest information in an image is at boundaries where there is a sharp change either of intensity or colour and the way the ganglion cell reacts to light falling on the retina has the effect of emphasizing such boundaries. To see how this happens, we give a one-dimensional illustration, shown in Figure 1.10(a). We consider a ganglion cell that in the dark gives a rate of spike discharge of one unit in the central region, represented by BC and one half unit in the peripheral regions represented by AB and CD. However, if the total area is illuminated then the central region is excited to give a response of 5 units and the peripheral regions are inhibited to give no response. Now, in Figure 1.10(b), we show ganglion cells at positions a, b, c, d, e and f where the illumination of the retina sharply changes from darkness to full illumination as shown by the black and white background. The total response of each ganglion cell is shown, dependent on the extent to which it is influenced by dark and illuminated regions of the retina. When these responses are plotted in Figure 1.10(c) it is seen that the response curve shows a peak and a trough

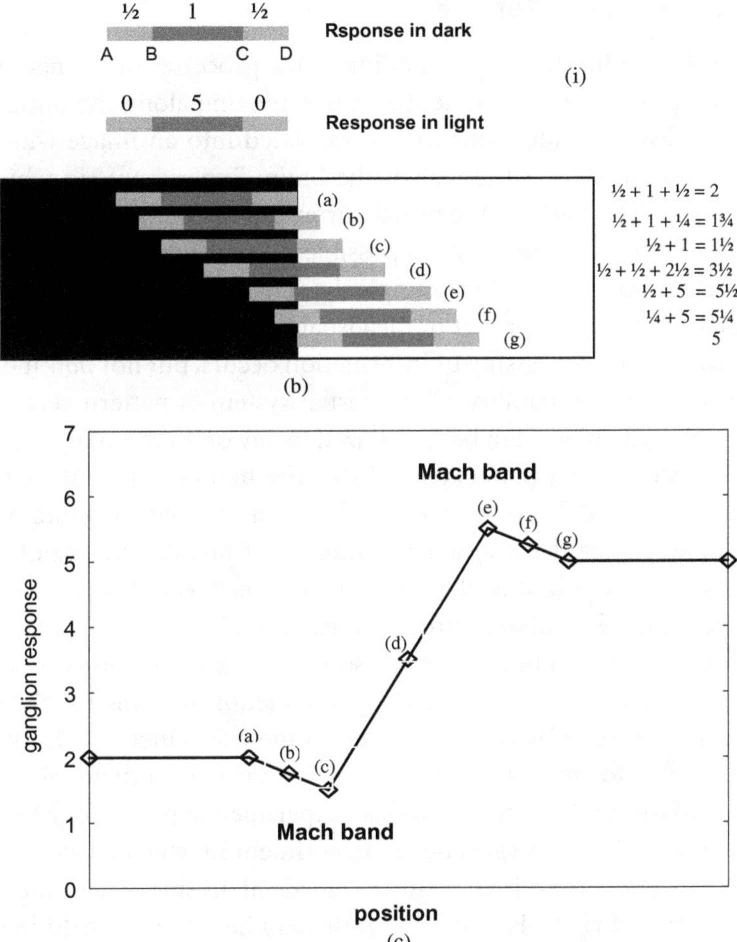

Figure 1.10   (a) Ganglion-cell response in the dark and in uniform illumination. (b) The responses for ganglion cells in different position in relation to the boundary. (c) The formation of Mach bands.

that has the effect of emphasizing the boundary. These peak and trough features are known as *Mach bands*; where there is a gradual variation of intensity the Mach-band effect amplifies the effect and makes the variation more evident. A similar, rather more complex, effect enables the eye to distinguish slight changes of colour.

1.2.5 The visual cortex

While we have a limited understanding of the processes in the neural network that give a stream of potential spikes moving along the optic nerve fibres, we have little idea how this is translated into an image within the visual cortex situated at the rear of the brain. Experiments in which the activity of various parts of the visual cortex are measured when subjected to various kinds of stimuli make it possible to identify regions that specialize in certain activities — for example, in detecting motion or in processing signals from the lower half of the visual field. In this way we are able to find out *where* the processing of information occurs, but not *how* it occurs.

An important capability of the visual system is pattern recognition whereby viewed objects can be recognized in any orientation or even when highly distorted. Every person has a distinctive handwriting but, nevertheless, the postman delivers virtually all letters addressed by hand. A word processor will offer the user a large number of possible fonts but all the following are recognized as the same letter — e, **e**, e, e, e, e, e and would still be recognized if rotated through various angles.

Related to pattern recognition in some ways is a phenomenon known as *perceptual adaptation*. This is the phenomenon by which if the visual cortex is presented with a distorted view of the world then it will compensate for the distortion and will present the viewing individual with an undistorted image. A pioneer American experimental psychologist, George Stratton (1865–1957), carried out an experiment in which he wore spectacles that inverted the visual field, i.e. made it upside-down and interchanged left and right. For the first four days he saw the world inverted, exactly as the spectacles presented it to the retina, but on the fifth day the perception of the visual field was restored to normal as though he was not wearing the spectacles. By concentrating hard he could return to the inverted view. Other experiments in which the visual field is artificially modified in various ways have confirmed the strength of the phenomenon of perceptual adaptation. It is clear that the visual cortex is not just a processor for presenting an image as it is actually presented to the retina. Within the processing there is an element that works to present the image in an acceptable and expected form by removing whatever is distorting the actual image. In Section 6.2 we shall meet another form of visual adaptation that applies to the way we see colour.

Chapter 2

The Evolution of the Eye

2.1 The Nature of Darwinian Evolution

Those who reject the idea of Darwinian evolution will sometimes point to the eye as an example of intelligent design, an organ that could not have arisen by an evolutionary process. It is sometimes difficult to grasp the power of evolution, operating over vast periods of time to effect changes that give an end product so far removed from its starting point that there seems to be no possible connection between the two. Let us consider an analogy, using the visible spectrum that stretches from a electromagnetic wavelength of 4000 Å[1] (blue light) to 7000 Å (red light). Starting at the blue end we compare light of wavelengths 4000 Å with that of wavelength 4001 Å and there is no discernible difference. This is then repeated for wavelengths 4001 Å and 4002 Å, again with no discernible difference, and the process repeated until wavelengths 6999 Å and 7000 Å are compared. After 3 000 steps, each with no discernible difference, the end point is starkly different from the starting point. So it is with evolution. The first simple life form began on Earth about 3 800 million years ago and with a simple almost imperceptible change every 100,000 years there would be 38,000 evolutionary steps to the present day. To take another example, this number of steps is greater than the number of days in a centenarian's life.

---

[1] 1 Å (angstrom unit) is 10^{-10} m.

From the time of his birth, each day he would look indistinguishable from his appearance the day before — but there is a huge difference between a new-born baby and a very old man.

Another point of interest is that, as we have seen, the eye is an example of *faulty design* leading to a blind spot, and the eyes of a much less well developed creature overall, the octopus, has a better designed eye than humans. It is to be wondered why the eyes of man and an octopus took two different evolutionary paths — but somehow and for some reason they did.

Reactions to visible light radiation, or even radiation outside the visible range, varies from just the ability to detect radiation to that of being able to create a detailed image of distant objects. We will now explore this range of reactions and indicate in a very general way how an evolutionary process could have led from crude detection to image formation. The steps in the evolutionary process described here may seem to be large and by no means indiscernible, but we must imagine that in going from one step to the next there were many tiny changes.

2.2 The Reaction of Plants to Light

The basis of Darwinian evolution is that if a change in an organism, however it occurs, is beneficial then that change, expressed in the genetic structure of the organism, will give it a competitive advantage. That advantage will be passed on to its progeny and, eventually, the modified organism will displace the unmodified form from which it originated. The replacement of an organism by a modified one better equipped to cope with its environment is usually summed up in the phrase 'Survival of the fittest'.

Plants develop and grow by the process of photosynthesis, carried out by the green chemical *chlorophyll* that is present in the leaves of plants. The process, which uses the energy provided by sunlight, takes in carbon dioxide from the air, combines it with water, drawn up from the soil by the plant's roots, and produces cellulose, the main structural component of plants, and releases oxygen, essential for most animate lifeforms, into the atmosphere. The ability to receive as much sunlight as possible is clearly an advantage and plants have evolved a mechanism that enables this to occur.

Many plants move when exposed to light and they do so to give the maximum exposure of their leaves to sunlight. Charles Darwin was particularly interested in this phenomenon, known as *phototropism*, i.e. movement in plants, and wrote a book with title *The Power of Movement in Plants*. Now it is known that this movement is mainly caused by the chemical indole-3-acetic acid (IAA), one of a class of plant hormones known as *auxins*. When light falls on a plant on one side, the IAA on the opposite side of the plant causes an elongation of the plant fibres in its vicinity. The effect of this is to bend the plant towards the light and hence increase its exposure to radiation (Figure 2.1).

Light energy was also very important for many early animate life forms and we will now describe how this dependence led from very simple light-detecting mechanisms to something that could be called an eye in the sense that it formed a crude image. Going from that point to the complexity of the vertebrate eye, involving the development of neural networks and different kinds of photoreceptor, is much more difficult to describe and explain.

2.3 The Evolution of an Image-Forming Eye

When life first formed in the very hostile environment of the early Earth, it had many problems to overcome. The Sun emits a wide range of electromagnetic radiation, including ultraviolet radiation, the high energy of which can disrupt organic molecules and so kill the organism of which

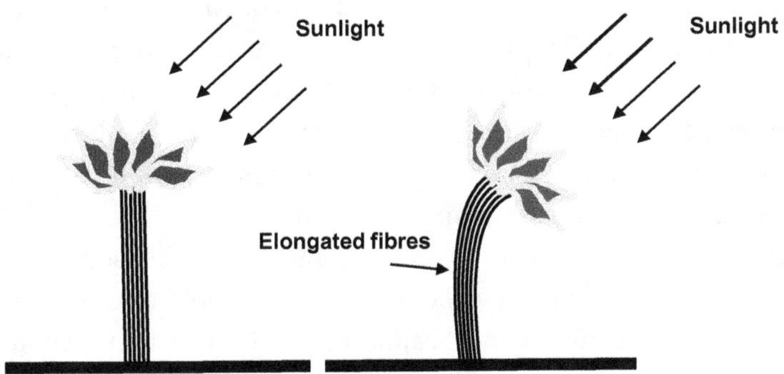

Figure 2.1   The bending of a plant towards light

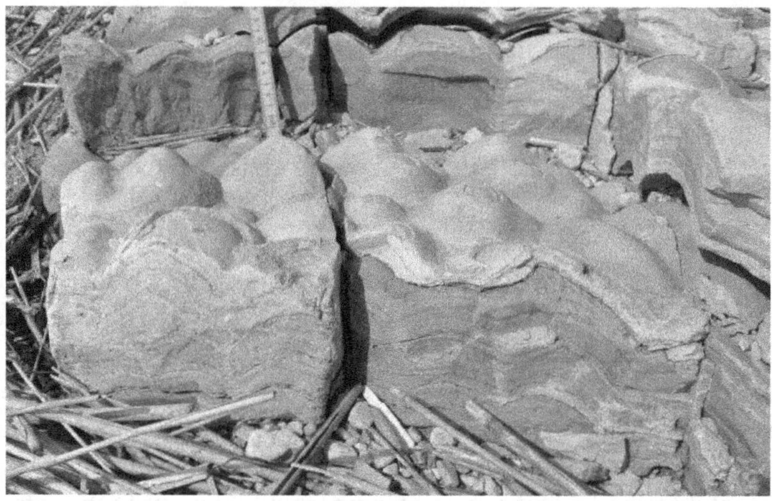

Figure 2.2   A billion year old stromatolite

they are a component. Life on the present Earth is protected by the *ozone layer*, formed high up in the atmosphere, which absorbs ultraviolet radiation. Ozone is a molecule consisting of three oxygen atoms bound together to form a triangle but, since on the early Earth there was no oxygen, there was also no ozone layer.

A very early life form on Earth was *cyanobacteria,* a common green–blue bacterium that forms clumps and mats in shallow water or on damp rocks. There are fossil records of this bacterium going back 3.8 billion years. Figure 2.2 shows a fossilized cyanobacteria mat, known as a *stromatolite,* dating from about one billion years ago. An important feature of cyanobacteria is that, like plants, they carry out the process of photosynthesis and they were probably responsible for first introducing oxygen into the terrestrial atmosphere. Early cyanobacteria could only have flourished in sheltered environments such as in water, which would filter out most harmful radiation, or within damp rocky crevasses.

Until an effective ozone layer had built up, the somewhat more complex organisms that followed cyanobacteria would also have needed to protect themselves from harmful radiation. To do this they would need to detect the radiation, in particular the direction from which it was coming, and then propel themselves in some way into a shady environment.

The organisms that could do this most effectively would have the greatest chance of survival — the condition required for Darwinian evolutionary theory to operate.

The early means of locomotion were very primitive. Bacteria have whip-like appendages called *flagella* (singular flagellum) that, when flexed, cause movement. At a more advanced level bringing together hinged surfaces in water can produce an outflow of water that gives motion in the direction opposite to the flow. However, whatever the means of propulsion the first requirement is to detect light and determine from which direction it is coming so that evasive motion can be produced in the opposite direction.

The crudest light detector would have been patches of photosensitive pigment on the surface of the organism (Figure 2.3(a)). This would give only a rough indication of the direction from which the radiation was coming but the organism would move in a direction opposite to points on the surface most strongly illuminated. Although used for a different purpose, an example of such a light-detecting system is found in *euglena*, small primitive unicellular creatures that form a green scum in pools of water. They are covered by a flexible membrane and contain chloroplasts, structures within which chlorophyll performs photosynthesis. In this case, like plants, the organism seeks the light. It possesses a flagellum at the base of which is an *eyespot*, a red photosensitive pigment that controls the flagellum so that the organism moves towards the light (Figure 2.4).

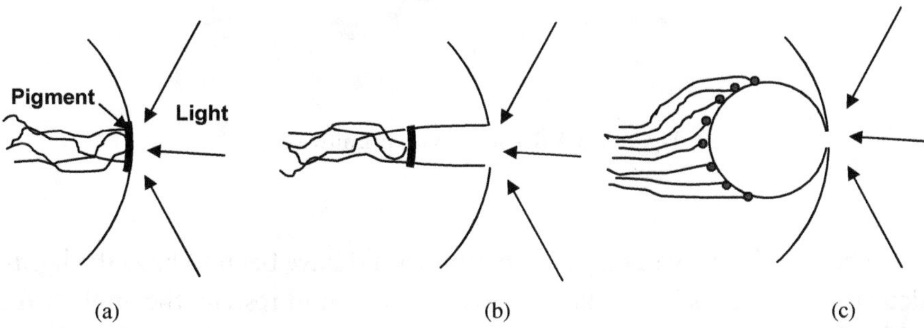

Figure 2.3   Three stages in the development of a primitive eye. (a) A pigment patch with poor directional discrimination. (b) Pigment within a hollow giving better directional discrimination. (c) A small aperture giving a pinhole-camera effect with several independent pigment patches

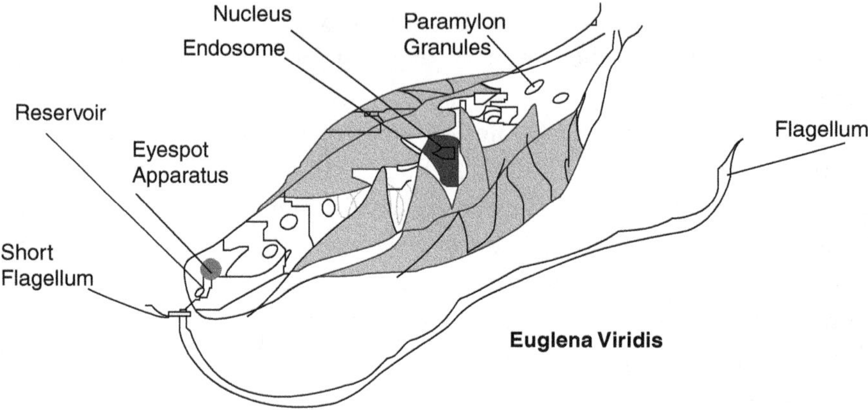

Figure 2.4   The structure of a euglena showing a red eyespot at base of flagellum

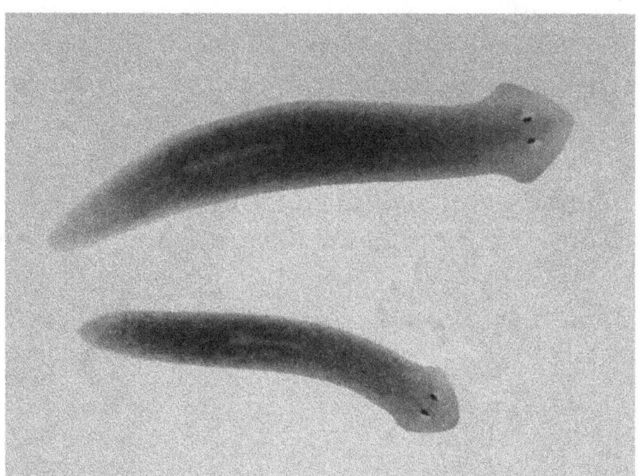

Figure 2.5 A flatworm with primitive eyes

The next improvement in detection would have been to have the light-detecting pigments in a hollow recess, which would restrict the angle from which light could come to fall on the pigment, hence increasing directional discrimination (Figure 2.3(b)). The *flatworm* (Figure 2.5) has two cups containing pigments on its head, which form primitive eyes. However, this is just a slight improvement of the light detecting system of euglena.

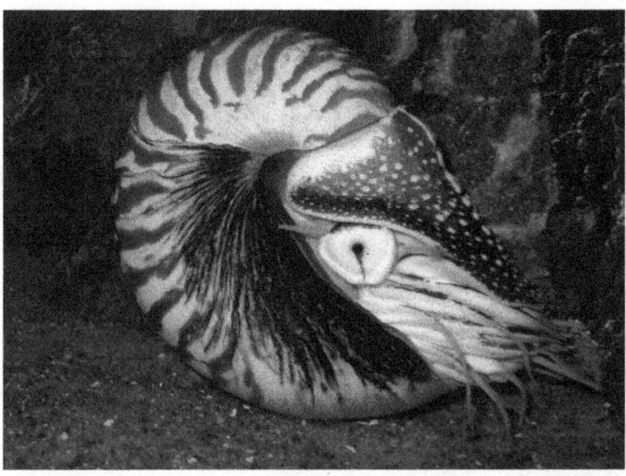

Figure 2.6 Nautilus showing the 'pinhole-camera' eye (Berlin Zoo)

A further improvement is to make the hollow recess into a deep recess, which would greatly improve the directional discrimination. Now a new development is possible; by widening the base of the recess and having several patches of pigment it is possible to give a sense of the distribution of light coming from different directions. Narrowing the entrance to the aperture and increasing the number of pigment patches is now giving something like a pinhole camera, a simple device for producing an image without using a lens (Figure 2.3(c)). The cephalopod *Nautilus* (Figure 2.6) has this type of eye, with a narrow aperture acting as a pinhole and with the interior of the cup open to the outside environment.

We have now moved from light detection to producing an image, albeit with very low resolution. More complex organisms, with better mobility and much more demanding requirements to survive, need something better. Covering the pinhole aperture with a membrane would protect the eye from contamination, and hence degraded performance, and then, to prevent the aperture collapsing and to strengthen the structure of the eye the enclosure could be filled with a clear fluid. Now we have the structure represented in Figure 2.7(a). The membrane covering the pinhole aperture would have to be transparent and if this thickened in the centre, as shown in Figure 2.7(b), it would act like a lens and give a clearer and brighter image.

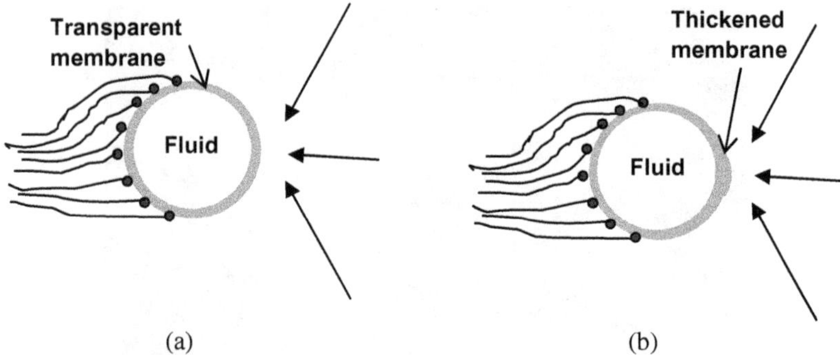

Figure 2.7   The beginning of the vertebrate eye. (a) A transparent membrane enclosing a fluid. (b) A thickening of the membrane to produce a lens.

The move from this stage to the vertebrate eye is not so easy to imagine. What is required is the development of an extra flexible crystalline lens behind the cornea with the mechanism to change the shape of that lens. The first stage, producing the crystalline lens might have come about by an initial splitting of the cornea into two parts, the inner one changing its composition as it evolved. We have to remember the gradual way that evolution operates with each change being a miniscule departure from what preceded it. Another necessary change is that the pigment patches would need to have evolved both in nature and number to give the array of photoreceptors that now exist.

We have not dealt with complex issues such as the way that patches of pigment eventually became individual photoreceptors of different kinds and how the neural system developed in such a way as to interpret the increasingly complex signals it receives. We have already noted that the eye structure of the octopus is superior to that of man and there are many other creatures that have eyes with properties different from those of humans with adaptations that have survival value. Thus some insects and birds can detect ultraviolet radiation; the extra ability enables the insects better to detect nectar-bearing flowers by their spectral emission and birds of prey to overcome the problem that, in the visible range alone, their prospective prey may be effectively camouflaged. Again, birds of prey have a much higher concentration of photoreceptors than ground-based animals, the greater visual acuity enabling them to resolve potential prey while flying or hovering at a great height. On the whole the evolutionary process seems to stop when further development serves no useful purpose. The ability of humans to survive would not be improved by a doubling of visual acuity but halving the visual acuity would be a distinct disadvantage. While there has been great development in brain power and general morphology between *Homo habilis*, a hominid human predecessor that lived two million years ago, and present humans, there is no evidence that there has been any improvement in visual function in the intervening period.

We began this chapter with the comment that there are some who claim that the eye is so complex and specialized that it is impossible to imagine that it is a result of evolutionary processes but rather supports the theory of creationism, i.e. intelligent design by a divine creator. However, while there may be some anatomical features that challenge evolutionary ideas the eye does not seem to be one of them. Indeed, Richard Dawkins, an eminent British evolutionary biologist and a strong advocate of evolution and opponent of creationism, points to the flawed structure of the human visual neural network, to which we have previously referred, as evidence *against* intelligent design.

Chapter 3
The Science of Colour

3.1 The Nature of Light

Ancient Greek and Roman philosophers had a number of theories about the nature of light. Some early philosophers thought that the ability to see depended on rays that left the eye and fell on the object being seen. This theory had so many flaws, for example, in explaining why one could not see in the dark, that it was soon discounted. The fact that light travels in straight lines and never takes a curved path in air convinced the Roman poet and philosopher, Titus Lucretius Carus (90 BCE–c.55 BCE), generally known as Lucretius, that light consisted of particles leaving the object being seen. In 55 BCE he published a treatise *De Rerum Natura* (On the Nature of Things) in which he wrote 'The light and heat from the Sun consist of tiny atoms that, when they are ejected, immediately move through the air in the direction of their ejection'.

This idea of light being particulate in nature was also proposed by the French priest and scientist, Pierre Gassendi (1592–1655) and was published shortly after his death. The English scientist, Isaac Newton (1643–1727; Figure 3.1), probably the greatest scientist of all time, similarly thought that light consisted of corpuscles — small particles — basing his argument on the fact that particles travel in straight lines. However, to explain the phenomenon of *refraction*, the change in direction of a light ray when it goes from one medium to another, e.g. air to glass, Newton had to assume that light travelled faster in a dense medium, which is not true. His idea

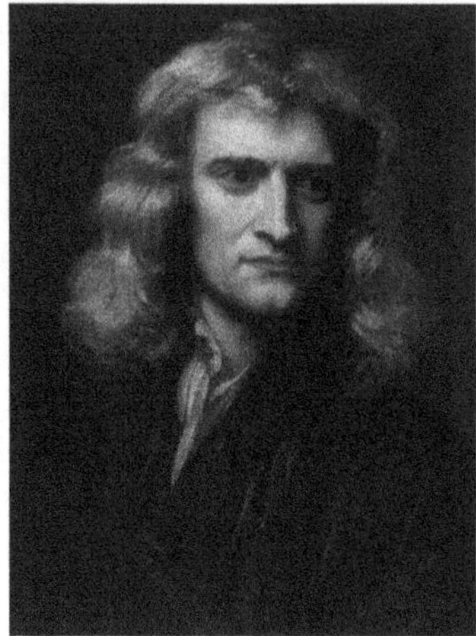

Figure 3.1   Isaac Newton

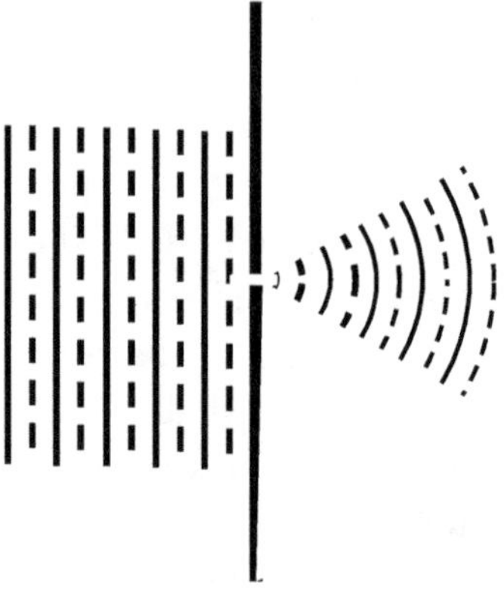

Figure 3.2   Diffraction of a plane wave falling on a small aperture

was based on the idea that the particles had mass and would be affected by the gravitational attraction of the dense medium. Again, he argued that waves tend to spread out as they travel; if a stone is dropped in a pond the resultant waves are seen to travel in all directions.

A basic property of waves is that they can be *diffracted*, a property that can be investigated in a water tank. Figure 3.2 shows what happens in a water tank when plane waves, in which the crests and troughs lie along

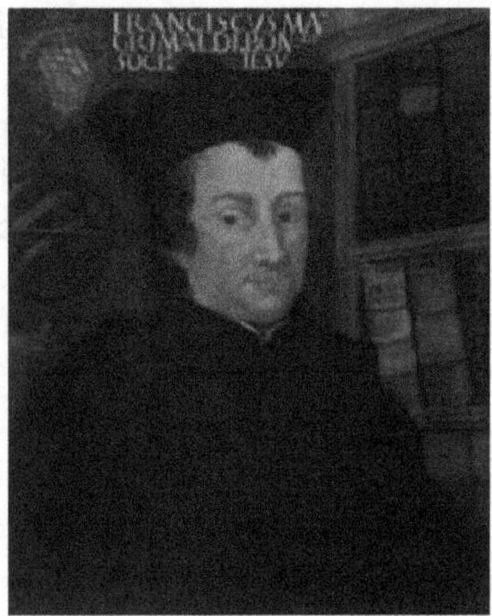

Figure 3.3   Francesco Grimaldi

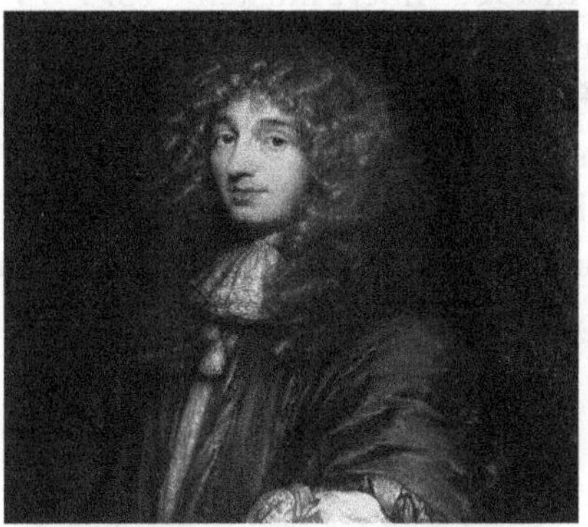

Figure 3.4   Christiaan Huyghens

straight lines, meet a barrier with a small gap. Waves are diffracted at the gap and move outwards over a wide range of directions. The Italian Jesuit philosopher, Francesco Grimaldi (1616–1663; Figure 3.3) noted that when a narrow object, such as a needle, was illuminated by a narrow pencil of light, the shadow was much broader than should occur if light travelled in straight lines, and he first coined the word *diffraction* to describe this phenomenon. Another strong supporter of the wave theory of light was the Dutch scientist Christiaan Huyghens (1629–1695; Figure 3.4) who also suggested that the speed of light was finite, something confirmed by the Danish astronomer Oleus Roemer (1644–1710) in 1679 by timing the appearance and occultation of Jupiter's Galilean satellites. The interval between the eclipses of the satellites became shorter as the Earth approached Jupiter, when the distance light had to travel to Earth was becoming less, and longer as the Earth receded from Jupiter.

The question of the nature of light was temporarily put to rest by the brilliant English polymath scientist Thomas Young (1773–1829; Figure 3.5) who devised a series of experiments illustrating the wave nature of light. The most famous of these experiments, one now carried out in all physics student laboratories, is 'Young's slits' in which light from a common source, passing through two narrow slits a small distance apart, produce an interference pattern of light and dark lines on a screen.

Considering the fierce debate about the nature of light, it is rather curious that we now known that light can manifest the properties of *both* particles *and* waves. In 1905 Albert Einstein (1879–1955; Figure 3.6) wrote a paper on the photoelectric effect, which had been discovered by the German physicist, Heinrich Hertz (1857–1894) in 1887. When light, or ultraviolet radiation, falls on some metal surfaces the energy contained in the light dislodges electrons from the metal atoms. The apparently strange result found was that, no matter how low was the intensity of the light,

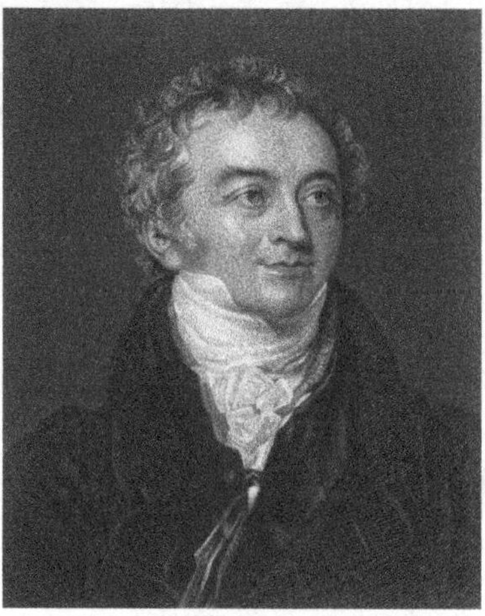

Figure 3.5   Thomas Young

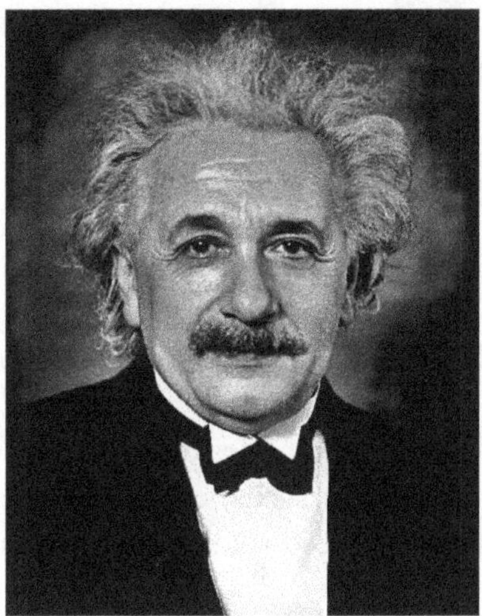

Figure 3.6   Albert Einstein

photoelectrons were immediately produced, the rate of production being proportional to the light intensity. On the generally-accepted assumption that light was a wave motion, with the energy spread evenly over the metal surface, it could be calculated that it might take minutes or even hours for an electron to receive enough energy to escape from a metal atom, after which a large number of electrons would leave the surface during a very short time interval. This conundrum was solved by Einstein who postulated that, in the photoelectric phenomenon, light consisted of a rain of particles, called *photons*, each with sufficient energy to dislodge an electron from the metal atom. Now, whatever the intensity of the light, photoelectrons would be produced immediately and the greater the rate at which the photons fell on the surface — proportional to the light intensity — the greater the rate of photoelectron production.

This ability of light to show the characteristics of both waves and particles is an example of what is termed *wave-particle duality* and another example is electrons that are normally thought of as particles but in an electron microscope take on the behaviour of waves and produce an image.

As a postscript to this account of Einstein's paper on photoelectricity, a phenomenon which is largely unknown outside the scientific community, it was for this work that he received his Nobel Prize for Physics in 1921 — not for his work on relativity for which he is known even by non-scientists.

3.2 The Scientific Nature of Colour

Along with the 17th century controversy about the nature of light there was also a great deal of uncertainty about the nature of colour. From the time of Aristotle (384–322 BCE) it had been believed that all light was fundamentally white, like light from the Sun, and colour came about as a result of mixing it with 'darkness' due to the interaction of the light with different substances. The colours of the rainbow were known and it was also known that a prism produced coloured light, although it was believed that the prism added 'darkness to the white light in varying degrees, the least addition being to bright red and the most to dark blue, the stage before complete darkness gave black.

This complete misunderstanding about the nature of light was resolved by Newton in a series of experiments, the results of which were published in 1672. In one experiment, illustrated in Figure 3.7 with red, green and blue representing the whole spectrum, he passed a fine beam of sunlight coming through a small hole in a window blind through a prism to produce a spectrum and then passed the spectral light into a second prism, in an inverse orientation to the first one, and recombined the spectrum to give white light. The idea that the first prism added darkness and the second prism removed it was clearly absurd. Newton's experiment showed clearly that white light was a combination of all the spectral colours; white light could be split up into a spectrum and the colours of the

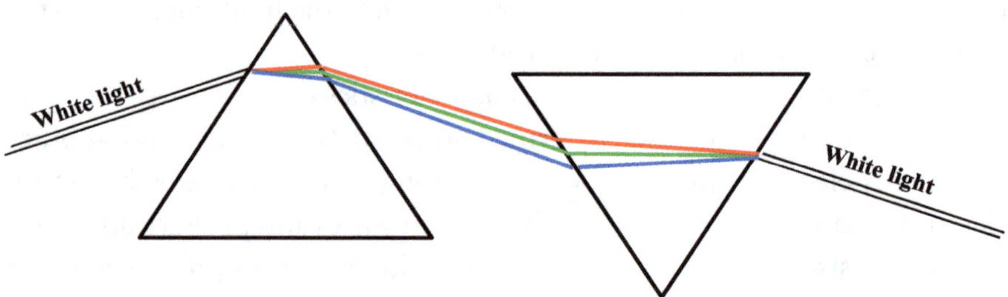

Figure 3.7   Newton's two-prism experiment

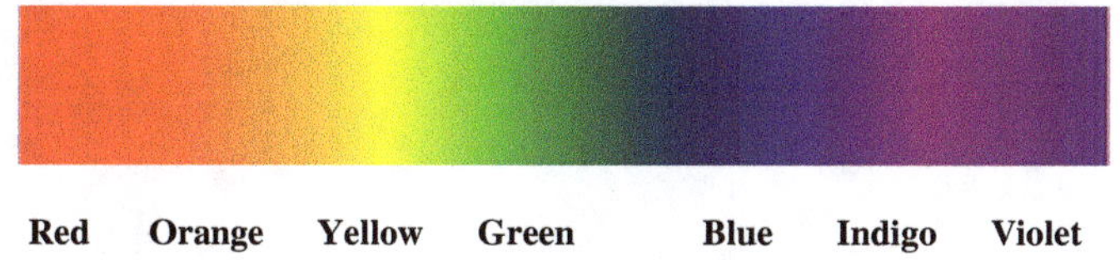

Figure 3.8   The visible spectrum

Table 3.1   Regions of the electromagnetic spectrum

Region of Spectrum	Typical Wavelength (m)
γ-rays	10^{-12}
X-rays	10^{-10}
Ultraviolet	10^{-8}
Visible	$4\text{--}7 \times 10^{-7}$
Infrared	10^{-5}
Microwaves	1
Radio waves	100

spectrum could be recombined into white light. In another experiment Newton isolated a narrow band of the spectrum from the first prism by passing it through a small slit in a screen and then passed it through a prism. Its colour was unchanged by passing through the prism, showing that no extra darkness had been added.

A full visible spectrum is shown in Figure 3.8 labelled with the colours that Newton introduced — red, orange, yellow, green, blue, indigo and violet. It is only a tiny part of the complete electromagnetic spectrum which stretches from γ-radiation with very small wavelengths to radio waves with very large wavelengths. The electromagnetic spectrum is continuous but names are given to regions with different characteristics although they merge into one another. Table 3.1 shows these regions with typical wavelengths.

Although the visible spectrum contains all the wavelengths contained in white light, nevertheless, it does not include the whole range of colours that can be perceived by the eye — something that we now discuss.

Chapter 4
The Range of Colour

4.1 The Chromaticity Diagram

The wavelengths that comprise the visible spectrum, ranging from 400 nm[1] for blue to 700 nm for red, do not contain all the colours that can be seen. Exceptions are colours linking red and blue, which are variously described as magenta or purple. In fact the complete range of colour that can enter the eye — although how they are perceived is another matter as we shall see — is contained in the 1931 CIE (Commission Internationale de l'Eclairage) colour diagram, shown in Figure 4.1.

The curved periphery of the diagram corresponds to pure spectral wavelengths and the point W corresponds to the colour perception we see as white. Although the point-W white can be defined as, say, a mixture of all spectral wavelengths with an equal intensity, there is a small region distributed around about the point W that would be judged to be white if seen in isolation. In Figure 4.2, the two rectangles seen side-by-side can just be distinguished as a blue-tinged white on the left and a red-tinged white on the right. Now if a tube is constructed by wrapping a sheet of A4 paper round a pencil and just one rectangle is viewed through the tube so that the colour is seen in isolation, then, after a short time, when the memory

---

[1] 1 nm (nanometre) is 10^{-9} metre or 10 Å.

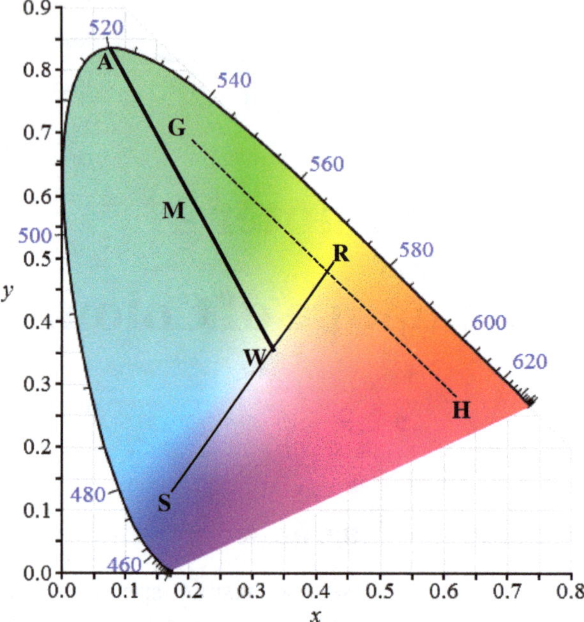

Figure 4.1   The 1931 CIE chromaticity diagram

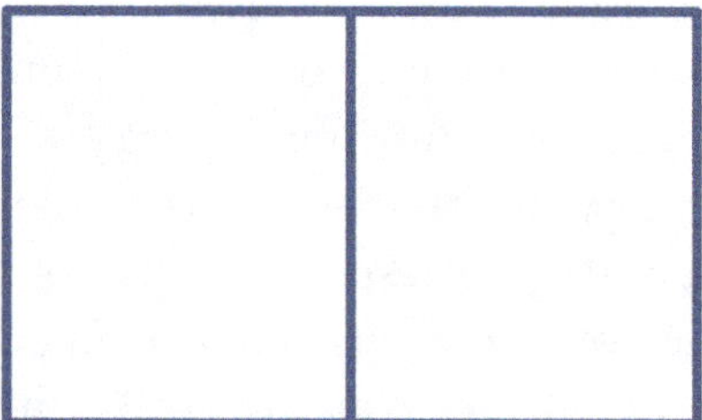

Figure 4.2   Two slightly different whites

of the comparison has faded, there would be little hesitation in judging it to be white. Retain the tube — it will be useful later.

In Figure 4.1, point A corresponds to the colour that is seen for the green spectral wavelength 520 nm. As we move from A along the line AW more-and-more white is added to the spectral green producing *pastel green* shades; the progression is shown more clearly in Figure 4.3. In technical language, the point A corresponds to a *saturated colour* and as

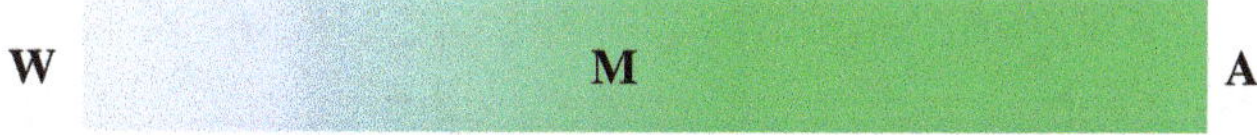

Figure 4.3   Increasing saturation of a green hue

one moves towards W the perceived colour is less-and-less saturated. The perception of colour difference, or saturation difference, depends on the way that the cone responses vary with intensity, so equal brightness changes of one component of a mixture of two colours may not produce equal perceptual differences. Nevertheless we can say that the point M, midway between A and W would roughly correspond to a mixture of spectral green and white with the same intensity.

In general, colour sensation can be described in terms of three parameters — hue, saturation and brightness. However, as previously mentioned, there is a part of the chromaticity diagram, bordered by the straight boundary, which cannot be directly described in terms of spectral wavelengths and corresponds to mixtures of blue and red — or, more precisely, mixtures of violet and red if we accept Newton's terminology for regions of the visible spectrum. Although these mixtures are variably, and seemingly interchangeably, described as either purple or magenta; we shall mostly use the term 'magenta' for any blue–red mixture.

4.2 Colour Addition

We are going to couch our discussion of the chromaticity diagram in terms of what would be seen on a white screen if two or more coloured beams of light were overlapped on it. In that case the eye is exposed to an addition of the wavelengths present in the beams, each of which is independently reflected without colour distortion from the white screen. As will be explained, this form of colour addition can be represented, although not perfectly, on a computer screen, and even less well in print, but the various colour effects will be reproduced here in print as well as possible with their deficiencies explained.

A general rule is that if two light beams, with hues and saturations represented by points P and Q on the chromaticity diagram, overlap on a screen, then by varying the relative intensities of the two beams one can reproduce every hue and saturation on the straight line between *P* and *Q*. We now look at some examples of colour addition.

In Figure 4.1(a), line GH is drawn between points of green and red hues. From the diagram it is clear that with a suitable mixture of two beams corresponding to those points it should be possible to produce somewhat-unsaturated green, greenish-yellow, yellow, orange and red, with gradual change from G to H. In Figure 4.4, we illustrate how an admixture of green and red can give yellow, but first we need to explain the difference between using lights and using either a computer screen or printing. If moderately intense lights were used then the appearance would be as seen in Figure 4.4(a). However, with a computer screen or printing, overlaying green with red gives red — the underlying green is blanked out. What can be done with computer word-and-image-processing facilities is to overlay green with *transparent* red. In the overlay situation at

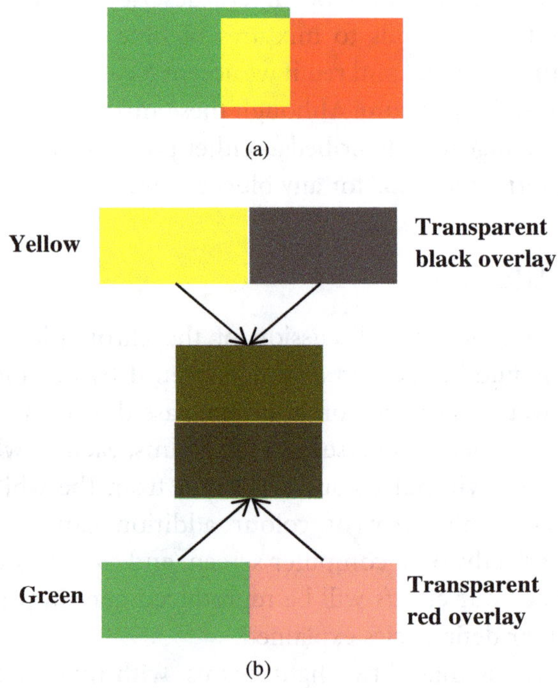

Figure 4.4   (a) Mixing red and green lights to give yellow. (b) A transparent red overlay on green and a transparent black overlay on yellow give similar dark yellows

the bottom of Figure 4.4(b) the transparency of the red is 60% so the effect seen in the overlay is 40% red plus 60% green, which is a very dark yellow. The yellow is very dark in the case of a computer screen or print because the intensities are so much lower than they would be with beams of coloured light. To emphasize that this is so, the top of Figure 4.4(b) shows the effect of a 44% transparent black overlay on yellow — suppressing the amount of yellow seen — giving a dark yellow that is similar to the green-red combination. Readers with computer facilities can reproduce these colour mixtures.

To those accustomed to using paint, the next addition-colour mix we consider might seem peculiar. In Figure 4.1 we show the line RS connecting a yellow region of the diagram to a blue one, which passes through the white region. In Figure 4.5(a), we see what would occur with the overlap of a suitable mixture of blue and yellow lights. The addition of blue and yellow gives white — not green as would occur with mixing pigments; we will deal with the pigment situation later. For the computer screen and printing the superposition of blue with 28% transparency on yellow gives 'dark white', the colour we recognize as grey Figure 4.5(b). A close-as-possible comparison grey is also shown and also black to emphasize the greyness, i.e. dark-whiteness, of the resultant of the colour addition.

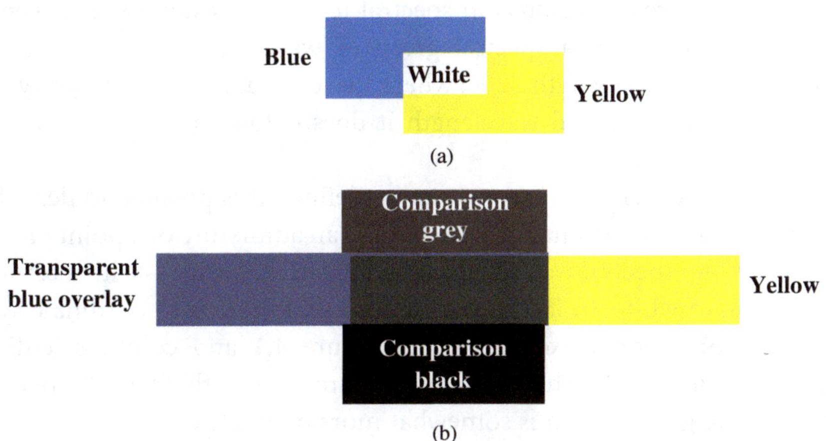

Figure 4.5   (a) The addition of blue and yellow coloured lights gives white. (b) Superposition of a partially-transparent blue on yellow gives grey (dark white)

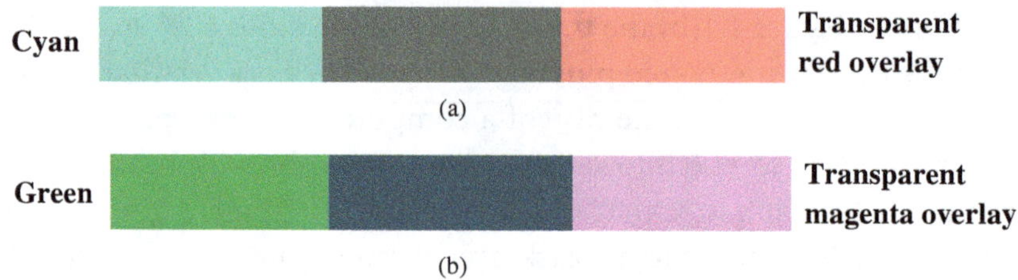

Figure 4.6   (a) The addition of cyan and red. (b) The addition of green and magenta. Both additions give what would be described as grey, although they are clearly different

Pairs of colours that when added can give white are known as *complementary colours*. Of course, just as there is a variety of 'whites' so there is a variety of 'greys'. If the mixed colours are not precisely complementary with respect to a perfect white, however that is defined, then the best grey one can achieve will be biased to a point away from 'perfect white'. Hence, when we say that the result of different screen mixtures or printed mixtures is grey, that is not to say that they are all the same grey.

It will be seen from Figure 4.1 that a blue–green, known as *cyan* and red are also complementary, the effect shown in Figure 4.6(a). Another interesting complementary pair is green and magenta, shown in Figure 4.6(b). The greys (dark whites) given in Figure 4.6 are different, but both are distinctly grey. The green–magenta combination gives a way of describing different magentas in spectral terms. For example, a magenta that gives white with a spectral green of wavelength 520 nm will be described as of wavelength 520c, where the 'c' means 'complementary to'. Although it is not a real wavelength it does define the magenta colour precisely.

Now that different magentas can be defined it is possible to describe every point on the chromaticity diagram as an admixture of a point on the boundary — a spectral wavelength or a defined magenta — with a certain proportion of white. In fact, it will be seen that there is a coordinate system with orthogonal axes shown in Figure 4.1 and colour scientists describe points on the chromaticity diagram differently from the definition we have given, which is somewhat more qualitative.

An extension of the rules of colour addition is that by varying the relative intensities of three beams represented by points D, E and F overlapping on a screen, all hues and saturations can be produced within the triangle DEF. If the three colours correspond to red, green and blue spectral wavelengths then it is clear from Figure 4.1 that every colour can be reproduced by a suitable mixture of the three, although, because of the curved nature of the boundary of the diagram, not all saturated colours. Red, green and blue are called *primary colours* and it is interesting to note that overlapping beams of spectral red, spectral green and spectral blue can give the perceived colour as white, as can yellow and blue, although only two or three wavelengths are present and not a complete spectrum as for white light coming from an incandescent source. The basis of this observation will become clear when the way that the cones respond to light is described in Chapter 5. Figure 4.7(a) shows a printable version of the overlap of pairs of primary colours and of all three of them and Figure 4.7(b) the corresponding image of what would be obtained with coloured lights. The main differences are that the printable version has a much darker yellow and the central white has come out grey — although in the context in which it is seen it may seem to be a purplish grey. If this central region is seen through the paper tube, used for the comparison in Figure 4.2, the fact that it is grey will be more apparent. Within the annular region defined by the black circles around the centre of Figure 4.7(a) is a comparison grey, which is a good match for what is obtained by overlapping the three primary colours.

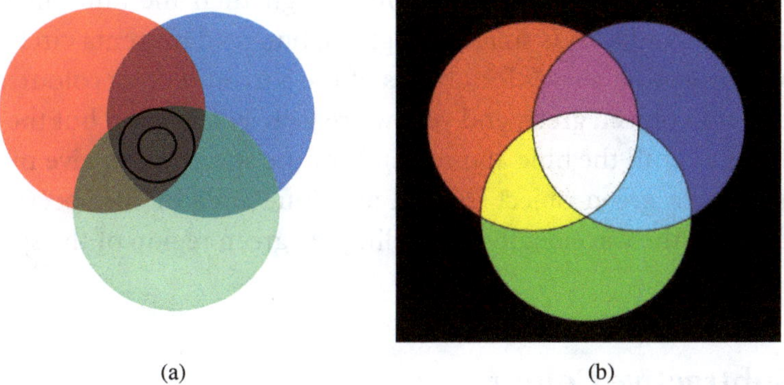

(a)   (b)

Figure 4.7   (a) The printable overlap of pairs and all three primary colours. (b) What would be seen with overlapping coloured lights

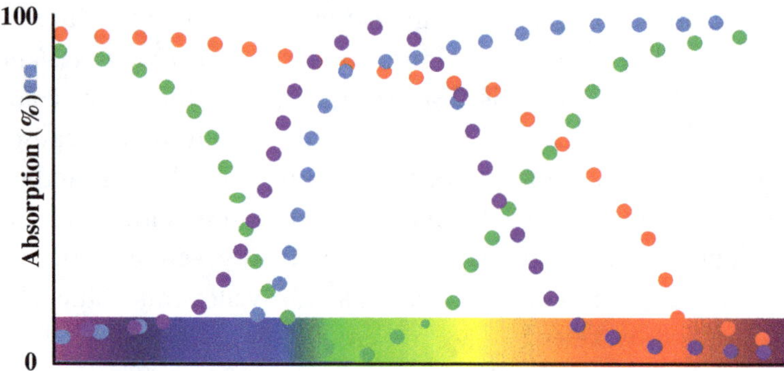

Figure 4.8   Absorption spectra for red, green, blue and magenta objects, shown by circles of the corresponding colour

4.3 Why are Objects Coloured?

When an object is illuminated with white light it is seen to have a distinctive colour. The object itself does not emit light — nothing would be seen if it were in a dark room — so what we see is clearly due to the interaction of the white light with the object. A red object is sending back into our eyes a distribution of wavelengths that we interpret as red and not the rest of the white-light spectrum. What is actually happening is that the object is *absorbing* the blue and green end of the spectrum quite heavily but re-radiating a range of wavelengths that give a perception of red. The absorption spectrum of the object may appear as shown in Figure 4.8 by the red circles. When the absorption is high then the amount of that wavelength re-radiated is small. The green, blue and magenta circles show possible absorption curves for objects of the corresponding colours. Thus, for a magenta object, green and yellow are heavily absorbed but the object re-radiates at both the blue and red ends of the spectrum to give magenta. Similarly, for a green object the red and blue ends of the spectrum are absorbed and the wavelengths straddling the green region of the spectrum are re-radiated.

4.4 Subtractive Colour

The phenomenon giving objects their coloration is known as *subtractive colour*, meaning that some wavelengths are removed, or subtracted, from the white light falling on the object and the colour we see is given by the remainder. A similar effect occurs with a coloured filter. The light seen through a transparent red plastic sheet is red because the filter has absorbed, i.e. subtracted, the blue and green parts of the spectrum so that a preponderance of wavelengths passing through the sheet are at the red end of the spectrum. Now we imagine what happens if we look through a combination of two filters of different colours. The first lets through a range of wavelengths; those enter the second filter and some of them are further absorbed. Let us consider what we would see if blue and yellow filters were superimposed. A particular wavelength in the white light, say of unit intensity, falling on the first filter would have a fraction a_1 absorbed and its intensity reduced by a *transmission factor* t_1 and so come through with intensity t_1. The transmission factor and the absorption factor are linked by $t + a = 1$, meaning that the particular wavelength is either absorbed or transmitted and that nothing else happens to it, for example, none of it is reflected backwards. The second filter would have a transmission factor t_2 for that wavelength so the final intensity passing through the two filters would be $t_1\,t_2$. Now, in Figure 4.9, we show some representative transmission factors for a blue and yellow filter and the resultant intensity of the wavelengths passing through the two filters. It will be seen that the resultant peaks in the green region of the spectrum and this mixture of blue and yellow to give green is familiar to every painter.

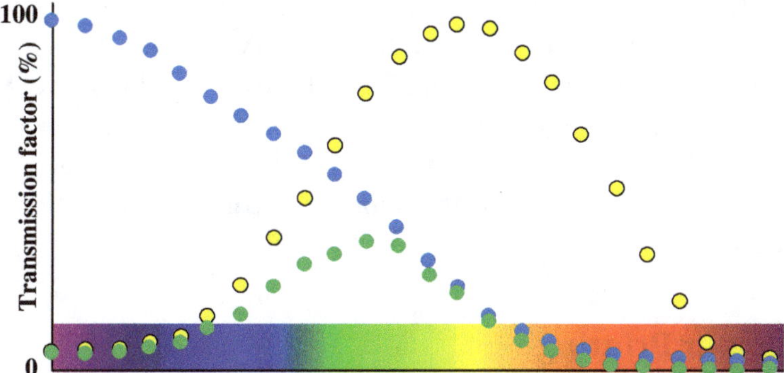

Figure 4.9   Transmission through a combination of a blue filter and a yellow filter gives transmitted green radiation

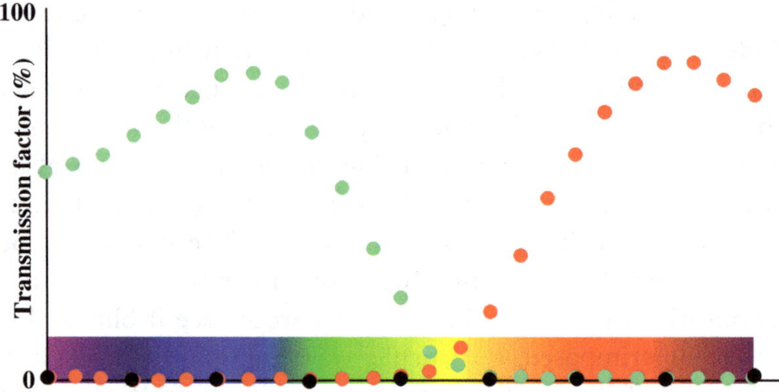

Figure 4.10   A combination of cyan and red filters give black. The combination shown here does give a very small intensity in the yellow region of the spectrum

If a filter were cleaved into two filters, such that the sum of their thicknesses equalled the thickness of the original filter, then their transmission factors, t_a and t_b would be related to the transmission factor of the un-cleaved filter, t_c. by $t_a t_b = t_c$, i.e. the splitting the filters would make no difference to their combined transmission factor. Pursuing this line of reasoning a little further, if two different filters were fragmented into small particles and then combined together in a random mixture of the fragments in the form of a sheet with thickness equal to the sum of the thicknesses of the original filters, then the transmission factor would equal that of the combined original un-fragmented sheets.

As a further example we consider the effect of the combined transmission through a cyan filter that lets through very little on the red side of green and a red filter that lets through very little on the blue side of yellow. The result, seen in Figure 4.10, is that very little light gets through the combined filters. With the addition colours as seen with overlapping lights, cyan + red gives white; with a subtractive colour combination cyan + red gives black.

4.5 Colour Printing

Many homes with either desktop or laptop computers will also have a printer and it would have been noticed that the colour cartridges provided are cyan, magenta and yellow and that the printer can provide a complete range of colours. This involves a subtractive colour process. It is similar to what occurred with coloured filters; each ink absorbs each wavelength to a different extent. The difference is that instead of the remaining radiation being transmitted, as for a filter, it is reflected backwards. In place of a transmission factor we now have to consider a *reflection factor* to describe what comes back from the inked surface. If green is required then a combination of cyan and yellow inks is deposited on the paper. The intimate mixture of the two inks behave like the intimate mixture of granulated filter material previously described and the reflectivity factor of the combined inks is the product of the reflectivity factors of the two inks if they were deposited alone. Figure 4.11 shows the effect of combining cyan and yellow inks to give green.

Cyan, yellow and magenta are known as *secondary colours* and a diagram showing subtractive combinations of these colours, similar to Figure 4.7 for primary colours, is shown in Figure 4.12. It will be seen that combinations of pairs of secondary colours gives the three primary colours — red, green and blue — and a combination of all three gives black. Most printers are four-colour printers with ink cartridges for cyan, yellow, magenta and black so for printing black type, or a black region in an image, only the black ink is used.

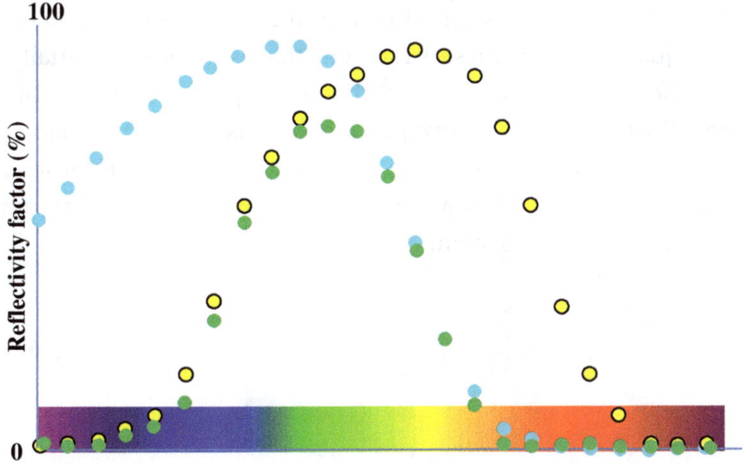

Figure 4.11   A combination of cyan and yellow inks gives green

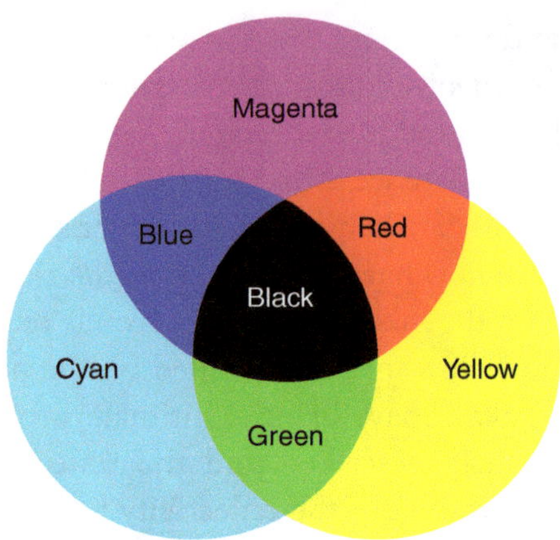

Figure 4.12   A combination diagram for secondary colours in subtractive printing

By varying the proportions of the mixture of the three secondary colours it is possible to reproduce all the colours in the chromaticity diagram, although many of them will be somewhat unsaturated. For example, by steadily increasing the amount of yellow relative to magenta in a two-ink combination it is possible to produce a wide range of colours from magenta through reddish-purple, red, orange and yellow. For subtle unsaturated colours it is usually necessary to use all three inks. It has previously been pointed out that it is impossible to reproduce on a computer screen or in print what is seen with coloured lights, the difference being ascribed to just the intensities of the light that is involved. Actually, there is even a difference between the way that a computer produces colour on its screen, which is by an additive process described for a television screen in Section 13.5, and the subtractive combination of colours produced by a printer. Nevertheless, what a printer produces is not too far removed from what is seen on the screen.

Chapter 5
The Visual System and Colour

Most individuals can distinguish the complete range of colour present in the CIE diagram although, sometimes, different individuals may describe the same distribution of wavelengths presented to them in different ways. For example, cyan may be described by one individual as a greenish-blue while another would say it was a bluish-green. This may reflect a slight difference in what they see, but both individuals could be described as having normal colour vision. Each of them would see a complete spectrum running from red to violet, but the spectra would be slightly distorted versions of each other. Here we first describe the characteristics of normal colour vision, with the caveat just given, then the different types of colour vision present in creatures other than hominids, and finally the various kinds of colour blindness that occur.

5.1 Rods and Scotopic Vision

It is a familiar visual experience that when going to bed at night and turning off the light the room seems extremely dark at first but after a few minutes the room seems much less dark, perhaps faintly illuminated by the low intensity of a street light percolating through the curtains. This adaptation to dark conditions and the ability to see under very low light conditions — *scotopic vision* — is due to the rods densely distributed all over the retina. There are about 20 rods to each cone in the retina — about 120 million rods to 6–7 million cones.

The rods contain a pigment, *rhodopsin*, which is very sensitive to light, under the influence of which it undergoes chemical changes. It is a purplish-red colour, because it most strongly absorbs light from the green to yellow part of the spectrum, and its name derives from Greek — *rhodon* (rose) and *opsis* (light). The reaction of a rod to light closely parallels the action of a physical device called an *image-intensifier* that is used to amplify the intensity of light in night-vision devices. The faint image is projected onto *photocathode*, a plate coated with a photoelectric material, such as an alkali metal, which releases an electron when it absorbs the energy of a photon. The single electron produced by a photon striking the plate then passes into a fine channel, a few nm in diameter, coated with a secondary electron emitter that releases several low-energy electrons when struck by a high-energy electron. The channel, about 0.5 mm long, has a potential difference of 1 kilovolt between its ends so the low-energy electrons are accelerated, become high-energy electrons and release more low energy electrons when they impact on the walls further along the tube. This process is repeated many times along the tube with the number of electrons increasing exponentially with distance travelled. A single photon striking the photocathode gives rise to many thousands of electrons that, when accelerated after they leave the tube, produce a bright spot on a fluorescent screen. In this way a faint image projected onto the photocathode becomes a bright image on the fluorescent screen. It has been shown that a single photon can activate a rhodopsin molecule and change it to a form where it transforms many thousands of a different protein molecule within the rod that, in their turn, activate other molecules and so on in a cascade effect — very like the image-intensifier. Eventually the electrical potential in the rod reaches the level at which a neurotransmitter is released towards either a horizontal cell or a bipolar cell. Several rods are connected to a single neuron — either horizontal cell or bipolar cell — and their combined effects again serve to amplify the signal that is passed on.

When rhodopsin is exposed to light it changes into an inactive form and is unable to respond to further illumination. Hence, in bright surroundings the rods become inoperative but when dark conditions are restored then the rhodopsin begins to reform. It takes several minutes before it completely recovers and this is the time it takes to adapt fully to dark conditions.

An interesting example of the importance of dark adaptation in a practical situation is that submarines on active duty at night will use red-light illumination within the vessel. This stimulates mainly the red cones so objects are seen in a monochromatic red. However, as we previously mentioned, the reason that rhodopsin is purplish-red is because it preferentially absorbs light in the green to yellow part of the spectrum — hence rhodopsin is virtually unaffected by red light. For this reason, dark adaptation from a red-illuminated environment takes only a short time so the submarine commander can more quickly observe the external night scene through his periscope.

5.2 Cones and Photopic Vision

Scotopic vision is essentially monochromatic and a scene viewed under those conditions is seen in shades of grey, although in some circumstances — and it may be a subjective phenomenon — there seems to be a tinge of blue superimposed on the grey. Under higher-intensity light conditions the rhodopsin in the cones becomes bleached and inactive and vision is then mediated through the cones. This is *photopic vision*, which gives visual images in full colour. Taking scotopic and photopic vision together, the eye can operate to produce images over an intensity range with a maximum-to-minimum intensity ratio of 100 million.

Although there are many fewer cones than rods, in the foveal region of the retina cones are very densely packed and greatly outnumber rods there. Hence, the resolution of photopic vision is very high in the centre of the field of view, although it falls off quite sharply with distance from the fovea. At the periphery of vision one is aware of the presence of objects but not what they are. Another feature of photopic vision is that it gives higher time-discrimination than scotopic vision. This is associated with a phenomenon known as *persistence of vision*, described more fully in Section 13.1. In hominids, which include humans, the cones are of three types, each of which responds differently to the range of wavelengths in the visual spectrum. The more they absorb the higher is the response to the light of that wavelength and the response curves all have a bell shape with peaks in different regions of the spectrum. The three kinds of cone are designated as L-type (L for long wavelength) peaking at about 570 nm, which is in the yellow region of the spectrum, M-type (M for medium wavelength) peaking at about 540 nm in the green part of the spectrum and S-type (S for short wavelength) peaking at about 430 nm in the blue to violet part of the spectrum. The response curves, scaled to give unit response at their peaks, are shown in Figure 5.1. Although the L-type cones do not give a peak response in the red part of the spectrum the cones are often referred to as being red cones, green cones and blue cones.

First we consider the response to light consisting of a single wavelength, say that corresponding to the dashed line in Figure 5.1 in the yellow part of the spectrum (shown as orange for clarity). The red cones would be most stimulated, the green cones less so, but still substantially stimulated, and the blue cones would give no response. In a small part of the visual field illuminated by this wavelength the relative response of the three types of cone would be interpreted in the visual cortex as that particular saturated yellow colour. Every wavelength gives a different mixture of the three responses and each mixture would be interpreted as the associated saturated spectral colour.

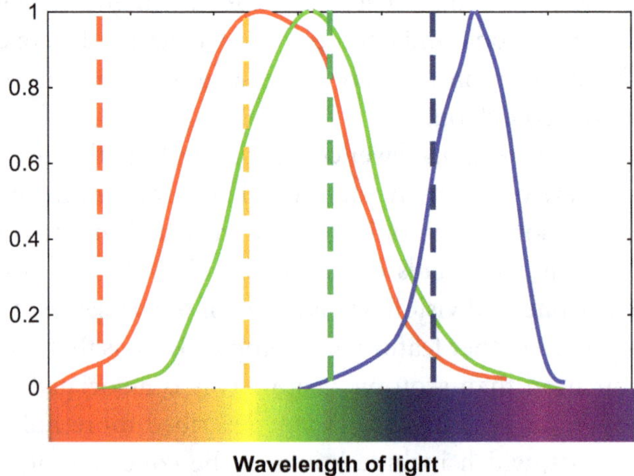

Figure 5.1   The relative sensitivity for each type of cone in the retina, each normalized to a maximum of unity

Now we consider what the effect would be for white light, which we will take as an equal mixture of all the spectral wavelengths. The response of each of the types of cone would then be proportional to the area under the curve for that type of cone and, on receiving that mixture of responses, the visual cortex would register the perception of white. From the curves the ratio of responses would be approximately red:green:blue = 1.0:0.75:0.5.

Next we consider the response of the different types of cone when simultaneously exposed to two wavelengths of light, corresponding to both the yellow dashed line and the blue dashed line in Figure 5.1. The responses to the individual lines are shown in Figure 5.2, together with the sum of the two responses that give the ratios red:green:blue = 1.00:0.77:0.53, very close to our approximate estimates for producing the colour perception of white. This demonstrates the way that the eye would perceive both an equal mixture of all visual wavelengths and also a mixture of two wavelengths corresponding to complementary colours, as white. We have assumed here that the response to a number of wavelengths is the sum of the responses taken separately but at not-too-intense light levels this seems to be true. Another assumption we have made here is that the yellow and blue lights have equal intensity. To achieve the perception of white with complementary colours, or the perception of a different colour from a mixture of two or more colours, often requires an unequal mixture of the components. For example, the wavelength corresponding to the red dashed line in Figure 5.1 gives the response ratios red : green : blue = 0.08 : 0.00 : 0.00, although the green response may be very small rather than zero. The green dashed line gives response ratios red : green : blue = 0.87 : 0.97 : 0.02. By adding eight of the red responses to the green responses and then normalizing to unit red response we have the resultant red : green : blue = 1.00 : 0.64 : 0.01, which

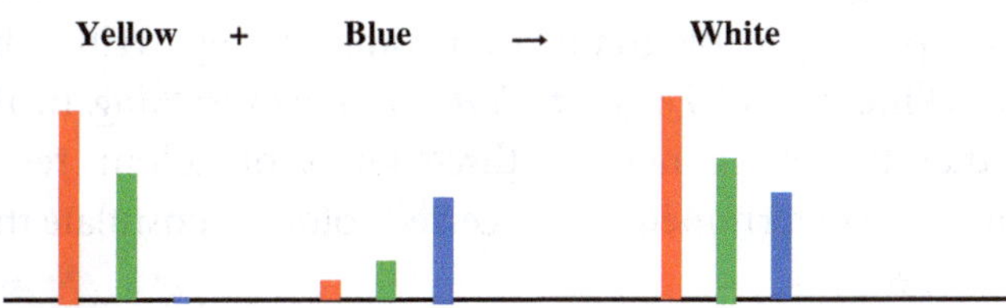

Figure 5.2   The sum of responses to a yellow wavelength and a blue wavelength gives the response for white

is very close to the response rations for the yellow dashed line –
red:green:blue = 1.00:0.64:0.00 – showing that a suitable mixture of red and
green can give yellow.

Now let us suppose that a particular mixture of spectral wavelengths
gives a relative red:green:blue response 2.87:2.45:1.00. Examining Figure
5.1 we find no spectral wavelength corresponding to those responses.
However, we may break up the responses as

$$2.87:2.47:1.00 = 2 \times (1.00:0.75:0.5) + (0.87:0.97:0.00).$$

The first bracketed mixture on the right-hand side corresponds to a
white light response and the second bracketed mixture corresponds to the
green dashed line in Figure 5.1. Hence the total response is equivalent to
an unsaturated spectral green. This example was chosen to be a simple one
but any combination of relative responses can be interpreted in this way.
Of course, this is not a mathematical exercise of any practical value; the
visual cortex is automatically doing the analysis and conveying the appropriate colour perception.

Not too much credence should be placed on the precise numerical
values used here in illustrating the way that the response curves for the
three types of cone can explain what is seen in colour mixing experiments.
Rather these examples should be taken as indications of the general way
that the response curves can explain what colour is seen.

5.3   The Young–Helmholtz Theory of Colour Vision

The first notable contribution to theories of colour vision was made by the
remarkable English physician and scientist, Thomas Young (Figure 3.5).
Despite his short life he made contributions over a vast range of subjects —
wave theory of light, vision processes, psychology, mechanics, language,
music and Egyptology. A biography of Thomas Young, written by Andrew
Robinson, is tellingly titled *The Last Man to Know Everything*. In 1802 Young
postulated that the eye contained three kinds of colour receptors, the
responses of which determined the perceived colour, a postulate that we now
know to be correct.

Young's idea was picked up and developed in 1850 by another
remarkable scientist, the German physician and physicist Hermann von

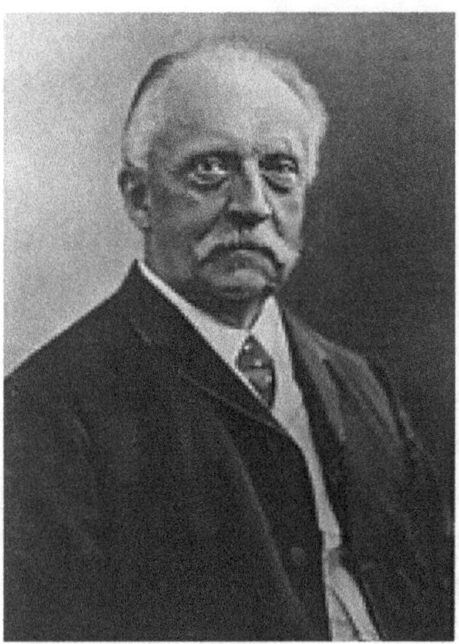

Figure 5.3   Hermann von Helmholtz

Helmholtz (1821–1894; Figure 5.3). The combined work of these two men, both grounded in the fields of medicine and physics, became known as the Young–Helmholtz theory of colour vision. It is basically the model for the way that colour is seen as described in the previous section. Helmholtz established the convention of describing the receptors as L, M and S (long, medium and short wavelengths). In this model the *relative* responses of the three kinds of receptor determine the perceived colour but the intensity of what is seen is determined by the pattern of the spike discharges to the brain. Because there are ON and OFF bipolar cells it is the relative response of these two kinds of neuron that determines the perception of intensity and not the rate of spike discharges to the visual cortex.

It is remarkable that it was not until 1956 that direct evidence was found for the existence of the three kinds of receptor. The Swedish–Finnish–Venezuelan physiologist Gunnar Svaetichin (1915–1981) examined fish retinae and found that they showed sensitivity to wavelengths grouped around the red, green and blue regions of the visual spectrum. Later research has been able to determine the detailed absorption curves at different wavelengths of individual photoreceptors. Although Figure 5.1 shows the response curves of the three receptors there are in fact small variations in the peaks and detailed shapes of the curves for different individuals — but this does not change the general description of the colour vision process that has been described.

5.4 The Hering Theory of Colour Vision

The Young–Helmholtz model suggests that the information from the three kinds of cone is individually fed into the visual cortex via the optic nerve and there it is processed to give a perceived colour and intensity corresponding to each part of the retina. This idea was challenged by the German physiologist, Ewald Hering (1834–1918; Figure 5.4) whose main area of research was on colour vision. He proposed an alternative model called the *opponent-process theory* in which information was pre-processed, in bipolar cells and ganglion cells before being passed along the optic nerve. In this model the information passed on was differences in the output from various types of cone. These differences are between red and green, yellow and blue and white and black, shown in Figure 5.5. The two pairs of colours are separated in the spectrum by other distinctive

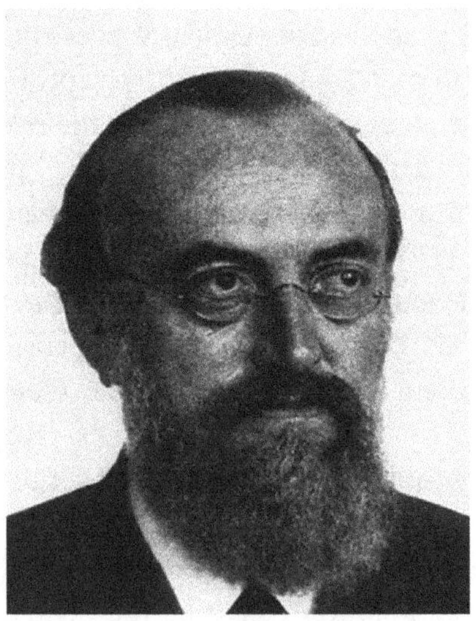

Figure 5.4   Ewald Hering

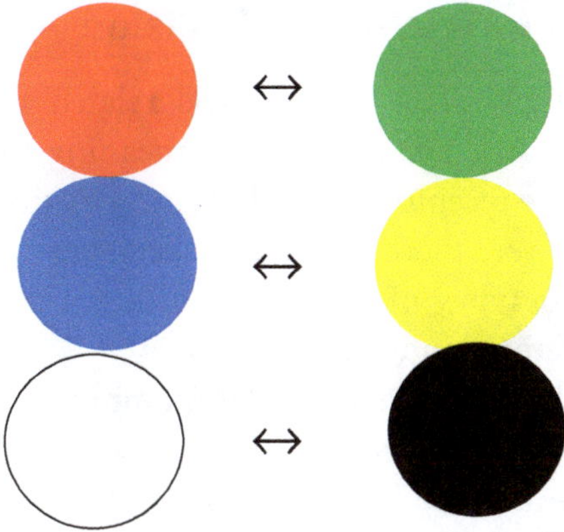

Figure 5.5   The opponent colours in Hering's opponent-process theory

colours; yellow is between red and green and green is between blue and yellow so they are distinctive pairs in the sense that there is no such colour as a yellowish-blue or a reddish-green. Finding the difference between red and green is simply a matter of comparing the responses from the L and M cones. The blue–yellow difference is found by comparing the combined responses of the L and M cones with that of the S cones. These comparisons are thought to be made in bipolar cells, and then passed on to ganglion cells. Ganglion cells fall into two main types, the first of which is *parvocellular*, which are small and comprise about 80 percent of all ganglion cells. They receive information from relatively few bipolar cells and many are attached to *midget bipolar cells* that, in their turn, are connected to single photoreceptors. The other type of ganglion cell, *magnocellular* or *P-cells*, are large and seem to be responsible for the majority of the processing of the colour information from the bipolar cells to a form that can be passed along the optic nerve — remember, it is only ganglion cells and some amacrine cells that give spike discharges, the only way to communicate with the visual cortex. Some P-cells handle the red-green information, others the blue–yellow information and a third type assesses the total amount of response of all the cones in a particular retinal region thus assessing the luminosity, or brightness, which is equivalent to a white–black comparison. Current evidence from physiological experiments seems to support the opponent-process theory.

5.5 Alternatives to Trichromatic Vision

Humans and most primates, i.e. animals related to humans such as monkeys and great apes, are *trichromats*, meaning that they have three different types of cone receptor from which information is conveyed to the visual cortex. However, there are some creatures that are *dichromats*, possessing only two types of cone, and others that are *tetrachromats*, possessing four different kinds of cone.

Among the dichromats are placental mammals, i.e. mammals giving live birth where the foetus is protected by a placenta — with the exception of most primates — and many New World monkeys. Dichromats do not see the full range of colour experienced by trichromats and those they do see can be matched by the outputs of two types of cone. It is estimated that each type of cone can pick up about 100 different gradations of colour so that with three cones there are about one million (100^3) different colours that can be distinguished. It is therefore likely that dichromats can distinguish about 10,000 (100^2) different colours.

It has been suggested by some researchers that dichromatic vision increases the ability to distinguish colours in dim light. The first mammals came into existence at a time when dinosaurs dominated the Earth. Mammals survived by virtue of their small size and the fact that they were nocturnal, so avoiding contact with dinosaurs. For these early mammals dichromacy would have had survival value but for hominids, which developed much later and adopted a diurnal lifestyle, the evolution of trichromatic vision was clearly an advantage.

The development of different kinds of colour vision would, like other characteristic of living organisms, have been driven by the principles of Darwinian evolution. There are creatures, such as some birds, insects, fish and reptiles, which are tetrachromats, meaning that they have four different types of cone. The range of the spectrum that can be seen by tetrachromats often extends into the ultraviolet region, down to about 300 nm. This increased range of colour perception is useful to pollinating insects as it enables them better to recognise different flowering plants, some of which emit ultraviolet radiation. Again, birds with a much greater visual acuity due to a higher density of cones in the fovea, needed when viewing the ground from a great height, and much greater colour discrimination,

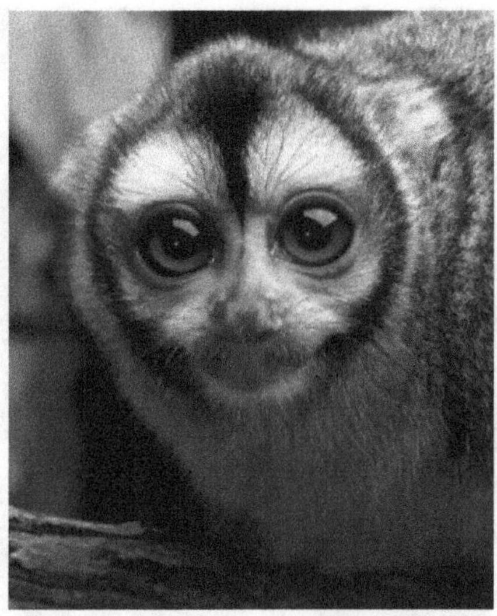

Figure 5.6   The owl monkey. Large eyes and monochromatic vision are an advantage for a nocturnal creature

would be able to resolve potential prey and also to see them in situations where humans could not see them because, with trichromatic vision, they would be effectively camouflaged, merging with their backgrounds.

There are some animals that are monochromats, i.e. they only have one type of cone and see the world in shades of grey from black to white. Creatures with this characteristic include sea mammals and the owl monkey, a South American nocturnal monkey (Figure 5.6). Because they only have the one kind of cone they can probably only distinguish about 100 gradations of colour, meaning that if presented with a complete spectrum, with a uniform intensity over the spectral range, they would be able to distinguish about 100 different shades of grey. However, an intense light of one wavelength might give the same effect as a lower intensity light of another colour. Just as dichromatics are more efficient then trichromats in distinguishing colour gradations at very low light conditions, the monochromats may be even more efficient in this respect. For the nocturnal owl monkey and sea mammals hunting in dim conditions in the depths of the oceans, this type of vision may be an advantage.

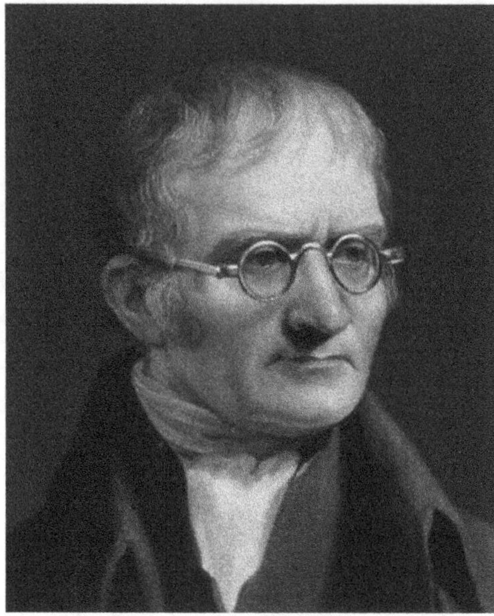

Figure 5.7   John Dalton

5.6 Colour Blindness

The first person to describe colour blindness in a scientific way was the eminent British scientist, John Dalton (1766–1844; Figure 5.7) who, together with his older brother, suffered from red–green colour blindness in which that range of the spectrum all appeared as different shades of brown or yellowish brown. In 1798, he described the phenomenon in a book, *Extraordinary Facts Relating to the Vision of Colours,* and concluded that the problem was due to a blue colouration of the vitreous humour, the jelly-like substance that fills the eyeball. Now we know that this explanation is untrue and the actual cause of this and other kinds of colour blindness is due to abnormality in the cones. In recognition of John Dalton's contribution in recognizing and describing red–green colour blindness this condition is commonly referred to as *Daltonism.*

Some forms of colour blindness are genetic in origin and the frequency of occurrence is gender related. All humans have 23 pairs of chromosomes each of which consists of a large number of genes, strands of deoxyribonucleic acid (DNA), which control specific characteristics of the individual. One chromosome of each pair is provided by the father and the other by the mother. In each chromosome there will be a gene corresponding to some characteristic. If they both relate to the individual having, say, brown eyes or blue eyes then the eyes will be, respectively, brown or blue. However, if one gene indicates brown and the other blue then the individual's eyes will be brown; The brown-eye gene is *dominant* and the blue-eye gene is *recessive,* So it is with other characteristics. For 22 chromosome pairs it would be impossible to tell the gender of the individual from the contained genes. For the 23rd pair the chromosomes can be of two distinct types, X or Y; a female will have two X chromosomes and a male one X and one Y. When an offspring is produced the female can only provide an X chromosome and the sex of the new individual is controlled by which kind of chromosome, X or Y, the male provides. When Henry VIII disposed of some of his wives because they did not provide male heirs he was unaware that the fault was his.

The X chromosome contains some genes that control the colour pigments in the cones, although some other chromosomes also contain genes that influence the pigments. For a male, if the X chromosome is faulty in that respect then some form of colour blindness will result. However, even if one of the X-chromosomes is faulty in a female, if the other one is normal then it will control pigment production and there will be no colour blindness — although the faulty gene may be passed on to give colour blindness in future generations. The good gene is dominant and the bad gene recessive. Because of this extra protection for the female — both X-chromosome genes have to be faulty for colour blindness to occur — colour blindness is more common in males than females. As an example, if a faulty gene is present at the 10% level in the X-chromosome of a population then 10% of all males will have the associated colour blindness. However, for a female to have that form of colour blindness the genes in *both* X-chromosomes would have to be faulty and there is only a 1% probability for that to happen.

There are a number of different reasons for colour blindness to occur. These are:

Cones of one or more types do not form or do not function.
Cones all form but in one or more the pigments are abnormal.
Damage occurs in the retina or in the brain.

We now discuss the possible forms of colour blindness due to the first two of these reasons; the effect of trauma in some part of the visual mechanism is very variable and difficult to describe in a systematic way.

5.6.1 Missing cones

Here we consider the effect of one or more types of cone being absent. Missing red cones lead to a condition called *protanopia*. As we can see from Figure 5.1 there is no response, or very little, of the green and blue cones at the extreme red end of the visible spectrum and an object emitting a near spectral red in that region would seem to be black, or nearly so. An object emitting wavelengths in the green to red part of the spectrum is getting very little response from the blue cones and hence it is difficult to distinguish between red and green since, with no red cones, there is virtually only a green response over the whole range. The effect of protanopia is illustrated in Figure 5.8 which compares the spectrum seen by someone with normal colour vision with that seen by someone suffering from this form of colour blindness. In addition to the dominant red–green distinction problem there are also difficulties in the green–blue part of the spectrum and magenta would look like blue since the red part of the emission from the object would not be recorded.

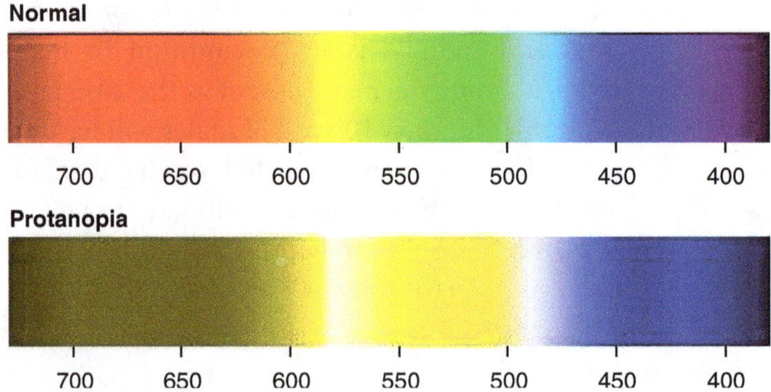

Figure 5.8   A comparison of the visual spectrum seen normally and by someone with protanopia

If the green cone is absent then the condition is known as *deuteranopia*. The effect of this on the perceived spectrum is shown in Figure 5.9. Again there is an inability to distinguish red and green and the resolution of different colours throughout the spectrum is seen to be very poor. As for protanopia the frequency of this form of colour blindness is gender-dependent and occurs in males at about the 1% level.

The final type of one-cone-loss colour blindness is *tritanopia,* where the blue cones are missing. Unlike protanopia and deuteranopia it is not dependent on genes in the X-chromosome and hence is not gender-dependent. Figure 5.10 shows the effect on the perceived spectrum and it

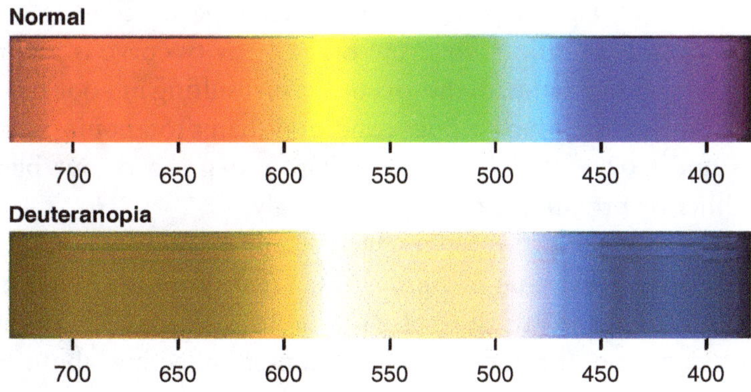

Figure 5.9   The effect of deuteranopia on the perceived spectrum

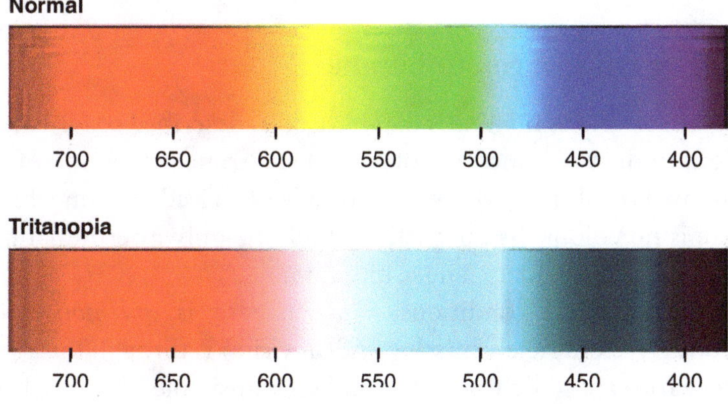

Figure 5.10   The appearance of the spectrum for someone with tritanopia

is seen to affect all but the red end of the spectrum. Colour perception at the blue end of the spectrum is dependent on the relative responses of the red and green cones, both of which are small. The blue end of the spectrum is diffused with green and in the region of yellow and orange a pinkish hue is seen. Magenta appears to be red since the blue component is not recorded.

5.6.2 Malfunctioning cones

Sometimes all three types of cone are present but one of the three pigments has an anomalous spectral sensitivity. There are three passible types of *anomalous trichromacy* depending on which type of cone is affected. *Protanomaly* is a condition when the red sensitivity curve is anomalous and has a greater overlap with the green curve, resulting in poor red–green discrimination. It is a much milder condition than protanopia. About 1% of males and 0.02% of women suffer from red–green colour blindness caused either by protanopia or by protanomaly.

Of similar effect to protanomaly is *deuteranomaly*, where it is the green sensitivity curve that is anomalous, again giving a greater overlap with the red curve and giving similar poor red–green discrimination. It is the most common form of colour blindness, affecting about 5% of European males. Anomalous blue cone pigment sensitivity gives the rare condition, *tritanomaly*. Its effect is similar to that of tritanopia but is less severe.

5.6.3 Other types of colour blindness

All the types of colour blindness that have been described so far have given distortions in the perception of colour but still some perception of colour. There are two conditions where the world is perceived as monochromatic and there is no colour discrimination at all; the only discrimination is in intensity, like seeing a black-and-white film.

The first of these conditions, which is rare, is *rod monochromacy*, where cones are completely missing and all vision is through the agency of rods. Since rods are so light sensitive and rhodopsin bleaches and becomes inactive in medium-to-strong light, sufferers from this condition must wear dark glasses to reduce the intensity of what they see down to the level where rods can operate effectively. The quality of vision is very poor and is usually accompanied by oscillations of the eye known as *nystagmus.*

The second condition, *cone monochromacy,* is quite rare and can result from having two of the three types of cone absent. The remaining cone type will give vision under the same general conditions of illumination as for normal vision — unlike rod monochromacy — but since there is only one colour pigment involved it is not possible to distinguish colours. All colours will appear the same but with different intensities — rather like as seen by a monochromat. If only the green cones are present then it would be impossible to distinguish a very dark green from a very bright blue, since they would both give the same green-cone response.

Chapter 6

Perceived Colour
and Environment

It might be thought that the colour, saturation and intensity perceived due to the light falling on any small region of the retina, of a size that could just be resolved, would depend only on the responses of the three types of cone in that region and on nothing else. However, that is not the case and the perception of colour and saturation in any small region depends on the stimulation of other parts of the retina, even those quite far from the region of interest. Another factor affecting what is seen at any instant is what the eye has been exposed to in the past. We now describe some of these effects.

6.1 Background Effects

The effect of background on perceived saturation, where only different saturations of one colour are used, is illustrated in Figure 6.1(a). All the colours used are different saturations of a particular red and the two small squares are similar. It is strikingly clear that the small square in the darker background is perceived to be less saturated than the square seen against the lighter background. The two small squares are large enough to be well resolved so it is evident that the colour of surrounding regions is affecting the perception of their saturation. The perceived difference of saturation is less discernible in Figure 6.1(b) when the background is reduced to a

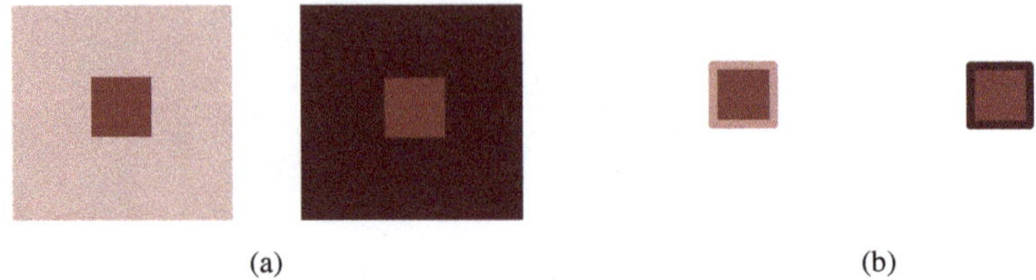

(a)   (b)

Figure 6.1   (a) A medium-saturation dark red square superimposed on larger squares of lesser and greater saturation. (b) The same with backgrounds reduced to narrow rims

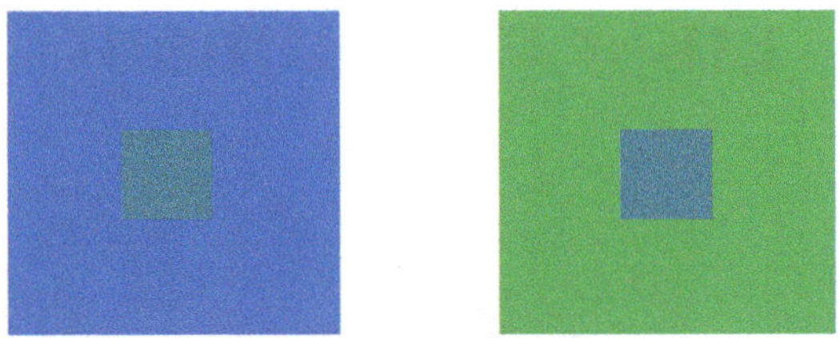

Figure 6.2   A small cyan square superimposed on blue and green backrounds

thin strip of colour surrounding the small square. This illustrates that the saturation of more distant regions is affecting the perception of the small square, not just the very close surroundings. It seems that the less saturated background is enhancing the perceived saturation of the small square while the more saturated background is reducing the perceived saturation.

Similar effects, but involving perceived colour, can be seen when the backgrounds are different in colour from the small squares. In Figure 6.2, small similar cyan squares are superimposed on blue and green backgrounds. On the blue background the perception of cyan veres towards green while on the green background the perception veres towards blue.

In both the cases illustrated in Figures 6.1 and 6.2 we may see a tendency to what we may describe as 'repulsion'. When the saturation of the background is less that that of the object being viewed, then the perceived saturation of the object colour is greater than its true saturation; there is an enhancement in the perceived difference in saturation of object and background. The converse is also true so that a greater saturation of the background colour leads to a perceived lower saturation of the object colour, again enhancing the apparent difference of saturation between object and background. For Figure 6.2 with a blue backround the small square is greener and so the perceived colour is pushed further towards green. Similarly, with a green background the square is bluer so the perceived colour of the small square is pushed further towards blue.

The repulsion principle can also operate in a black-and white situation. In Figure 6.3 the grey in the small square is intermediate between the greys of the backgrounds and is seen as lighter on the darker backround and darker on the lighter background.

In all the cases considered so far, the coloration of the small square has been intermediate between that of the backgrounds, approximately what would result from some mix of the backgrounds — i.e. mixing background colours green and blue would give cyan. However, this is not a necessary condition for the small squares to be perceived as different. In Figure 6.4, a light-brown square is shown agains dull-orange and dark blue backgrounds and a mixture of the two background colours would not give brown. Against the dark blue the brown square seems less saturated. In this case the distinction between the colours of the backgrounds and the small squares is their relative brightness, with those of the backgrounds straddling that of the small squares.

Figure 6.3   Similar small grey squares on lighter and darker grey backgrounds.

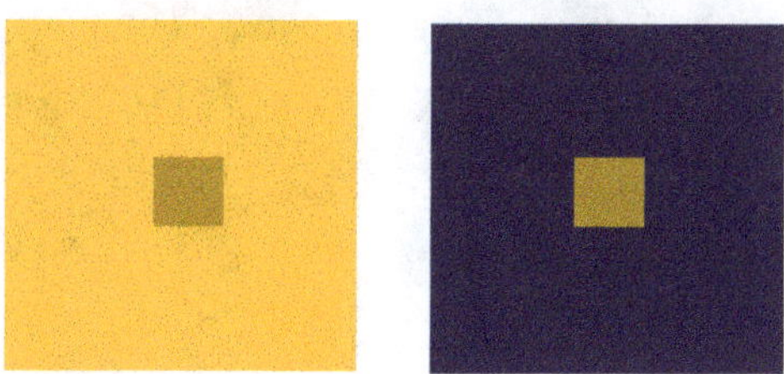

Figure 6.4   A light-brown square seen against dull orange and dark blue backgrounds

6.2 Colour Constancy

Imagine that you and a friend are dining out in an expensive restaurant, with artistic décor and soft candlelight as the primary means of illumination. Being of a scientific bent you happen to have a portable spectrometer in your pocket and pointing it at the candle flame you see that the wavelengths emitted are strongly concentrated in the yellow part of the spectrum. You suspect that the restaurant is meticulous in laundering its white tablecloths and, since a white object reflects back all incident wavelengths equally, the tablecloth should look yellow. You check this with your spectrometer and, sure enough, the light coming from the tablecloth is just a less intense version of what was previously seen for the candle flame.

After a short time, with spectrometer measurements out of mind, you realise that the tablecloth looks white, not yellow. Indeed, all the colours you see in the restaurant seem little affected by the yellow illumination and are much as you expect them to be. What you are experiencing is the phenomenon of *colour constancy* in which if a scene is illuminated by other than white light we compensate for the colour of the overall illumination and see colours more-or-less as they would appear under white-light illumination.

An example of colour constancy is shown in Figure 6.5. The snow scene on the left-hand side is seen on the right hand side through a pale-red filter. We still judge the snow to be white and the trees to be bluish-green and the sky to be blue. The perception of colour constancy in this case is somewhat weakened by having the original scene and the surrounding white of the

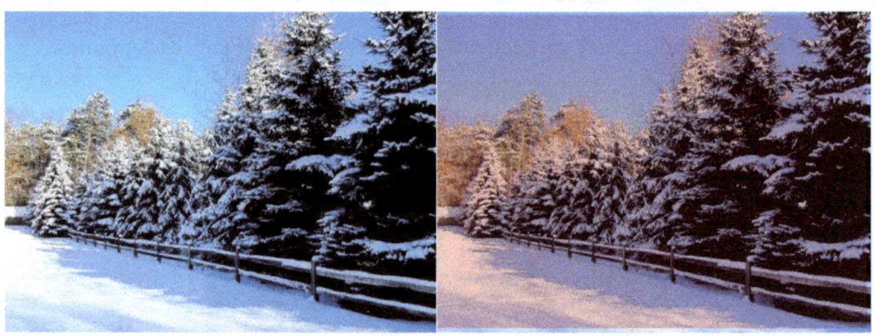

Figure 6.5　A snow scene in white light and seen through a red filter

page in sight. Looking at the right-hand image in isolation for a few minutes — preferably surrounding it with a black surround, or looking at it through a tube made by putting two hands together, so that just the reddened image shows — strengthens the colour constancy effect.

The colour constancy effect is seen most strongly if a filter of some pale colour, say pale green, is held close to one's eyes so that the whole scene ahead is seen through the filter. A white object is seen as white, yet if the filter is now placed close to that white object it is clearly seen through the filter as green. The light entering the eye in both cases has the same chromatic content.

Colour constancy does not operate if the illumination is either monochromatic or contains a very narrow band of wavelengths. Some cities and towns use low pressure sodium lamps to light their streets at night. The light is an almost monochromatic yellow and it is impossible to distinguish colours; since only yellow light is falling on objects, which is all they can reflect back so they all appear to be yellow of various shades from bright yellow to black.

Colour constancy can be a useful phenomenon for some types of creature. Thus diurnal animals will be able to distinguish colours correctly in the full light of day or at sunset when light becomes reddish. For fish it is a useful attribute since seawater in particular acts as a strong filter for sunlight and the chromatic illumination in the sea will change with depth. Assessing the correct colour of another fish may help to determine whether it is predator or prey.

6.3 Colour, Intensity and Saturation

In describing colours, terms are often used that are not part of the spectral range plus magenta. One such colour is grey, which we have recognized as dark white, but there are others that usually refer to normal standard spectral colours but at a low intensity. For example, brown is just a very dark orange; this is illustrated in Figure 6.6 that shows a gradual change in the intensity from what is clearly orange at the left-hand end to what we would call brown at the right-hand end.

There is a lecture demonstration with coloured lights that shows in spectacular fashion the relationship between orange and brown. First a

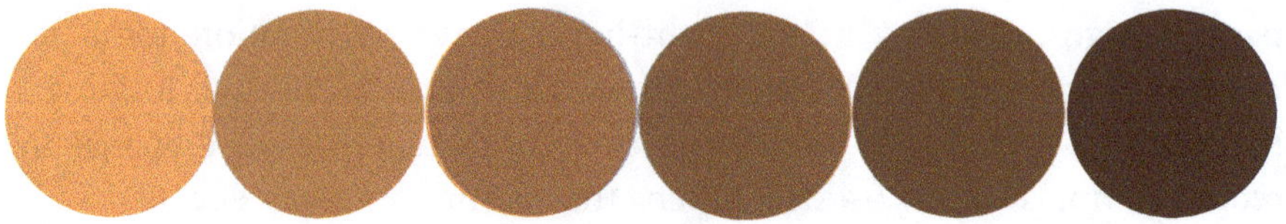

Figure 6.6   A gradual change in the intensity of orange to brown at low intensity

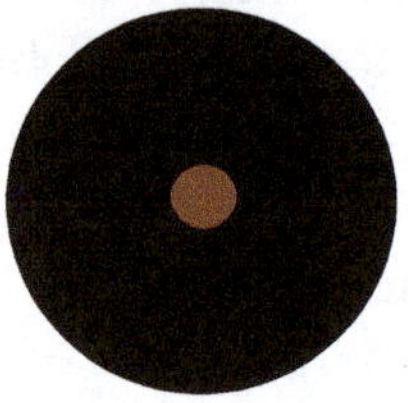

Figure 6.7   A brown circles with black surround

low intensity orange circle is projected onto a screen in a darkened room. It is seen clearly and unambiguously as orange. Then, with another projector a low intensity white surround is projected round the orange circle. The intensity of the surround is slowly increased and by the time the surround is an intense white the orange circle has turned into a deep chocolate brown. The centre of the field of view has not changed but the perception of it has changed significantly.

While we cannot reproduce such an experiment on a printed page we can reproduce the essence of what it shows. To do this we need the paper tube, the construction of which was described in Section 4.1. With Figure 6.7 strongly illuminated, look at the brown circle with the black surround through the tube so that in the field of view there is only the brown circle and black. The brown circle will look distinctly orange–brown. Without the tube the dominant ambient lighting is white — it is like the light-projection experiment with the white surround and the small circle is brown. When looking through the tube it is like the centre circle being in the dark, so the small circle will take on a more orange hue.

The everyday language of colour in the world of art and design describes colours with various adjectives and special names that correspond to different shades, degrees of saturation and intensity. In Figure 6.8 there is shown a collection of 20 varieties of red. Some, when seen at some

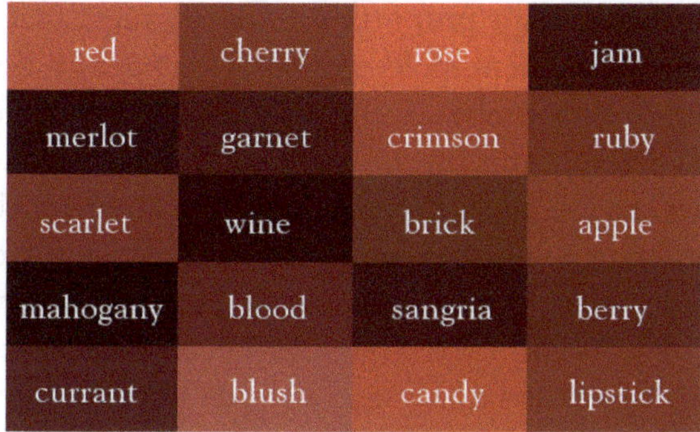

Figure 6.8   Twenty varieties of red

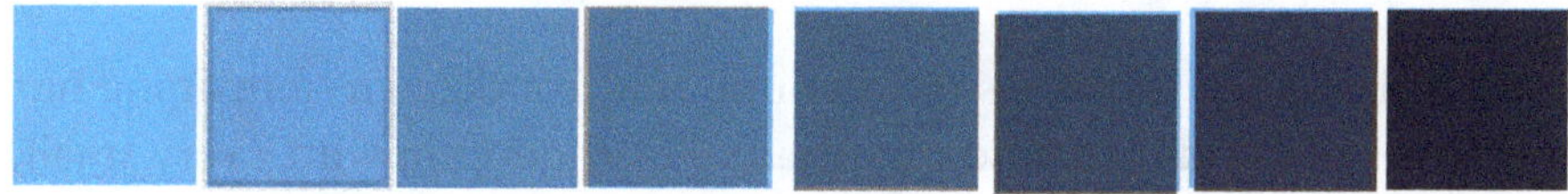

Figure 6.9   The progression from sky blue to navy blue

distance apart, are indistinguishable — for example, jam and merlot — but when placed side-by-side they are seen to be slightly different. The same kind of diagram could be produced for any other of the named colours of the spectrum — pea green, Lincoln green, emerald green, olive green and many others greens for example. To illustrate this Figure 6.9 starts with what would be called *sky blue* on the left and by successive darkening it becomes *navy blue*, a colour seen almost as black, on the right.

6.4 The Decay and Recovery of Pigments

When visual pigments are exposed to light they undergo a chemical transformation that, after several stages of neuron processing, generates part of the visual signal. In the transformed state they become inactive — that we can consider as in a state of decay —but immediately start to regenerate themselves back into the active state, regardless of whether or not the exposure to light is continuing. Here we are going to do some very simple mathematics. We take the total amount of pigment, be it active or inactive, as one unit and the proportion of the pigment that is active as p. Then the number of pigment molecules decaying per unit time is going to be proportional to the number in the active state, p, and the intensity of the light, I. We represent this rate of decay as $R_D = d \times I \times p$, where d is a constant that we call the *decay constant*. Now the rate at which the decayed molecules regenerate will just be proportional to the number of decayed molecules, $1 - p$, and we represent the rate of regeneration as $R_R = r \times (1 - p)$, where the constant r is the *regeneration constant*. Once the proportion of pigment has settled down into a steady state the rate of regeneration must equal the rate of decay so that

or
$$r(1-p) = dIp \qquad p = \frac{r}{r+dI}.$$

The larger is I the less is the amount of active pigment remaining but the values of r and d are also important. For rhodopsin with I very small, corresponding to dark conditions, there is a large value of p but p quickly falls with increasing I. In an intermediate stage both rods and cones are active, a state of what is known as *mesopic vision,* which operates in light conditions such as those of a well-lit night-time city street.

The equations governing the level of active rhodopsin from the time it is first exposed to light can be solved and some schematic, but typical, results are shown in Figure 6.10. These are for

Scotopic vision: $r = 0.1$ second^{-1}, $d \times I = 0.01$ second^{-1}
Mesopic vision: $r = 0.1$ second^{-1}, $d \times I = 0.1$ second^{-1}
Photopic vision: $r = 0.1$ second^{-1}, $d \times I = 5.0$ second^{-1}

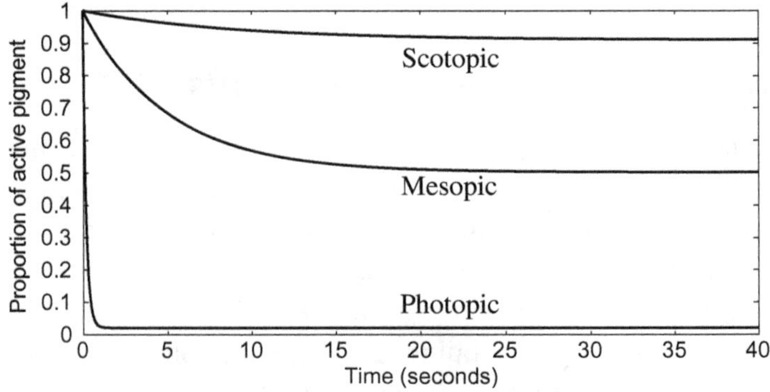

Figure 6.10   Some schematic curves for rhodopsin decay

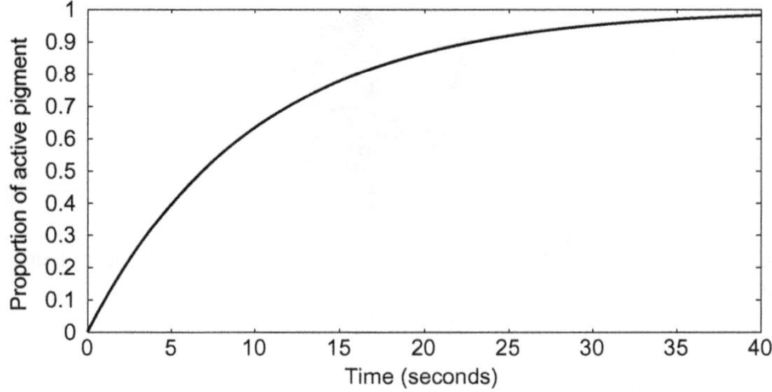

Figure 6.11   A schematic regeneration curve for rhodopsin

For very intense illumination ($d \times I = 5.0$) it is seen that the rhodopsin decays quickly and almost completely.

Using the same model we can look at the regeneration of rhodopsin once dark conditions are restored. Starting with $p = 0$ and with $r = 0.1$ and $d \times I = 0$ the regeneration curve is shown in Figure 6.11.

What we have illustrated for rhodopsin applies equally to the pigments in cones, although the various constants of proportionality are very different.

6.5 Afterimages

If the eye is exposed to a bright source of light under the conditions for photopic vision then the pigment levels in the cones will fall to an extent that depends on the intensity and duration of the illumination. If, for example, the intense light was predominantly red then the level of red pigment would fall greatly, the green pigment less so and the blue pigment would be hardly affected. This can be demonstrated by the following experiment. Strongly illuminate the red circle in Figure 6.12 and stare fixedly at it for about 30 seconds. The first thing you notice as you stare at it is that with time the red circle seems to become less saturated. Although the circle is red it is not completely saturated so the green and blue cones are also activated. However, with time the red pigment is being decreased more than the green and blue, so the red response is diminished more than the green and blue responses. The net result of this is to give the perception

Figure 6.12   Fixating on the red circle causes preferential decay of the red pigment in a portion of the retina

Figure 6.13   A yellow circle giving a blue afterimage

of a less saturated red. Next, if you transfer your gaze to the white space to the right of the red circle you will see a cyan circle. There is less red pigment in a circular region of the retina so that in that region the green and blue pigments dominate and you see an *afterimage*, a cyan circle — the complementary colour to red — in a position corresponding to the affected region of the retina.

The principle that the afterimage has the complementary colour to that of the object that has been viewed can be confirmed by repeating the experiment with the yellow circle shown in Figure 6.13. Again the perceived saturation of the yellow circle is seen to fall and the afterimage is blue, the complementary colour to yellow.

6.6 Flicker Colour

A German physicist and experimental psychologist, Gustav Fechner (1801–1887) and Hermann von Helmholtz found that if the eye was exposed to a black and white flicker then sometimes faint colours could be seen. The colour depends on the frequency of the flicker, the relative duration of exposure and non-exposure, and also on the individual viewing the effect, since not all individuals see precisely the same colours. This phenomenon can be explained by the decay and recovery characteristics of the cone pigments as described in Section 6.4. During exposure both decay and regeneration are taking place but during the period of non-exposure only regeneration is taking place and the concentration of pigment increases. Hence there is a fluctuating amount of pigment in the cones, with a certain average, but if the flicker rate is fast enough then the cones will effectively just have the sensitivity appropriate to the average concentration.

Figure 6.14 shows the simulated effect on three pigments where repeatedly there are exposures to light for 0.05 seconds followed by darkness for 0.1 second. The constants used were:

$$\text{Red } r = 0.1, \quad d \times I = 0.1;$$
$$\text{Green } r = 0.1, \quad d \times I = 0.15;$$
$$\text{Blue } r = 0.15, \quad d \times I = 0.1;$$

The fluctuation in the concentrations of the pigments is not evident, although it is there, and the colour seen would be a very unsaturated bluish-magenta.

A demonstration of this effect was devised by Charles Benham (1860–1929) a British journalist and amateur scientist who invented *Benham's top*. This is a disk, as shown in Figure 6.15(a) that, spun on an axis through its centre like a top, shows various colours in circular bands. An alternative disk for showing the effect is given in Figure 6.15(b). An effective

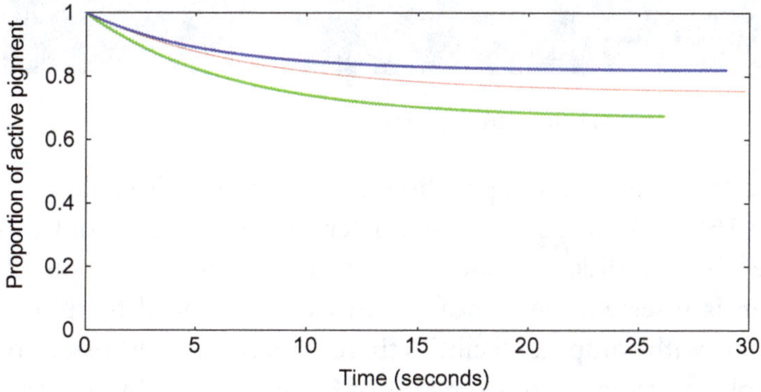

Figure 6.14   Concentrations of pigments for a modelled black-and-white flicker

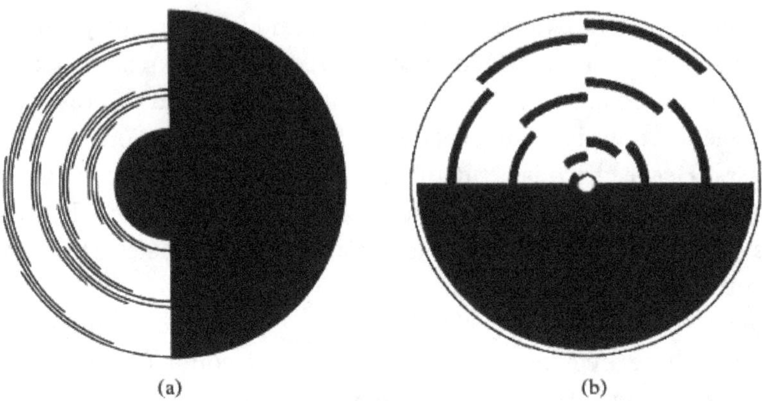

(a)   (b)

Figure 6.15   (a) Benham's disk. (b) An alternative version of the disk

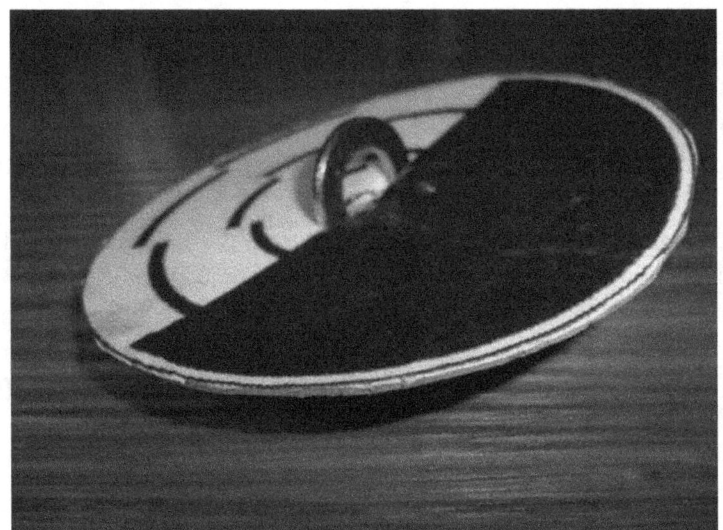

Figure 6.16   A homemade Benham's top

homemade version of the top is shown in Figure 6.16. An enlarged copy of
Figure 6.15(b), about 10 cm in diameter, is pasted onto stout cardboard
and the circular disk cut out. Then a coin or washer, about 2 cm in
diameter, is inserted, the top of which can be gripped to spin the disk.
For readers with computer facilities there are also many websites that show
flicker colours using various versions of Benham's disk, but they are not as
clear as those obtained with the top shown in Figure 6.16.

Chapter 7
Painting and Painting Pigments

In this chapter and the next, we are going to describe the development of *pigments*, mostly used in an artistic context and *dyes*, mostly used for colouring textiles or other everyday objects. Pigments are usually inorganic materials, very often derived from naturally-occurring minerals and are in the form of a suspension of fine particles in a fluid in which they are insoluble. By contrast a dye is either liquid in form or is disolved in some solvent in which it is used and it is usually an organic compound. It is sometimes possible to convert a dye to a pigment by precipitating a soluble dye by adding a metallic salt; the resultant is then called a *lake pigment* — for example, *crimson lake*.

7.1 Cave Paintings

There are examples of cave paintings from all over the world, many of which date back to 30,000 to 40,000 years. The oldest cave painting known is a red disk from El Castillo in northern Spain, with an estimated age of 40,800 years. Related to cave paintings are rock paintings by aboriginal artists in Australia. The oldest of these go back 28,000 years; because of the dry desert climate in which these paintings were produced they have survived in the open air. We cannot know whether all these paintings reflected some inherent desire by our species, *Homo sapiens*, for artistic expression or whether the depiction of hunting scenes and the game being hunted

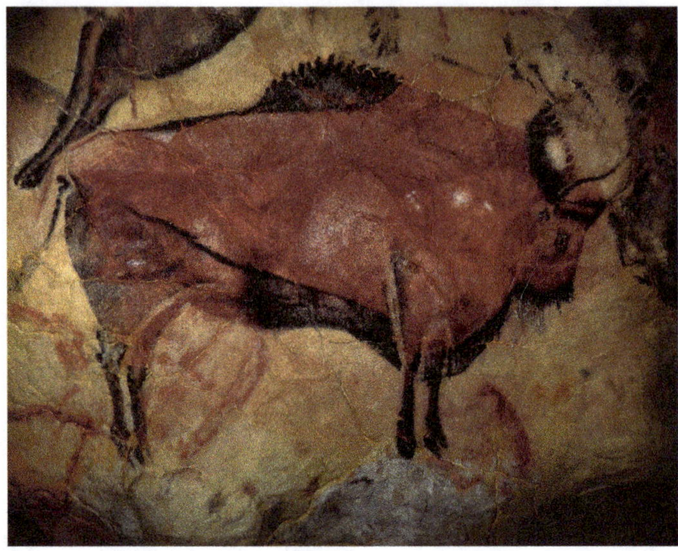

Figure 7.1   Cave painting from the Cave of Altamira in Northern Spain

(Figure 7.1) had some ceremonial, possibly religious, significance. Another common form of cave decoration, again found throughout the world, is of producing outlines of human hands, made by blowing a suspension of pigment in human saliva over a hand held against the cave wall (Figure 7.2). The occurrence of cave paintings in widely separated locations suggests either that worldwide communications, perhaps by slow osmosis from one region to a neighbouring one over thousands of years, was better than might be expected or that artistic expression, for whatever reason, is an inevitable accompaniment to human existence and takes similar forms wherever it occurs.

While the use of pigments in cave paintings has been traced back to 40,000 years or so, there is evidence for the use of pigments a long time before then. Figure 7.3 shows a chunk of the mineral limonite, used as a yellow pigment, from the Twin Rivers region of Zambia. It is one of a number of similar pieces of the mineral that have been ground flat on one face and it is thought that they might have been used by early man, rather like a piece of chalk, to ornament their bodies. They have been dated as 250,000 years old, a time close to the beginning of *Homo sapiens* and close to the time when Neanderthal people appeared in Europe.

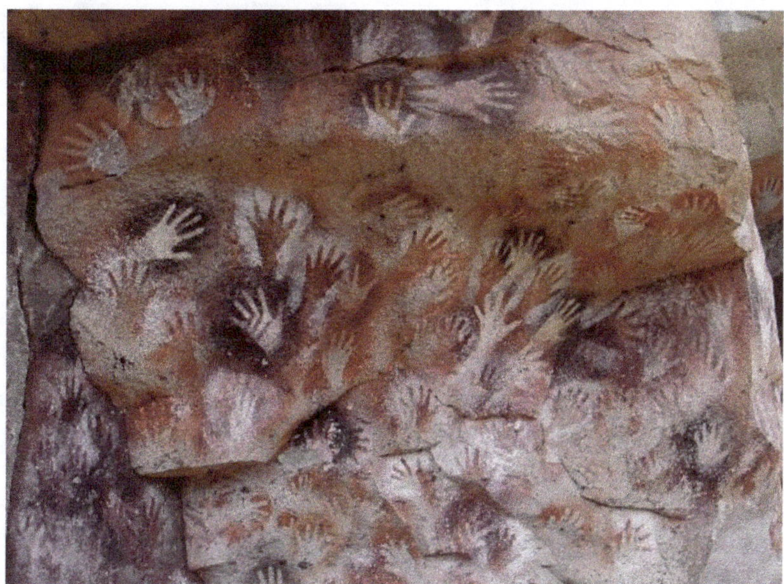

Figure 7.2   Outlines of hands from the Cueva de las Manos, Santa Cruz province, Argentina

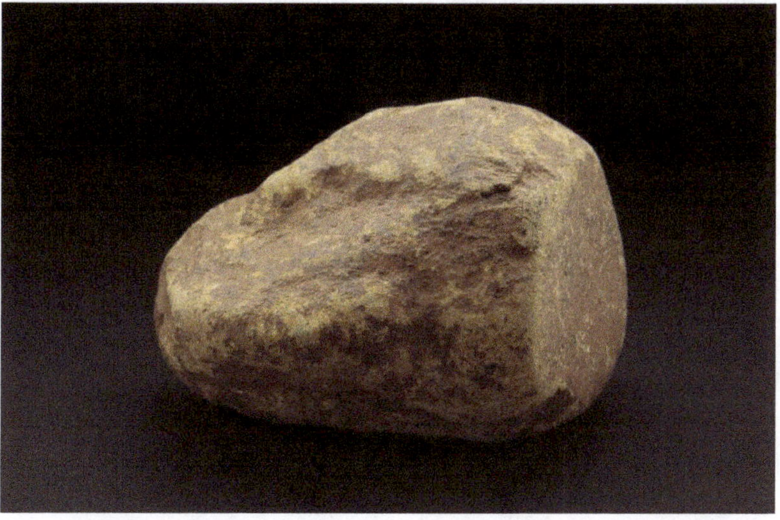

Figure 7.3   Limonite ground flat on one face from Twin Rivers, Zambia (Chip Clark, Smithsonian Institute)

The pigments used in cave paintings are all at the yellow to red end of the spectrum plus black and white. The yellow to red pigments are usually *ochre,* a generic name for a family of pigments that are mixture of clay and iron hydroxides or iron oxides. These include:

Yellow ochre	(limonite; $FeO(OH)nH_2O$) is a hydrated iron hydroxide.
Brown ochre	(goethite: $FeO(OH)$) is an iron oxyhydroxide.
Red Ochre	(haematite,: Fe_2O_3) an iron oxide.
Purple ochre	haematite with a larger particle size.
Sienna	limonite plus a small amount of manganese oxide (MnO), which gives a darker yellow.
Umber	limonite with more than 5% of manganese oxide that makes it dark brown.

If sienna and umber are heated then some of the limonite is dehydrated and converted to haematite. This imparts a more reddish tinge to the pigments giving rise to *burnt sienna* and *burnt umber,* common colours in the modern artist's palette.

White pigment was usually *kaolin,* also known as *china clay.* It is a soft white mineral and prehistoric artists found that by heating kaolin they could make it harder, and hence more durable, and at the same time increase its whiteness. Black pigments were usually some form of manganese oxide that could be *groutite,* which is black, *hausmannite,* which is very dark brown or *manganosite,* which varies from grey to black in colour. These pigments were crushed into a fine powder and then mixed with a *binder* — water, saliva or animal fat. They were then applied in various ways, by finger, feathers or a primitive brush made from horse-hair.

It must not be thought that mineral pigments are some rather primitive form of colouring material with their use restricted to prehistoric times. Although new synthetic colouring agents are available, mineral pigments still have their uses today.

7.2 Art Pigments Used in Ancient Egypt

The ancient Egyptian civilization left behind a great legacy of art in many forms — in great sculptural works and, of particular interest in the

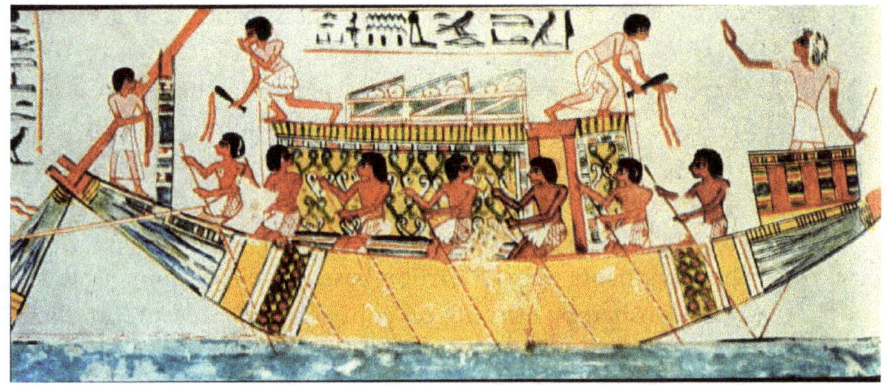

Figure 7.4   An Egyptian painting from 1450 BCE

consideration of colour, numerous wall paintings, particularly within tombs. Figure 7.4 is a splendid example, from 1450 BCE; it shows a rowing boat and uses a wide range of coloured pigments.

The Egyptian palette of colours was limited by modern standards but sufficient to cover the spectral range. Their main pigments were:

Red: Most of the red pigments used were the natural earth minerals, based on iron oxide, and used by prehistoric artists. However, they also had access to *cinnabar*, mercury sulphide (HgS), which is a red mineral found in the vicinity of Giza in Egypt.

Orange: The pigment used for red–orange colours was the mineral *realgar*, a compound of arsenic and sulphur (As_4S_4), which is highly toxic, to the extent that it has been used to kill rodents.

Yellow: The yellow pigment used was the bright yellow mineral *orpiment*, which is another arsenic sulphide (Ag_2S_3), related to realgar and also extremely toxic.

Green: This colour was derived from the copper ore *malachite*, copper carbonate hydroxide ($Cu_3CO_3(OH)_2$).

Blue: There were two commonly-used blue pigments. The first was *azurite*, another form of copper carbonate hydroxide ($Cu_3(CO_3)_2(OH)_2$) found together with malachite. A dark blue pigment, *Egyptian Blue*, is thought to be the first ever synthetic pigment. It was made by first producing blue glass (calcium copper silicate ($CaCuSi_4O_{10}$) and then grinding it to a fine powder.

White: These pigments were either *chalk*, calcium carbonate ($CaCO_3$) or the mineral gypsum, calcium sulphate dehydrate ($CaSO_4 \cdot 2H_2O$), Gypsum is the material now used for plastering broken limbs and the manufacture of plasterboard, used in construction.

Black: These pigments were all carbon based — either *lamp black*, the soot deposited by burning oil lamps or *carbon black*, produced by burning wood or bone.

Examples of the use of many of these pigments can be seen in Figure 7.4.

7.3 The Pigments of Ancient Rome

The two main kinds of Roman art with which we are familiar are *mosaics* — producing pictures by an assemblage of small pieces of coloured glass or stone — and *frescos*, painting on lime plaster, either when still wet or very newly dry. A fine example of a Roman mosaic, found in Tunisia, is shown in Figure 7.5.

Figure 7.6 shows a charming fresco, found in the ruins of Pompeii, of a young woman holding a stylus, a writing instrument for use on wax tablets. It shows a wide range of colours with red lips, green tunic and a blue background.

When Roman frescos were produced, the patron of the artist was required to pay for the materials used. This meant that cost was often an important factor in the choice of pigments and sometimes cheaper alternatives were used instead of better, but more expensive, pigments. The pigments most commonly used by Roman artists were as follows:

Red: Romans used the natural earth minerals, based on iron oxide, and cinnabar, as used by the ancient Egyptians. They also treated cinnabar by washing and heating and obtained a bright vermillion colour. However, it was very expensive so, for that reason, it was often used as a mixture with natural earth red pigments. Modern spectroscopic techniques have shown that the Romans sometimes used extracts from the plant *madder* (*Rubia tinctorum*) and

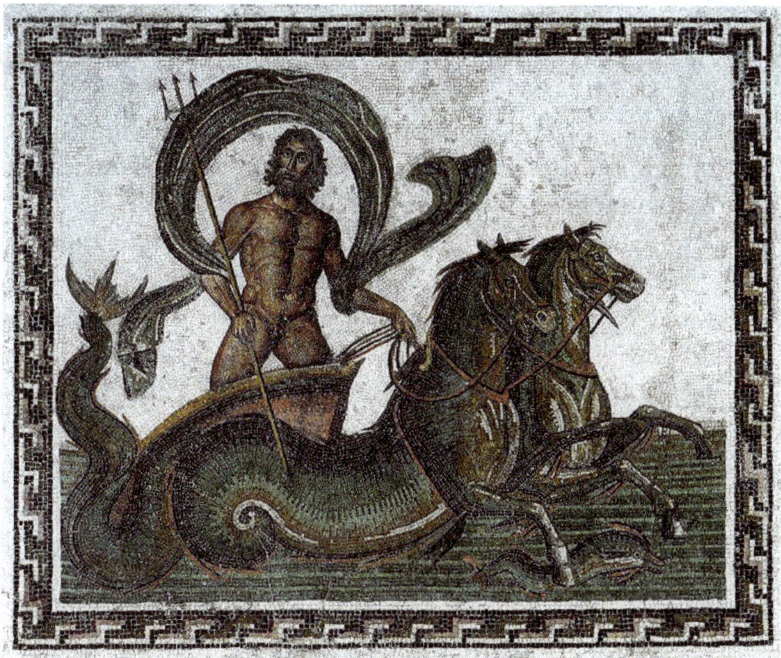

Figure 7.5   A 3rd century Roman mosaic of Poseidon (Neptune) in his sea chariot

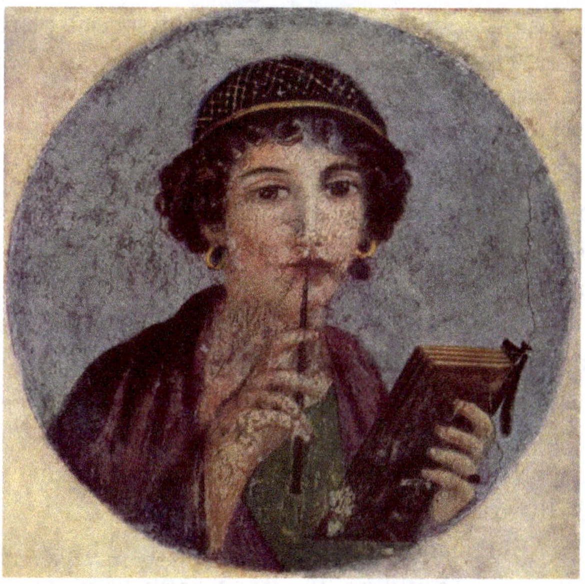

Figure 7.6   A fresco of a young woman, stylus in hand, found at Pompeii

crushed insects to produce red pigments for their frescos. Madder was also known to the Egyptians who mainly used it to dye fabrics.

Yellow: The main yellow pigments were limonite and yellow ochre. By mixing with other pigments various shades of yellow and brown (dark orange) could be produced.

Green: The most common green pigment used by Roman artists was *green earth*, a mixture of minerals that occurred near Verona and was mentioned by the author and naturalist, Pliny the Elder (23–79 AD). The individual minerals are hydrosilicates, one of which is *celadonite* ($KMgFeSi_4O_{10}(OH)_2$. This gave a rather grey-tinged green but a much more vivid green could be produced by mixing the blue dye extracted from the plant *woad* (*Isatis tinctoria*), known as *indigo*, with the yellow dye extracted from a plant known as *dyer's greenweed* (genista tinctoria). Other ways of producing green were occasionally used — for example, by mixing Egyptian blue with yellow ochre.

Blue: Egyptian blue was the most commonly-used pigment for this colour but there were some alternatives — for example, by dyeing chalky materials with indigo.

Purple: The colour purple (magenta) had a special place in Roman society. The source for the best purple dye was a secretion from the sea snail *Bolinus brandaris* that had the unusual characteristic that, instead of fading when it was exposed to light, as happens with most dyes, it became even stronger and brighter. However, this dye, known as *Tyrian purple*, was very expensive and its use restricted to the garments of the rich and powerful, particularly emperors and royalty. There were other, cheaper and inferior sources of purple dye. One such, suggested by the 1st century BCE author, architect and engineer, Vitruvius, was to dye chalk with madder root and *hyaginum*, a blue extract from a bulbous plant that grew most prolifically in Gaul (modern France). Other purples could be made by mixing red dyes and blue dyes, for example, madder and indigo.

White: Most Roman white pigments were derived from some source of chalk, which could be limestone or shells of some kind. Pliny also mentions the production of a white lead pigment, made by placing lead, soaked in vinegar, placed over burning wood shavings. Some Pompeian frescoes have been found with this white pigment. A device to make the whites seem brighter was to add a dash of Egyptian blue to the white pigment.

Black: The Romans manufactured a black pigment from soot, burning resinous pinewood and preventing the smoke from escaping to trap the soot particles. Cheaper alternatives were for painters to burn their own pitch pine or to use roasted wine lees, a recipe repeated on a manufacturing scale in some parts of Germany and France in the 19th century.

7.4 The Pigments of Mediaeval Europe

In this period, from about 500 AD to 1400 AD, most of the mineral pigments used by earlier artists continued to be used. These included red ochre, umber, yellow ochre, orpiment, green earth (known then as *Verona green*), malachite, azurite, chalk-based whites and sooty blacks. They also used *verdigris* as a green pigment, which contained several different compounds and was made by treating copper oxide (CuO) or copper carbonate ($CuCO_3$) with acetic acid (CH_3COOH). It is the green coloration seen on old copper-roofed buildings.

The colour blue had a particular significance in mediaeval Europe since it was taken to signify purity, and representations of the Virgin Mary were often clad in blue garments (Figure 7.7). The most important blue pigment in mediaeval times was ultramarine, made by grinding the mineral *lapis lazuli* (Figure 7.8) into a fine powder. The main source of lapis lazuli was Afghanistan so it was very expensive, but was appropriate for use in representation of the mother of Christ. Figure 7.7 is part of a much larger 14th century painting showing the death and assumption (rising to heaven) of the Virgin Mary; her ultramarine garment stands out vividly from the rest of the painting.

During this period the commonest binder for the various pigments used was a water–egg mixture. Paint was usually applied in successive thin layers as it was found that applying thick layers of paint led to cracking.

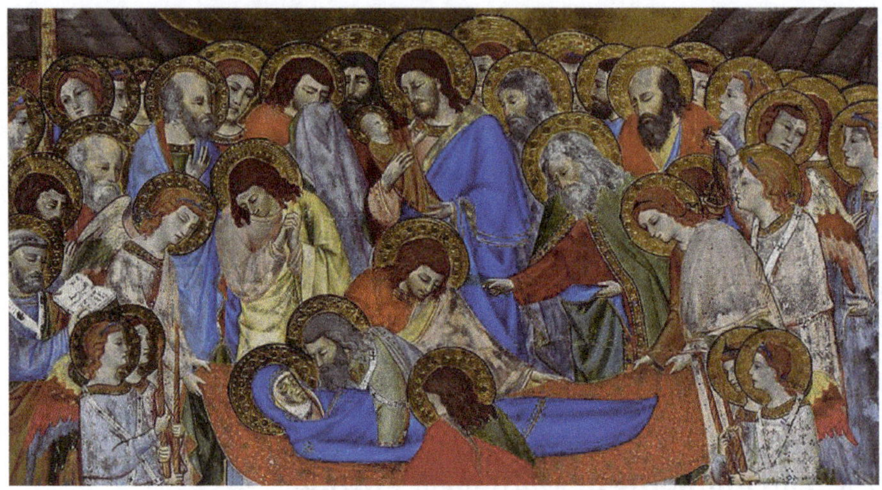

Figure 7.7   Portion of a 14th century painting showing the death and assumption of the Virgin Mary

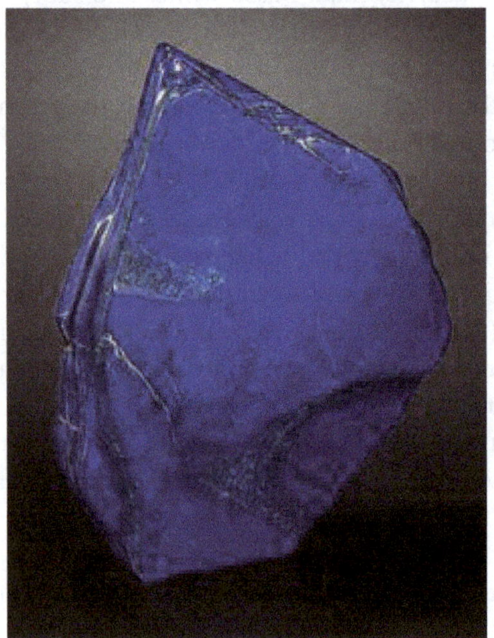

Figure 7.8   A polished piece of lapis lazuli

7.5 Renaissance and Baroque Painting and Pigments

The renaissance period, which lasted from the early 15th century to the end of the 16th century was a period when there was a great flowering of arts and science in Europe, artistically particularly in the Italian peninsula. Among the great painters of the time were Leonardo da Vinci (1452–1519), Michelangelo (1475–1564), Raphael (1485–1521) and Titian (circa 1489 –1576), and there were many others. The baroque period, which lasted throughout the 17th century and into the 18th century, saw the European centre of gravity of artistic enterprise shift northwards, particularly to the low countries with artists such as Rubens (1577–1640), Hals (1580–1665), Van Dyke (1599–1641), Rembrandt (1606–1669) and Vermeer (1632–1675)

While there were great improvements in painting techniques between the mediaeval and these later periods there was not too much change in the materials available. Egg and water fillers were replaced either by linseed or walnut oil, which gave the paint greater plasticity. However, the pigments that were used were essentially those of the mediaeval period plus a few others. The most important additional pigments were *Naples yellow*, a synthetic pigment consisting of a mixture of two forms of lead antimonite, $Pb(SbO_3)_2$ and $Pb_3(Sb)_4)_2$ that could vary in colour from orange to bright yellow, *smalt*, which is similar to Egyptian blue and is made by powdering an intense blue cobalt glass, and *crimson lake*, a purplish red produced from the insects *cochineal*. If one should feel squeamish about insects as a source of colour it should be noted that cochineal is routinely added to give red coloration to some foodstuffs.

In these periods paintings were on canvas and paintings could be done in a greater variety of environments, which greatly improved the range of subject matters that could be dealt with. Improvements in the understanding of perspective gave greater realism to renaissance painting, without detracting from that quality of painting that distinguishes it from the realism of photography.

An example of a painting by one of the great Italian masters is *The fall of man*, painted by Titian in 1570 and shown in Figure 7.9. It shows Eve picking an apple from the tree of knowledge and so embarking humankind on the path of a hard demanding world away from the paradise that preceded it.

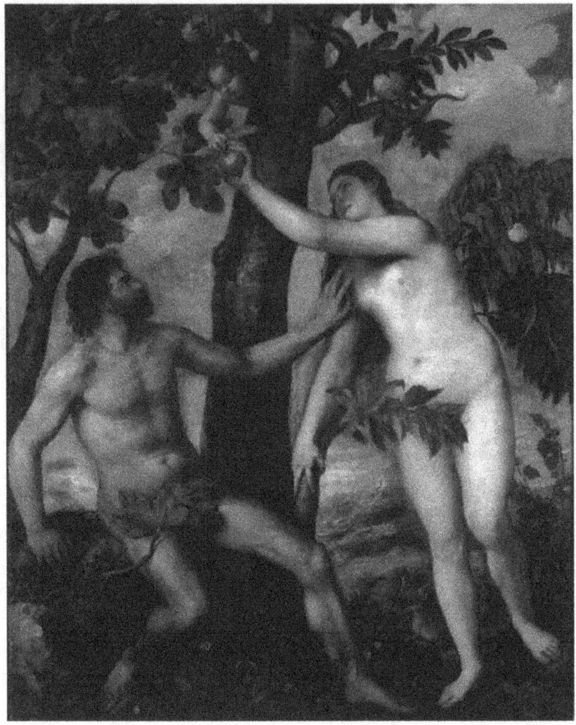

Figure 7.9   *The fall of man*, sometimes called *Adam and Eve* (Titian 1570)

As an example of the baroque period, Figure 7.10 shows the portrait *Old woman selling eggs* by Frans Hals. Portraiture flourished in the baroque period, not only in the Low Counties but all over Europe. It became fashionable for wealthy people to commission artists to paint portraits of themselves and their families, much as modern generations take family photographs.

7.6 Painting in the 18th Century

In the 18th century, painting took a new turn when it became a hobby for people wealthy enough to acquire the relevant equipment and pigments. This new aspect of painting was assisted by the ability to buy readymade pigments, in particular for watercolour, which was the main hobbyist's medium. In 1766, William Reeves set up the first shop selling watercolour

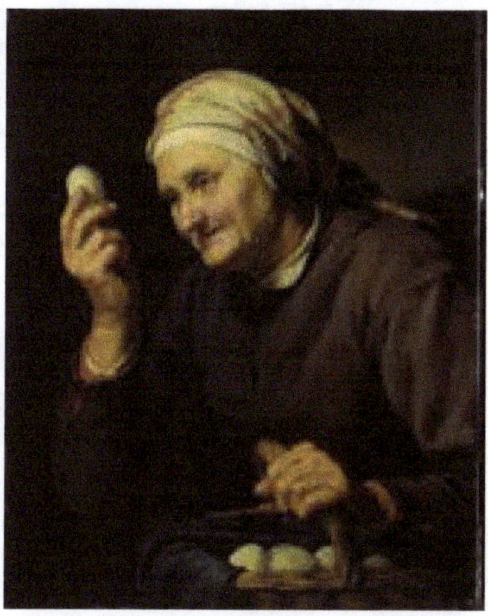

Figure 7.10   Portrait of *An old woman selling eggs* (Frans Hals)

supplies near St Paul's Cathedral in London. The pigments were sold in the form of small blocks that provided colour to a wetted brush. The blocks of pigment contained a small amount of honey that prevented them from cracking when they were stored. Another source of painting material was the Rowney Company. This was set up in London by Thomas and Richard Rowney who abandoned the wig trade, which was fast declining, and in 1783 began trading in artist's pigments. Among their distinguished clients were the landscape painters John Constable (1776–1837) and Joseph Turner (1775–1851). Figure 7.11 shows a painting by the English portrait and landscape painter, Thomas Gainsborough (1727–1788), of his two daughters, Mary and Margaret, a typical portrait of this period.

The palette of pigments used by artists in this period was largely what had been used previously plus two new colours, the first truly synthetic pigments to enter the world of painting — *Prussian blue* and *cobalt green*. Prussian blue, with chemical formula $Fe_7(CN)_{18}$ was produced by the German company Diesbach in 1706. It is dark blue and was used as a replacement for the much more expensive lapis lazuli. The very intensely coloured cobalt green was produced by a Swedish chemist, Sven Rinman,

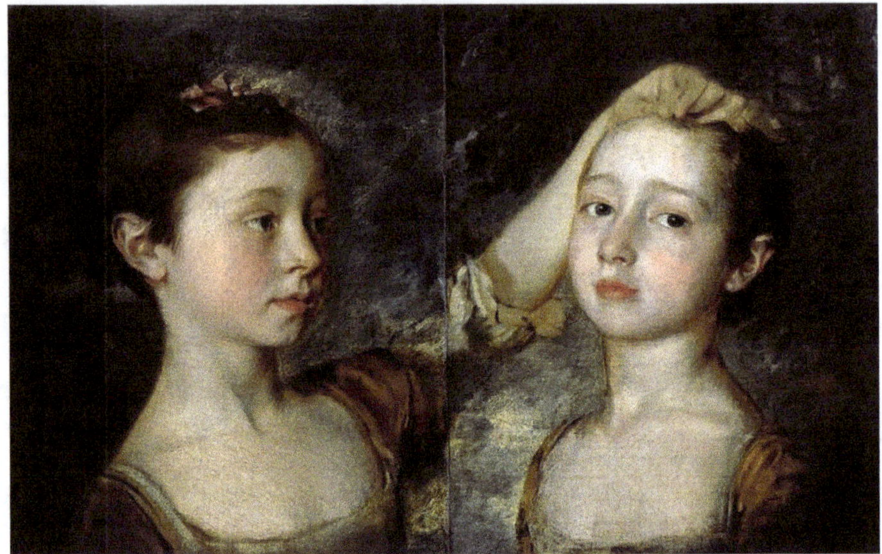

Figure 7.11   Mary and Margaret Gainsborough (Thomas Gainsborough, 1758)

in 1780 by heating together cobalt oxide, CoO, and zinc oxide, ZnO, to give $CoZnO_2$.

7.7 Painting from the 19th Century to the Present

The 19th century marked a watershed in painting technology. The combination of increased industrialization, in particular in the production of textiles, and the need to colour those textiles, led to an explosion in the production of new synthetic dyes, some of which found their way into the realm of painting. Another improvement was that paint companies found methods to suspend pigment particles in linseed oil, removing the need for painters to mix ground pigment with fillers while they were painting. Yet another notable advance was the introduction by John Rand (1801–1873), an American painter and inventor, of the flexible tin paint tube from which a controlled amount of paint could be extracted while leaving the bulk of the paint protected from the harmful influence of being exposed to air. This advance made open-air painting much more practical and much easier.

Some of the new pigments, with the years of introduction, available to painters, both with oils or watercolours were:

Cobalt blue (1801)	calcium aluminate ($CaAl_2O_4$), lighter than Prussian blue.
Cadmium yellow (1820)	cadmium sulphide (CdS), a brilliant yellow.
Viridian (1838)	chromium oxide (Cr_2O_3), a blue-tinted green.
Cerulean blue (1850)	cobalt stannate ($CoSnO_3$), a green-tinted blue.

Other pigments introduced in the 19th century were, *French ultramarine*, a synthetic and cheaper version of lapis lazuli, *zinc white* (zinx oxide, ZnO) and *cobalt violet* (cobalt phosphate, $Co(PO_4)_2$).

The 19th century saw the rise of *impressionism*, introduced by Parisian artists, who broke away from the realism of previous artistic endeavour and introduced new factors such as emphasis on lighting and the creation of the impression of movement. A typical product of this movement is shown in Figure 7.12, a painting called *Haystacks* by the French painter, Claude Monet (1840–1926).

The most important pigment introduced in the 20th century was *titanium white*, titanium dioxide (TiO_2), a very brilliant white. It is sourced

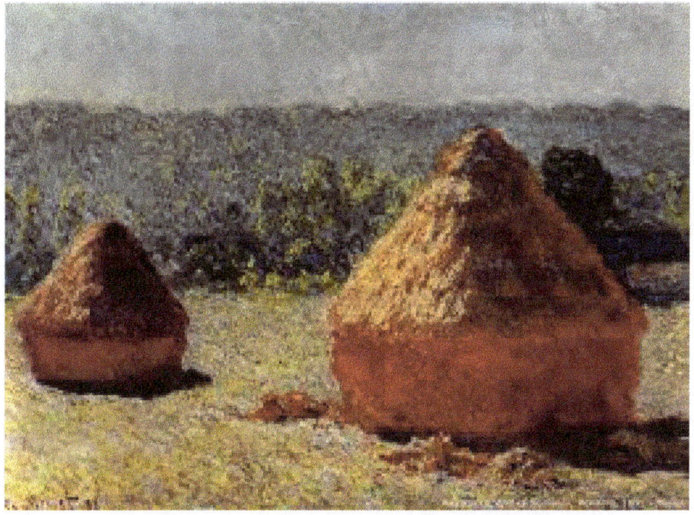

Figure 7.12   *Haystacks* by Claude Monet

from various minerals, but in particular from *ilmenite*, titanium iron oxide ($TiFeO_3$). Another new introduction to the world of art was *acrylic paint* — pigment suspended in an acrylic polymer. These paints are water soluble but become water resistant when dry. The paint can be diluted with water and then its use gives the appearance of a water colour, Alternatively if mixed with acrylic gels, which can give either a matte or a gloss finish, the final product can resemble an oil painting or have a quality that cannot be obtained by any other type of painting medium.

Now we move on to considering dyes, related to pigments in that they bestow colour onto previously colourless objects, but completely different in their application.

Chapter 8
The Development of Dyes

8.1 Dyeing and Mordants

An obvious process for dyeing textiles, or other material such as leather, is to heat and agitate the material, or perhaps the yarn from which a textile will be made, in water together with the source of the dye until the colour is transferred. However, this simple procedure would not be satisfactory since the dye would not be *fast*, i.e. fixed to the material, and would be dissolved out when the material was washed or just became wet. Thus a red-dyed garment would become lighter and lighter shades of pink with successive washing.

To ensure that this does not happen, a *mordant* has to be used. This is a chemical that will attach itself to the dyestuff, forming what is known as a *coordination compound*, which is insoluble in water and also attaches itself to the fabric. Some common mordants are alum (hydrated potassium aluminium sulphate, $KAl(SO_4)_2 \cdot 12H_2O$), tannic acid ($C_{76}H_{52}O_{46}$), common salt ($NaCl$) — or other metallic salts — and urine. Urine was once an important industrial substance; in Ancient Rome large canisters were left in the street to collect it — very public toilets so to speak — and it was used for tanning leather. In Tudor England it was transported by ship from Hull to North Yorkshire where it was used to extract alum from alum-bearing minerals that were mined there. The alum, to be used as a mordant, was an important English export at that time. Actually, urine is still used in Fez in Morocco where they produce very high quality Moroccan leather!

Since the action of a mordant is to create a chemical compound different from the dye itself — although the chemical structure of the dye is maintained within the coordination compound — it generally has the effect of modifying the colour produced by the dye. Another factor that may affect the colour is the procedure for applying the mordant, which can either be pre-mordanting, where the mordant is applied to the textile before it is dyed, meta-mordanting, where the mordant is added to the dyeing vat while dyeing is taking place, or post-mordanting, where the textile is treated with the mordant after it has been dyed. Figure 8.1 shows the different colours that can be produced with the dye *madder* (Section 8.2) due to different mordants and procedures.

8.2 Natural Dyes

Humankind's fascination and interest in colour goes back as far as we can delve into the history of *Homo sapiens*. Since the use of colour occurred all over the world, at a time when communication over large distances was extremely difficult, if not impossible, it seems likely that a desire to impart colour to objects must be an innate characteristic of mankind. Various dyestuffs were used to colour the human body, the clothes that people

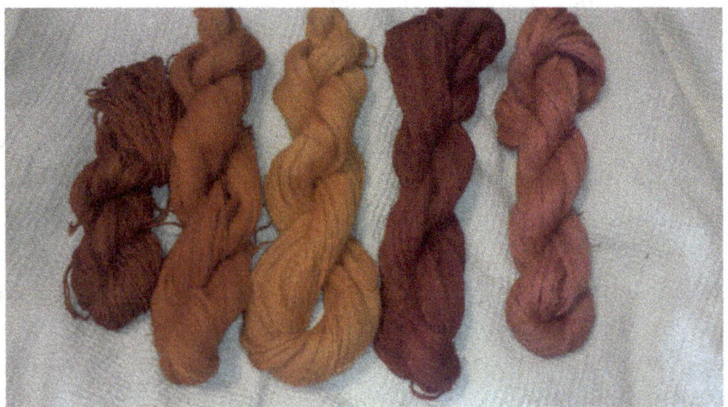

Figure 8.1   Colours that can be produced with the dye madder

wore and the artefacts, especially pottery, that were in everyday use. Ancient sources of colour were either pigments, as mentioned in Chapter 7, or dyes extracted from vegetable or animal sources, and such sources would vary from one part of the world to another. Dye sources available in Africa would differ from those of northern Europe, but human ingenuity would make full use of whatever was available locally.

The first dyes were probably of vegetable origin since many of the foodstuffs available to early people, such as wild berries, would have been strongly coloured and it would not have escaped their notice that anything that came into contact with the juice of a berry would be stained with its colour. Again, flowers offer a wide range of colours so attempts would have been made, many probably unsuccessful, to extract colour from them. The successful attempts would yield a dye and experimentation might give the best way to extract it to give a strong colour. By trial-and-error less obvious sources of dyes would also have been found, such as fungi, lichens, roots and the bark of trees. Extracts from insects were also used as dyes and, from scientific tests at archaeological sites, it has been estimated that something of the order of 1,000 different sources were used by prehistoric people to extract dyes. Here we shall just give a few examples of natural dyes from antiquity to comparatively recent times in various categories of colour.

Red

We initially mentioned madder as a source of a red lake-pigment in Chapter 7. The actual source plant, *Rubia tinctorum*, is shown in Figure 8.2. It stands about 1.5 metre high but it is the root, up to a metre in length and more than a centimetre thick, which is the source of the dye.

Madder, and a variety of related plants of the *Rubia* genus, were known to prehistoric people and madder-dyed linen was found in the tomb of Tutankhamun, dating from the 14th century BCE and also in wall paintings in the ruins of Pompeii. The plant grows widely all over Europe and in other temperate regions of the world and was cultivated as long ago as 1500 BCE in ancient Egypt and central Asia. Much more recently it was of great commercial importance, being used to colour military uniforms, until about 1869 when it was replaced by a synthetic dye.

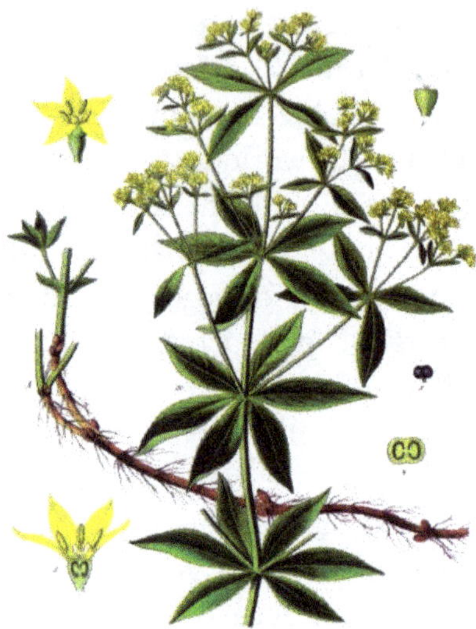

Figure 8.2   The madder plant

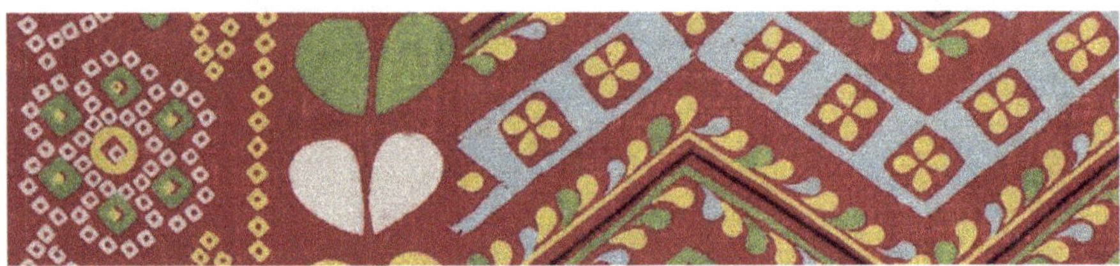

Figure 8.3   A fabric with a Turkey-red produced background

Madder was used to produce a very intense and fast red dye by the so-called *Turkey red process*, which was actually discovered in India but progressed by stages through to Turkey. The process was introduced into France by Greek workers from the Levant, where the dye was produced, but kept secret by the French dyers. Eventually, through what we now call commercial espionage, first Dutch and then British dyers discovered the secret and in the late 18th century the process was adopted in Manchester and Glasgow. The process, mostly applied to cotton textiles, was long and complicated and a single dyeing could take more than three weeks to complete. The main steps were:

- thoroughly clean, or bleach, the cloth,
- saturate the cloth, or yarn, in a mixture of rancid olive oil and sheep dung,
- apply alum mordant to the cloth or yarn,
- dye the cloth or yarn in a mixture of madder extract and bullock's blood,
- boil in a solution of tin chloride ($SnCl_2$) to clean and brighten the cloth.

Some of these steps were repeated several times. A revised version of the process, replacing some of the more unsavoury components with less odious ones, was being used in Manchester in 1784. A fabric with a background of red produced by the Turkey-red process is shown in Figure 8.3.

In a completely different part of the world, the native-American Navajo tribe, who produce beautifully coloured rugs and other textiles, use a fermented prickly pear from a cactus, *opuntis polyacantha*, as a source of a delicate pink dye. They also produced different shades of orange-tinted pink using red earth mixed with pure rainwater.

Orange

Many of the dyes that produce either yellow or red will, under particular circumstances also produce orange. This can be seen in Figure 8.1 where the centre skein has a distinct orange hue. However, there are a number of plants that primarily produce an orange dye, although with wide variations of shades of orange or brown or even yellows and reds, depending on the exact process used. One such vegetable source of orange dye is yellow onion skins. The recipe, used by amateur dyers, is as follows:

- boil onion skins in water and then leave to soak for a few days,
- strain off the dye from the onion skins,
- soak fabric or yarn in hot water before inserting in the dye, which has alum mordant added,
- heat dye-bath for one hour making sure that fabric or yarn is fully submerged at all times,
- allow dye-bath, containing fabric or yarn, to cool,
- wash fabric or yarn in water and then dry.

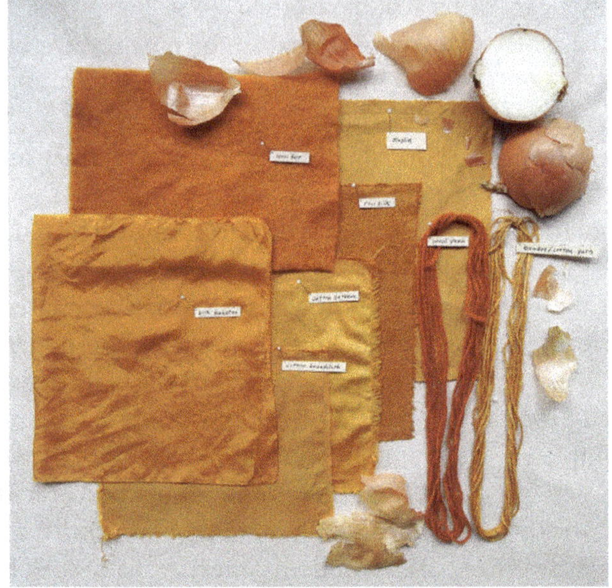

Figure 8.4   A range of orange hues from onion-skin dye

A range of oranges obtained by this process is shown in Figure 8.4

There are many other sources of orange dye. Navajo dyers use the bark and berries from the one-seeded juniper, *Juniperus monosperma*, or bark from the alder tree.

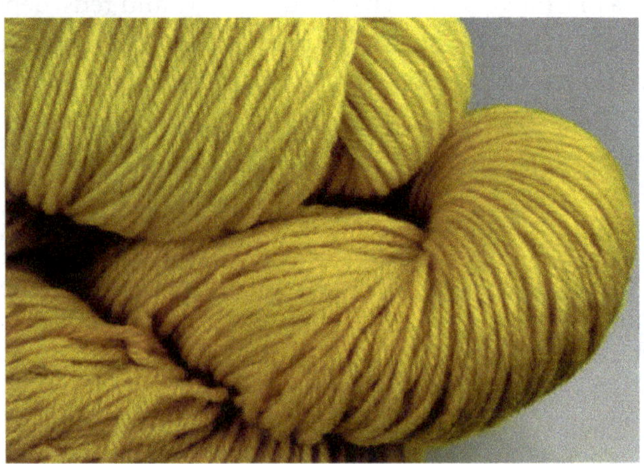

Figure 8.5   Yarn dyed with weld

Yellow

There are a large number of plants that yield a yellow dye — for example, saffron, the stigmas of a type of crocus also used as a spice, turmeric (*Circuma longa*) the rhizomes of which are also used as a spice as well as in Chinese and Indian medicine, and onion skins. A common weed in England, weld (*Reseda luteola*), also known as 'dyer's rocket', produces a bright yellow dye (Figure 8.5) and archaeological evidence suggests that it might have been used as a source of dye more than 3,000 years ago. An important commercial dye in Europe from the 18th century came from the yellow inner bark of the eastern black oak (*quercus velutina*), a native of eastern regions of the USA.

Navajo dyers use several sources for their yellow dyes — small snake-weed, which has a daisy-like yellow flower, rabbitbrush (*Chrysothamnus*), a shrub native to western parts of the USA, rubber plant (*Parthenium incanum*), which grows in the south-west of the USA and, once again, onion skins. They also use rose hips to extract an unsaturated-yellow dye.

Some comments about green

Away from desert or polar regions we live in a largely green world. The vast majority of plants contain the green pigment chlorophyll that is responsible for photosynthesis so it would be imagined that there was a plethora of green dye sources in nature. Curiously this is not true; grass and spinach can yield green dyes but they are neither very strong colours nor do they resist fading under sunlight. For this reason the most successful way to dye a material green is to combine dyeing with yellow with dyeing with blue. For that reason we leave our spectral sequence and move on to blue natural dyes.

Blue

The main sources of natural blue dye are essentially those plants that contain the chemical indigo ($C_{16}H_{10}N_2O_2$). The earliest centre for dyeing with indigo, and the main supplier of the dye to Europe from Roman times onwards, was India. The Romans used the word *indicum*, meaning *Indian* in Latin, for the dye, derived from a similar Greek word, and this eventually became the English word *indigo*. The colour of indigo is shown in Figure 8.6: Newton adopted indigo as a spectral colour situated between blue and violet.

Figure 8.6   Paper dyed with indigo

The indigo-bearing plants all belong to the genus *Indigofera*, which are widespread in tropical and subtropical regions. The main species in Asia is *Indigofera tinctoria*, known as 'true indigo', in South America the sources were Añil (*Indigofera suffruticosa*) and Natal indigo (*Indigofera arrect*), in Japan and coastal China indigo was obtained from dyer's knotweed (*Polygomum tinctorum*) and in West Africa the shrub *Lonchocarpus cyanescens*). The main source of indigo in temperate climates was woad (*Isatis tinctoria*), a native plant in the Middle Eat but cultivated in Europe for over 2000 years. When Julius Caesar invaded Britain in 55 BCE he was confronted by British warriors whose bodies were covered with blue war paint derived from woad.

Green

Although there are a few natural sources of green dye — grass, spinach, some lichens and some fungi — as previously indicated the commonest way of producing a strong and fast green is to use a combination of yellow and blue dyes. A famous green, linked in legend with the English outlaw Robin Hood, is Lincoln green (Figure 8.7(a)), produced by dyers in the cloth town of Lincoln in the Middle Ages. They first dyed wool with woad

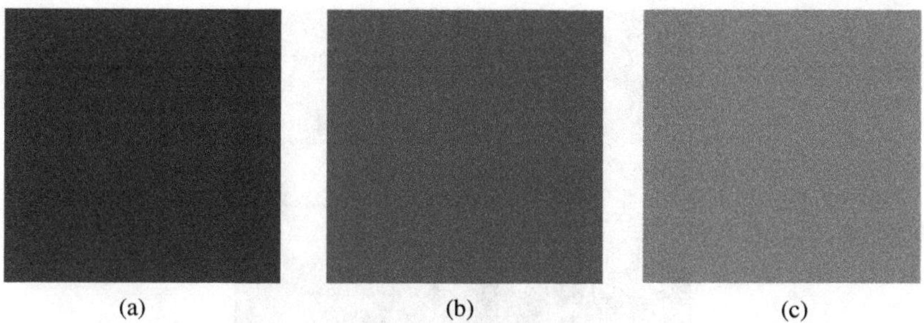

Figure 8.7   (a) Lincoln green. (b) Kendal green. (c) Saxon green

and then dyed it again with weld or another source of yellow dye, dyer's greenweed. Later, mordanting woollen cloth with alum, dyeing yellow with dyer's greenwood then dyeing again with indigo gave the very popular Kendal green (Figure 8.7(b)) but in the 18th century the brighter Saxon green (Figure 8.7(c)) was preferred, produced by dyeing with indigo and fustic, a yellow dye from the plant *Maclura tinctoria*.

There are ways of producing green other than by combining dyeing with a combination of yellow and blue dyes. Adding an iron-based mordant to yellow dye can produce an olive green and some Native American peoples have used lichen to produce green. Navajo dyers have also produced green dye, paradoxically from red onion skins.

Purple

The colour purple had significance above all other colours for many ancient civilizations. The derivation of one purple dye, Tyrian purple, was described in Section 7.3. The dye was probably first produced by the Phoenicians in the second millennium BCE; the country name Pheonicia means, in Greek, 'land of purple'.

In mediaeval Europe purple and violet were produced by mixing the effect of blue and red dyes, which were comparatively cheap and plentiful. Thus, first dyeing with woad and then over-dyeing with madder or cochineal could give a variety of purples and violet hues. Purple could also be produced from madder when used with an alum mordant.

Figure 8.8   One of the shades of cutch brown

Native American tribes used maple, lichens and various berries to produce dyes in the lavender to purple range of colours.

Browns

There are a number of natural vegetable products that give brown dye. The wood of acacia trees (*Acacia catechu*) gives a brown dye, *cutch brown* (Figure 8.8), giving a range of hues depending on the mordant used — greyish-brown with an iron-based mordant and greenish-brown with a copper-based one.

The native tribes of the USA have produced many brown dyes. As previously mentioned, Navajo dyers use one-seeded juniper to give orange dye but it can also give brown. They also produce brown dye from the hulls (outer covering) of wild walnuts.

Black and grey

A black dye can be produced using a source of tannic acid, and an iron salt. The tannic acid can be produced by placing ground acorns in water and leaving for some time. The item to be dyed is then placed in the acorn solution (tannic acid), left for several hours and then immersed in a

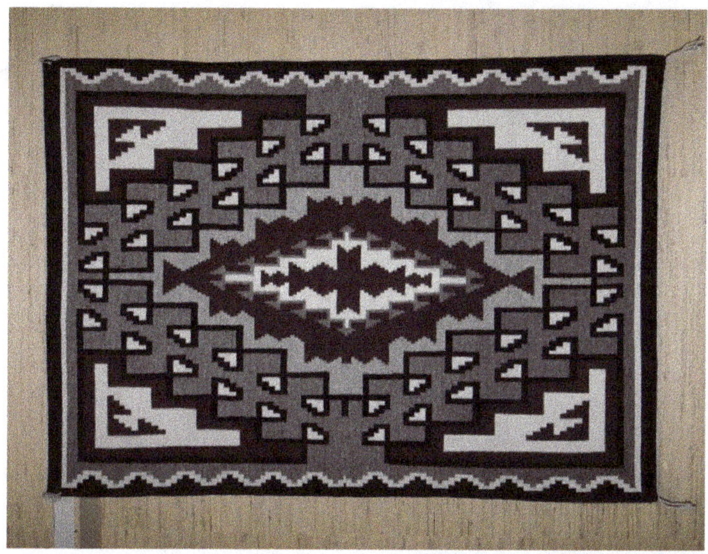

Figure 8.9   A Navajo rug mostly dyed brown and grey

solution of the iron salt. Depending on the time spent in the two solutions the resulting colour can be anything from light grey to deep black.

Navajo weavers create a black dye by mixing yellow ochre, pitch from the piñon tree (*pinus edulis*) and extracts from the shrub sourberry (*rhus trilobata*). They also produce a bluish-grey dye from blue lupin flowers and a yellowish grey from juniper mistletoe (*phoradendron juniperinum*), a flowering plant in the sandalwood family that grows in the south-west of the USA. Figure 8.9 shows a Navajo rug with large grey-dyed regions.

8.3 Synthetic Dyes

The first synthetic dye was produced in a serendipitous way, as a result of trying to do something else. In the 19th century there was a great expansion of the colonial empires of the European powers, mainly those of Britain and France. One of the hazards for the explorers, soldiers and administrators in this colonial enterprise was malaria, for which

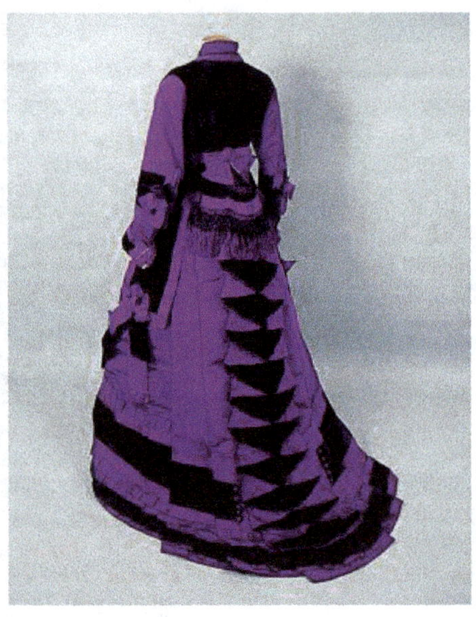

Figure 8.10   A mauveine-dyed gown from 1870

mosquitos, which abounded in wet tropical areas, were the carriers. The only effective treatment was *quinine,* extracted from the bark of the *Cinchona tree,* which grows in South America. In 1856 a young 18-year-old English chemist, William Perkin (1838–1907) was trying to prepare a synthetic form of quinine. He began with the compound aniline ($C_6H_5NH_2$) and at the end of the exercise he had produced a sticky black substance that clearly was not quinine. He found that by adding alcohol as a solvent he could extract an intense purple dye from the black substance. This was exploited commercially as the synthetic dye *mauveine* (Figure 8.10), which was the precursor of a huge industry for producing synthetic dyes, many of them aniline derivatives.

Although the initial discovery was made in England, by the end of the 19th century it was German chemical companies that were dominant in the field of producing synthetic dyestuffs. A chemical conglomerate *Interessengemeinschaft Farbenindustrie AG (Syndicate of dyestuff corporations),* generally known as I G Farben, was formed that eventually became a massive general chemical company.

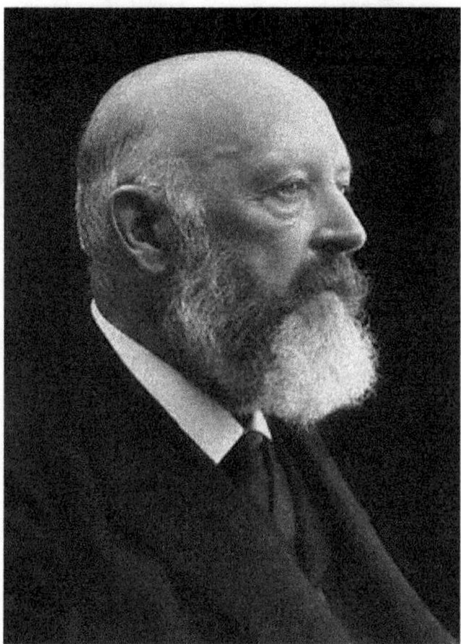

Figure 8.11   Adolf von Baeyer

The synthetic dyes provided a range of colours that the natural dyes could not match and, more importantly, they were cheaper to produce. For example, the German chemist, Adolf von Baeyer (1835–1917; Figure 8.11), who won the Nobel Prize for chemistry in 1905, first synthesized indigo in 1880, but it took the German chemical company BASF (Badische Anilin-und-Soda-Fabrik) until 1897 to produce an economically viable process. Shortly after that, the production of natural indigo in India, the main natural source, essentially ceased.

An interesting bye-product of the dyestuffs industry is that it had an impact on the development of pharmaceuticals. An early use of dyes was to stain biological microscope specimens; two components of a specimen might be difficult to distinguish under a microscope because of their similar optical properties but, if their take-up of a dye is different, the contrast is much improved. Paul Ehrlich (1854–1915; Figure 8.12) was a German physician who was a pioneer in the development of techniques for staining tissue. He developed the first effective treatment for

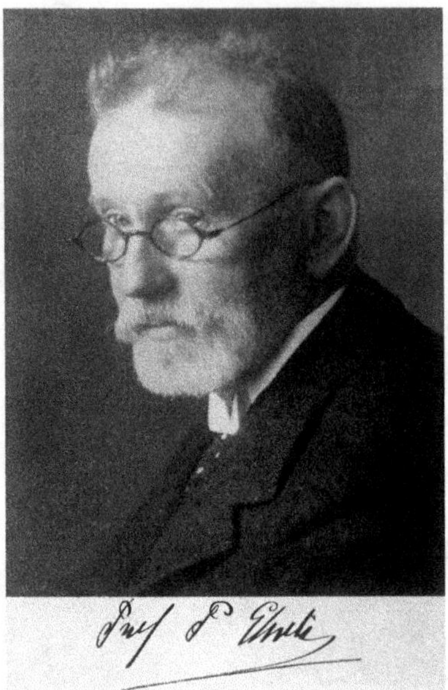

Figure 8.12   Paul Ehrlich

syphilis and also an antiserum for the treatment of diphtheria; he was awarded the Nobel Prize for Medicine in 1908. One of his discoveries was that the yellow dye *flavine* killed the bacteria that caused abscesses, which led to many other discoveries of useful drugs derived from chemicals in coal tar, the main feed chemical for the synthetic dye industry. Indirectly, the dyeing industry has helped to prevent people from dying!

Chapter 9
Colouring Pottery and Glass

9.1 The Origin of Pottery

The term 'pottery' includes a number of products with different properties, all made from clays of different types and characteristics. Clay is a fine-grained mineral material with a high water content that is plastic and soft and is capable of being moulded into various shapes. At its simplest, creating a pottery object consists of shaping the clay into the desired form, allowing it to dry and then subjecting it to a high temperature to drive out the remaining water content and change its composition. This transforms the clay into a hard and brittle form that will permanently keep its shape. However, that simple description conceals a great deal of detail in the process of producing a successful piece of pottery.

The art of producing pottery goes back far into pre-history, before the Neolithic period in which early man depended on stone for making tools, weapons and other artefacts. Some pottery objects in Europe, including figurines, date from before 25,000 BCE and the oldest pottery vessels in China date back to 20,000 BCE. Other old pottery objects, from the Neolithic period, have been found in Siberia, Japan, South America and Africa. Like the art of dyeing, the art of pottery existed all over the world at a time when communication between different groups of individuals must have been very tenuous.

The earliest and crudest form of pottery is *earthenware* that, outside the Far East, was the most common form of pottery until the 17th century. It is soft and of low mechanical strength so, although they are usually made quite thick, earthenware products still easily chip and break. Modern earthenware products include bricks, terracotta tiles used for roofing and flower pots. The temperature at which earthenware is fired, 900°C–1150°C, is not sufficient to vitrify (i.e. make glass-like) the surface and so make it impermeable to liquids. To make it impermeable requires an extra *glazing* process. However, permeable earthenware pots are used in many parts of the world as cooling devices. If water is held in such a pot then evaporation of the water than seeps through to the outside extracts heat from the remainder of the water inside and so cools it to below the ambient temperature. The most famous earthenware products are the terracotta soldiers, horses and chariots buried in 210–209 BCE near Xian in China, whose purpose was to protect the emperor Qin Shi Huang in his afterlife (Figure 9.1). Although there are many thousands of terracotta soldiers, no two are alike.

The next grade of pottery is *stoneware*, made from a different kind of clay, which is fired at a higher temperature, 1180°C–1280°C, and so acquires a glazed, or partially glazed, surface that makes it impermeable to liquids. It is quite hard, opaque and usually of a grey or light brown colour,

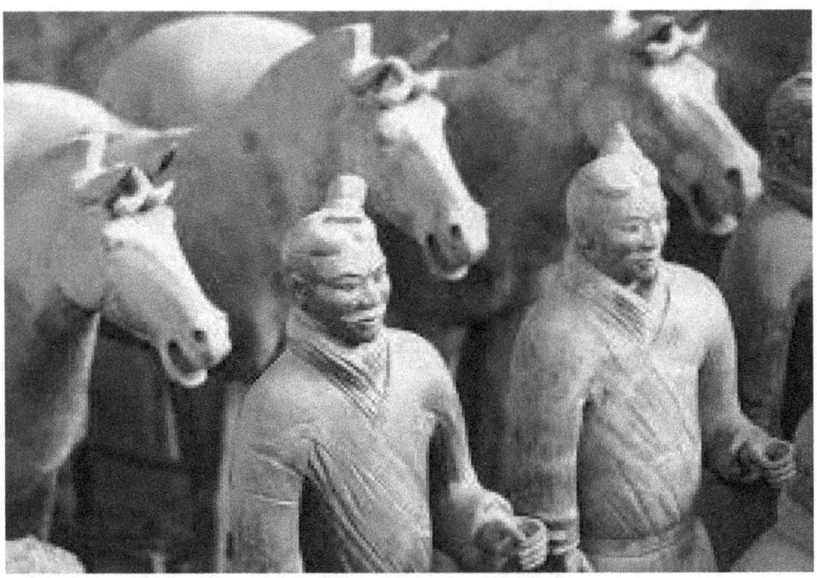

Figure 9.1   Terracotta soldiers near Xian

reflecting the nature of the material from which it is made. The earliest examples of stoneware come from India and China, dated between 1900–1600 BCE. In the 17th to 19th centuries it was the most common form of pottery in North America and Europe.

The most refined pottery is *porcelain*, made using white clay called *kaolin*, or, more popularly, *china clay*. Porcelain, which is fired at a very high temperature, 1200–1400°C, is highly glazed, mechanically strong so thin vessels can be made, and translucent. The earliest true porcelain originated in the early period of the Han Dynasty in China, about 200 BCE. Chinese porcelain was exported, first to the nearby Islamic world and later to Europe where it was highly prized. Eventually the secret of its production process became known outside China, and European manufacturers began to make high-quality porcelain products. The first European porcelain came from the German town of Meissen in 1710, based on local kaolin deposits. Early 17th century potteries in Staffordshire, England, which exploited local deposits of clay, coal and other necessary materials, began porcelain production when large deposits of kaolin were discovered in Cornwall in 1745. New types of porcelain were created by mixing kaolin with powdered glass, giving what was called *soft paste*. Another type of raw material gives *hard-paste porcelain*, first produced in China in the 7th century. The modern composition of the raw material for this type of porcelain is a mixture of kaolin, quartz (silicon dioxide, SiO_2) and feldspar, a common rock forming most of the Earth's crust that crystallizes from volcanic magma. Whereas soft-paste porcelain is fired at 1200°C, the hard-paste variety is fired at the higher temperature of 1400°C. The main advantage of hard-paste over soft-paste porcelain is that it withstands high temperature liquids better and is much less prone to cracking.

9.2 Coloured Decoration of Pottery

Adding colour to pottery occurs during a final firing which also adds glaze to the object. For earthenware the primary objective may be to render a vessel impermeable to liquids but for stoneware and porcelain the objective is usually decorative. Glazes normally include the mineral silica that, like quartz, is silicon dioxide, which turns into a glassy form when heated to high temperature. Adding metal oxides or hydroxides, such as those of sodium, calcium or potassium, produces the silicates of those metals and lowers the melting temperature.

If the pottery object is to be given a uniform colour then an aqueous suspension of the finely-ground glaze materials, plus some other metallic oxide that will give colour, is produced and the whole object is dipped into it. If cobalt oxide is used for colouring then the object will be a deep blue. Some other colours that can be produced are with iron oxide (brown), manganese oxide (black), copper oxide (green) and stannic (tin) oxide (white). A complete spectrum of colours, including quite subtle shades, is available to the potter. To produce a decorative piece, the pottery can have the pattern, or picture painted on it, using aqueous suspensions of oxides as the pigments. A colourless glaze is then superimposed over the whole object by one of, dipping in an aqueous suspension, spraying the suspension over the surface or applying the glaze as a dry powder. The final colour of the applied pigment after firing may not be the same as that when originally applied; cobalt oxide that gives a deep blue in the fired object is black when first applied. However, experienced pottery decorators know what the final appearance is going to be.

There is a kind of decorated porcelain, known as *blue-and-white*, which originated in China but had its copiers in Europe and elsewhere. Figure 9.2 shows a large Chinese blue-and-white jug with a floral pattern motif dating from about 1335.

Blue-and-white decoration also became popular with Islamic potters whose work very much mirrored Chinese designs; Figure 9.3 shows a 17th century plate from Persia (modern Iran) featuring a dragon motif that was very popular with Chinese potters. Examples of blue-and-white ware from Europe are shown in Figure 9.4. The first of these is a Delft biblical wall tile produced in Holland in the 17th century (Figure 9.4(a)) and the second an English *willow-pattern* plate, showing a Chinese scene, probably produced in the late 18th century (Figure 9.4(b)).

Although blue-and-white pottery was quite popular and produced all over the world, highly coloured pottery was also produced from quite early times. An early example of Islamic coloured pottery is shown in Figure 9.5(a), a 10th century plate from Persia, and Figure 9.5(b) shows a Chinese 'goldfish vase' from the 16th century. For European examples, Figure 9.6(a) shows a collection of early 18th century teapots from the Meissen factory

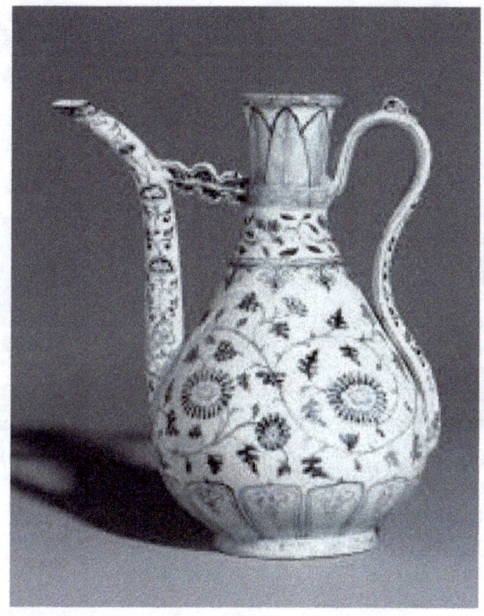

Figure 9.2   A blue-and-white jug dating from the late Ming Dynasty period

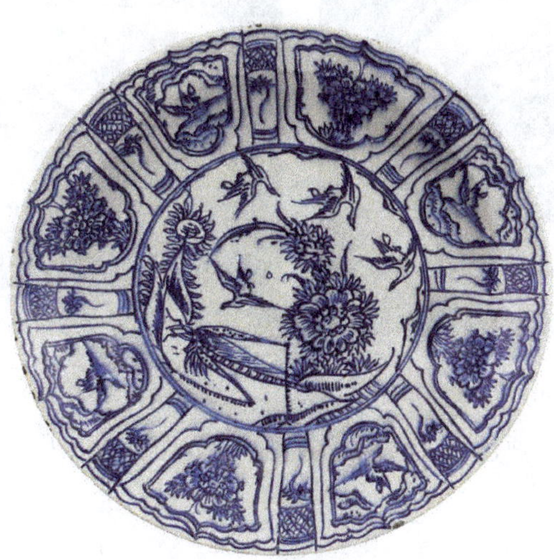

Figure 9.3   A Persian blue-and-white plate from the 17th century

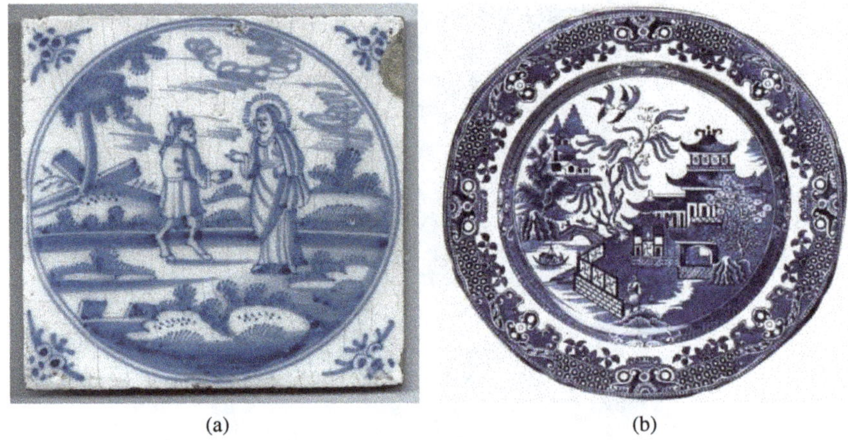

(a)   (b)

Figure 9.4 (a) A Delft tile showing *The temptation of Christ* (17th century). (b) An 18th century English willow-pattern plate

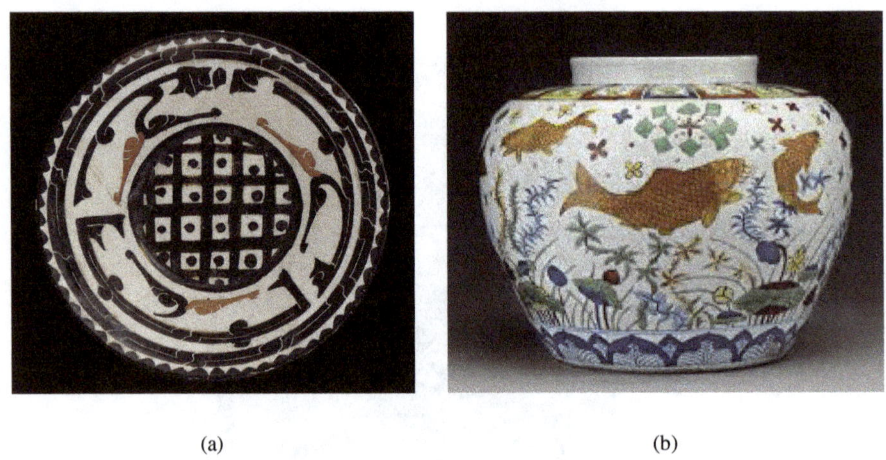

(a)   (b)

Figure 9.5 (a) A 10th century Persian plate. (b) a 16th century Chinese 'goldfish vase'

and Figure 9.6(b) a 20th century vase from the English Moorcroft factory in Staffordshire.

Apart from useful articles — such as plates, teapots, cups and saucers and vases — many purely decorative pottery objects are made, such as the Staffordshire figurines of spaniel dogs that were very popular in 19th century Britain and were often placed on mantelpieces or in hearths (Figure 9.7). During its long development from prehistoric vessels and

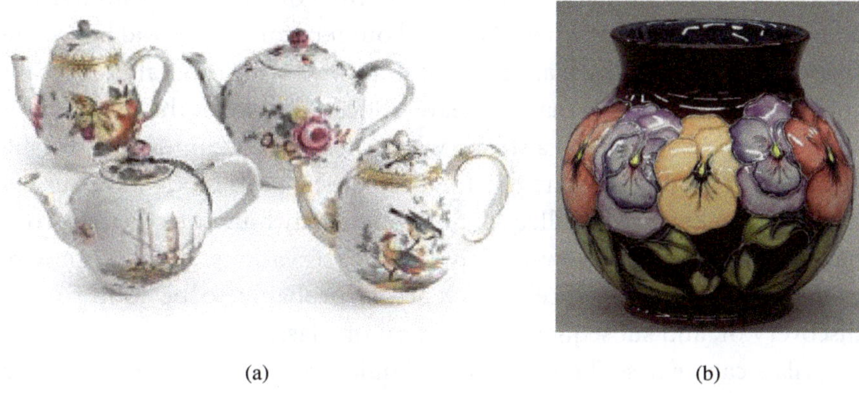

(a)   (b)

Figure 9.6   (a) Meissen teapots from the early 18th century. (b) A 20th century Moorcroft vase

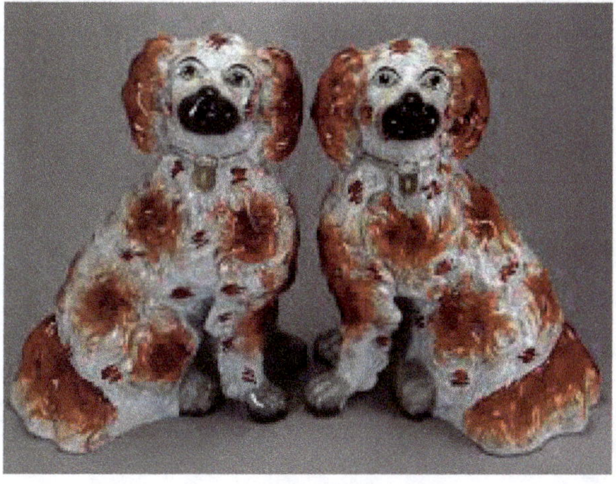

Figure 9.7   Staffordshire pottery dogs

figurines, pottery has now become a colourful and important art form in the modern world.

9.3 The Origin of Glass

Archaeology can often indicate the dates of the production of various artefacts but it is not usually possible to know exactly how and when the technology for producing those artefacts began. Plausible theories can be advanced but it cannot be known for certain. For example, primitive men could have noticed that when clay dried out it became hard and hence they shaped vessels from the plastic clay to hold water or to contain food being cooked over a fire. They may also have noticed that when the fire was unusually hot, perhaps due to a strong wind, the vessel became more durable. We must not underestimate our forebears; their technology was primitive but their intelligence equalled that of present-day humanity so they would have been able to follow-up on their observations. Another notable example of such a chance occurrence is probably to be found in the discovery of, and subsequent production of, glass.

Glass can be described as a 'frozen liquid'. In crystalline materials atoms are fixed in a regular pattern — like three-dimensional wallpaper — over distances that are very large compared with the repeat distances of the pattern. This contrasts with a liquid in which atoms or molecules are in constant motion. At any instant there is some approximate local order in the atomic arrangement, similar to that of a crystal, but this order does not persist over large distances. Figure 9.8 illustrates in two dimensions the

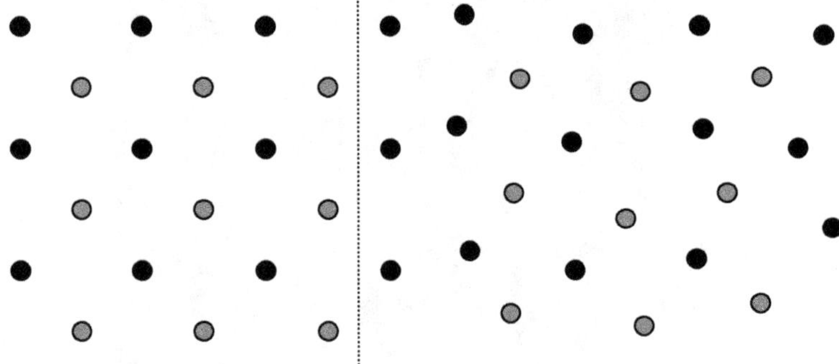

Figure 9.8   Representations of a crystal structure (left) and a liquid structure (right)

difference in the atomic arrangement in a crystal and, at some instant, in a liquid. In glassy materials the atoms are more-or-less fixed, as in a crystal, but have only local order in their positions as for a liquid. The term 'more-or-less fixed' to describe the positions of the atoms in glass was used for a reason. In reality glass is not a solid but is a liquid — but one that flows so slowly that for all practical purposes, over periods of time much greater than a human lifetime, it behaves like a solid. The liquid properties of glass can be confirmed by examining glass window panes in very old buildings. Under the influence of gravity the glass flows downwards and the glass at the bottom of the pane is found to be thicker than at the top. This is a manifestation of the flow of a liquid with a very large *viscosity*. Water, which easily flows, has a low viscosity, treacle, which flows less well, has a considerably larger viscosity. Tar, the material sometimes used in road building, flows very reluctantly and hence has a very high viscosity — although in unusually hot weather the tar becomes more fluid and the road surface may then become distorted. Glass has an extremely high viscosity — so great that its flow properties cannot be discerned over a short time span.

The chief ingredient of glass is sand that, in its very pale form, is almost pure silica. The mineral quartz that occurs in the form of large crystals is also silica and glass can be made of silica alone by melting sand or quartz at a temperature of more than 2300°C in an electric furnace and then allowing the melt to cool. This *silica glass* is too expensive for everyday use in making common objects like wine bottles, but it has its use in special circumstances, for example, in some laboratory equipment or to make lenses that transmit ultraviolet light. However, sand mixed with sodium carbonate, Na_2CO_3, produces a glass, *soda glass*, with a melting point of 1500°C, a temperature easily attainable with a bellows-assisted normal combustion furnace. A disadvantage of soda glass is that it is readily leached by water and so degrades over time. It can be made more durable, without greatly affecting the melting point, by adding small amounts of oxides such as calcium oxide (lime), CaO, magnesium oxide, MgO, or aluminium oxide, Al_2O_3, to give what is known as *soda-lime glass*.

Some glass occurs naturally, such as the mineral *obsidian* that is produced by the melting of some kinds of rock during volcanic activity with subsequent rapid cooling that prevents the formation of crystals. It can be ground to make very sharp knives and was used for this purpose by the various civilizations that flourished in South and Central America. Scalpels made of obsidian are sometimes used in modern surgery. One can only speculate about the origin of man-made glass. A fire lit in a sandy desert in the presence of soda, derived from the ash of burnt plants being used as fuel, with a strong wind that was funnelled through the fire to give a high temperature, could lead to globules of opaque glass being formed. Glassmaking probably originated in Mesopotamia — modern Iraq — about 2500 BCE, and was initially used for making beads and various decorative objects. About 1000 years later glass vessels were produced by covering a clay core with a layer of smoothed molten glass and then, when the glass had cooled, removing the brittle clay interior. Sometime later, in Syria or thereabouts, the art of glassblowing was invented. This involved placing a blob of molten glass on the end of a tube and then, by blowing through the tube, creating a glass bubble that could be fashioned into vessels of any required shape.

From its early origins as a rare and expensive material, glass has become a cheap throwaway product in the form of jars and bottles to hold food and drink. However, the fact that exotic high-quality glass can be produced, and that colour can be added, has led to glass, like pottery, becoming an artistic material.

9.4 Coloured Glass

Just as coloured glazes are added to pottery, coloured glass can be produced by adding metallic oxides, or other chemical compounds, to the mixture that is to be melted. A selection of important additives, and the colours produced, is

iron and chromium oxides	green
cobalt oxide	blue
titanium oxide	yellowish-brown
chromium oxide	dark green
metallic copper	dark red
various silver compounds	yellow to red
manganese oxide	reddish purple

When soda-lime glass is produced it usually has a very pale green tinge due to iron oxide impurity in the sand. This can be cancelled out to give a colourless glass by adding a small amount of manganese oxide that adds a purple tinge. The effect is like adding two filters, as described in Section 4.4. The pale green filter subtracts a small fraction of the red and blue parts of the transmitted white light and the purple filter subtracts a little of the green part. The net effect is a slight reduction of intensity but the transmission of white light.

9.4.1 Stained-glass windows

For more than 1,000 years, places of worship, such as churches and mosques, have used windows not only as a means of lighting the interior but also as a means of religious expression or decoration. Church stained-glass windows combine small pieces of coloured and painted glass, linked together by lead strips, to give either abstract artistic patterns or representations of biblical scenes. An example of church abstract art is the Rose Window in York Minster (Figure 9.9(a)), the great Norman church in northern England. In the same church, the Great East Window (Figure 9.9(b)) is the largest expanse of stained glass in the world, some 23 metres high and 9.5 metres wide — as large as a tennis court. It depicts scenes from the Book of Genesis and the Book of Revelations, the first and last books of the bible. Figure 9.10 shows a detail of the Great East

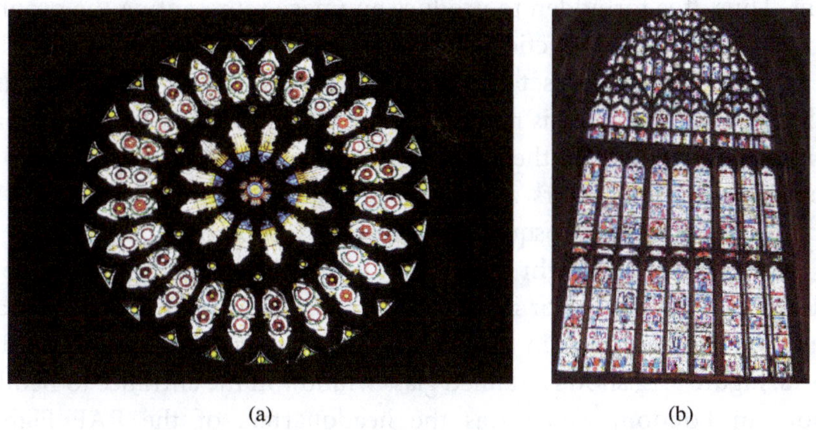

(a)   (b)

Figure 9.9   Stained glass in York Minster (a) The Rose Window. (b) The Great East Window

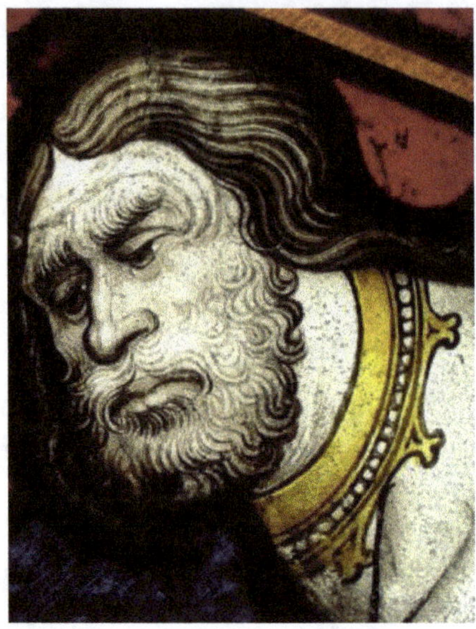

Figure 9.10   Detail from the Great East Window of York Minster

Window. The piece of glass has been painted and then fired, much as is done with the glazing process in pottery.

Islamic art is subject to a number of restrictions imposed by religious belief, although there are some examples of departures from these restrictions. Thus, it is forbidden to produce an image representing the prophet Mohammed and the depiction of the human form in a mosque is regarded by orthodox Muslims as tantamount to idolatry. Both in pottery and stained glass, Islamic art is noted for displaying intricate geometrical patterns, possibly reflecting the great contributions made to mathematics by mediaeval Islamic scholars. A beautiful example, illustrated in Figure 9.11, is in the Süleymaniye Mosque, the largest mosque in Istanbul.

It must not be thought that the art of making stained-glass windows belongs to a bygone age or is restricted to religious institutions. There are many modern examples in large houses and public buildings all over the world. Figure 9.12 shows a stained glass window in the entrance to Bentley Priory in London, which was the headquarters of the RAF Fighter Command in the Second World War.

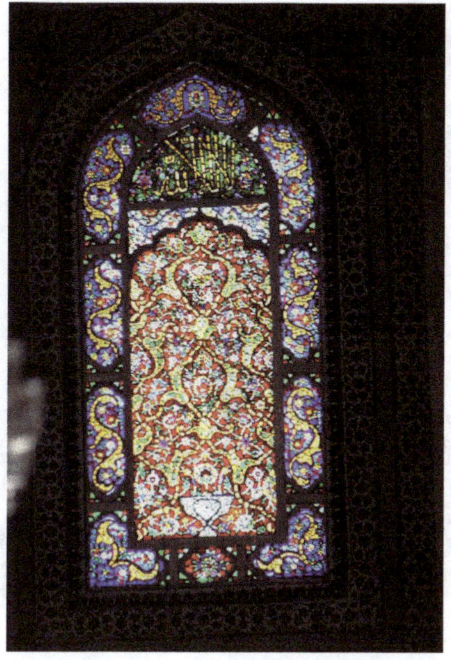

Figure 9.11   A stained glass window of the Süleymaniye mosque in Istanbul (José Luiz)

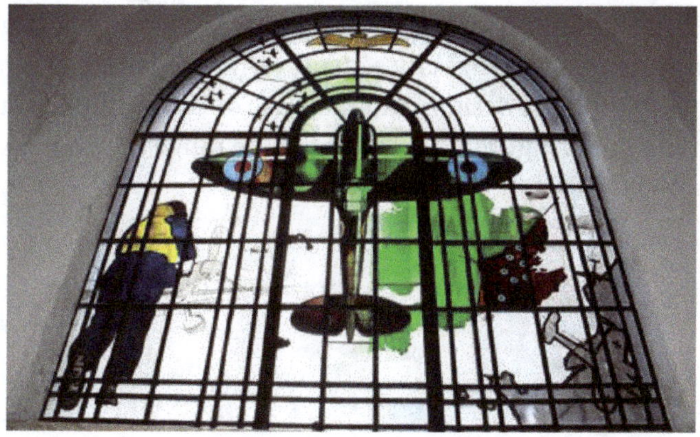

Figure 9.12   A stained-glass window in Bentley Priory, London

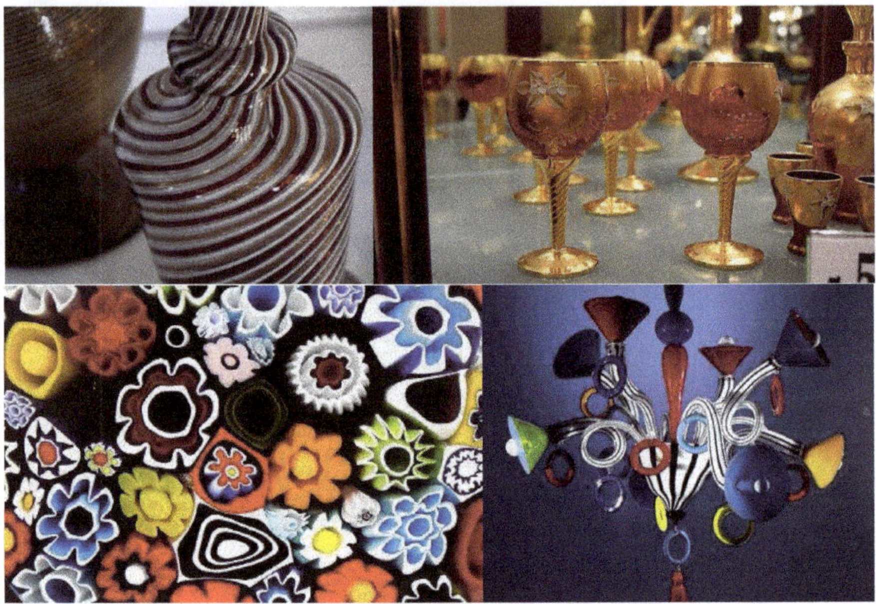

Figure 9.13   Some examples of Murano glassware

9.4.2 Decorative glassware

While glass is a substance of great utilitarian value it is, as we have seen with stained glass, a material that lends itself to the production of works of art. The most famous producers of artistic glass products, beginning in the 13th century, are based in Venice, mainly on the island of Murano. Both in the intricacy of theirs designs and their use of colour the Murano artists are world renowned. Figure 9.13 illustrated the range of products that they produce, some utilitarian but all artistic.

Chapter 10
Projecting Coloured Images

10.1 The First Projected Coloured Image

One of the giants of 19th century science was the Scottish physicist, James Clerk Maxwell (1831–1879; Figure 10.1) who, despite his short life, made seminal contributions in many areas of science. Indeed, it can be said that the whole edifice of modern physics stands on the shoulders of four giants — Newton, Maxwell, Einstein and Schrödinger. Isaac Newton established the rules that govern the material world of macroscopic, i.e. visible to the naked eye, objects and how they move. James Clerk Maxwell established the connection between electricity, magnetism and electromagnetic radiation. Albert Einstein formulated the theory of relativity that related time and space and, to an extent, his work supplanted some aspects of Newtonian mechanics. Finally, Erwin Schrödinger developed quantum mechanics that established the rules governing the behaviour of tiny objects, such as electrons, and established a connection between the world of particles and the world of waves.

Maxwell studied for his undergraduate degree in physics at Edinburgh University which was headed by the Scottish physicist James David Forbes (1809–1868). Forbes had invented a spinning disk with which the effect of adding colours could be seen. Three such disks are shown in Figure 10.2. Due to persistence of vision, when they are spun like a top about an axis through the centre they present to the eye a mixture of the individual colours on the disk similar to what is seen with overlapping coloured lights.

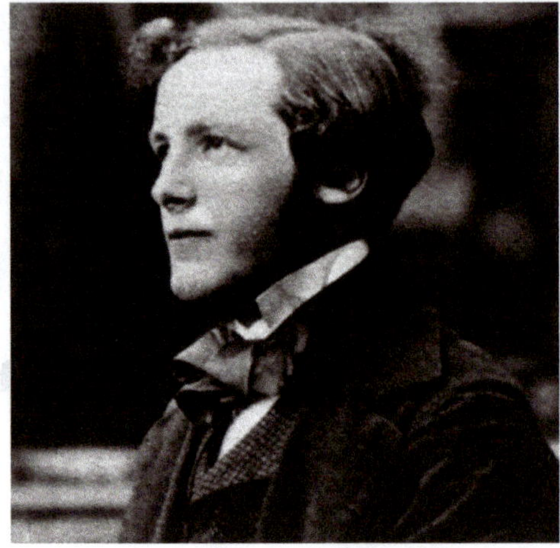

Figure 10.1   James Clerk Maxwell

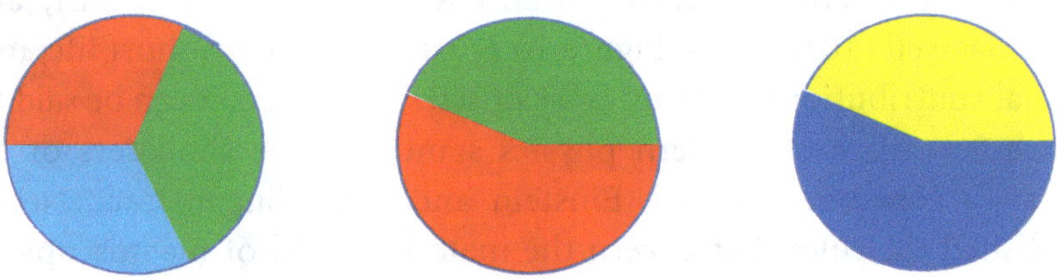

Figure 10.2   Three colour disks giving grey, yellow and grey, respectively

The left disk in the figure, with equal amounts of red, green and blue, gives grey (dark white), the centre one, with contributions of red and green, gives yellow and the right hand one, with the two complementary colours, yellow and blue, again gives grey. By copying enlarged versions of the disks in Figure 10.2, pasting the disks onto cardboard and then spinning, as indicated in Section 6.4 for Benham's disks, the reader may reproduce what Maxwell saw. The colours seen are not as bright as those seen with overlapped coloured lights, but the disks illustrated the principle of additive colour mixing quite well. Maxwell was fascinated by Forbes' disks, in particular by the result of the yellow-plus-blue combination, and this began his interest in colour and colour vision. He published a number of

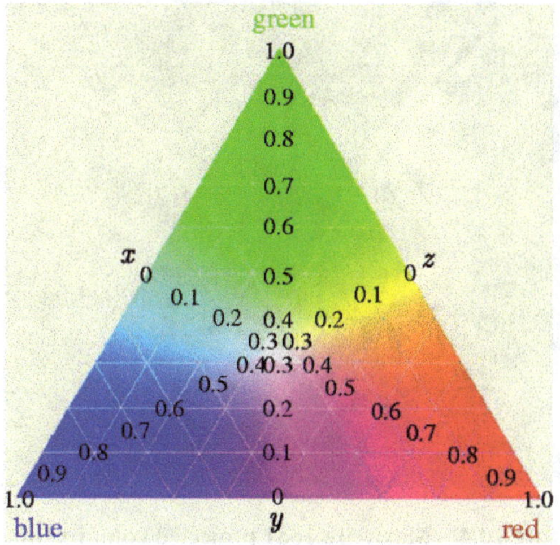

Figure 10.3   Maxwell's colour triangle

papers in the field and in 1860 he was awarded the Rumford Medal of the Royal Society for his paper *On the Theory of Colour Vision.*

Maxwell realized that it is possible to synthesize the perceived effect of any spectral colour at a wide range of saturation from mixtures of three primary colours, red, green and blue. He produced the *Maxwell colour triangle*, shown in Figure 10.3, which was a precursor of the more scientifically derived CIE colour chart displayed in Figure 5.1.

The first coloured projected image was displayed by Maxwell in a lecture to the Royal Society in 1861. At Maxwell's request, an English photographer Thomas Sutton (1819–1875) photographed a tartan ribbon three times, separately through red, green and blue filters, from the same point for each colour. The black-and-white negative for the blue-filtered negative was darkened according to the amount of blue light passing through the filter, which was greatest for blue parts of the scene, less dark for green parts and probably clear for red parts — but the darkening would also depend on the brightness of the colour. Actually, in general the light from any part of the scene would contain components of blue green and red. Producing a positive from the blue-filtered negative would then give a transparency roughly proportional to the intensity of the component of the blue radiation coming from each part of the

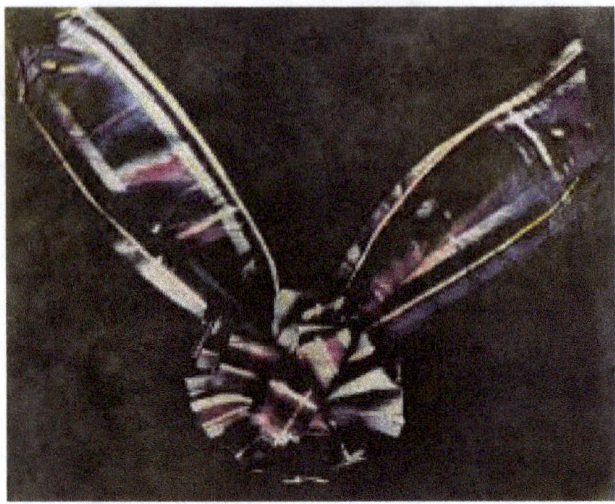

Figure 10.4   Maxwell's 1861 projected coloured image

field of view. Similar considerations should apply to the positives produced via the green filters and red filters. Maxwell used three projectors to give overlapping images — the first of the red positive with red-filtered light, the second of the green positive with green-filtered light and the third of the blue positive with blue filtered light. The result is illustrated in Figure 10.4.

By modern standards the colour rendition was poor and the reason for this is that the photographic plates used by Sutton — the only ones available at that time — were highly sensitive to blue light, less sensitive to green light and insensitive to red light, to the extent that red lights were used in photographic darkrooms because the plates would not be affected. Maxwell knew this and explained the poor colour quality as due to the nature of the colour sensitivity of the plates, but for many years people wondered how he obtained *any* red in the image; the red negative should have been transparent and the positive completely opaque so no red should have appeared in the projected image. This was explained in 1961, a century after Maxwell's lecture, when it was found that many red dyes, such as might have been used to dye the tartan ribbon, also emit some ultra-violet light, which could have passed through the red filter and to which the plates would have been sensitive.

Modern panchromatic emulsions, usually on film rather than plates, are almost equally sensitive over the whole visual range of wavelengths and had panchromatic plates been used the result of Maxwell's demonstration would have been vastly improved.

10.2 Land Projected Images

In 1959, in an issue of the journal *Scientific American*, an article appeared, written by the American scientist Edwin H Land (1909–1991), which claimed that full-coloured images could be produced with only two projection colours. Land's procedure was to produce red and green positives, much as Maxwell had done except with panchromatic film, but then to project them with some other colours, with the proviso that the red positive is projected with the longer wavelength colour. For example, the author has found that it is possible to use two yellow projection colours, one yellow from a sodium lamp as the longer-wavelength projection colour and the other from white light passed through a slightly-greenish yellow filter. While it is true that colours are perceived that are not predicted by the chromaticity diagram, the unexpected colours are very pale and sometimes barely discernible. Land also found that red and white were effective projection colours, where white light was used to project the green positive. From a classical point of view, projecting with red and white lights should only give red, through various unsaturated reds (pinks) to white. Figure 10.5 shows a red wedge, going bright to dark from left to right, and a white wedge going bright to dark going downwards. The white wedge is partly transparent and when superimposed on the red wedge the light from any point should just be a mixture of red and white. No unexpected colours are seen. The effect is much clearer with coloured lights for which to top right-hand corner would be white rather than grey.

In one of Land's experiments the original scene is shown in Figure 10.6(a) and the result of projecting the red positive with red light and the green positive with white light is shown in Figure 10.6(b). The light falling on the screen at any point in this case could only be white-plus-red, as was produced in Figure 10.5, yet the overall effect was as seen Figure 10.6(b). While the colours are nowhere near the colours in the original scene there is unexpected colour tendency towards the true colours.

An important element in the Land effect is that there should be some randomness or unpredictability in the scene being photographed. In Figure 10.5, where wedges were used and colours and intensities varied

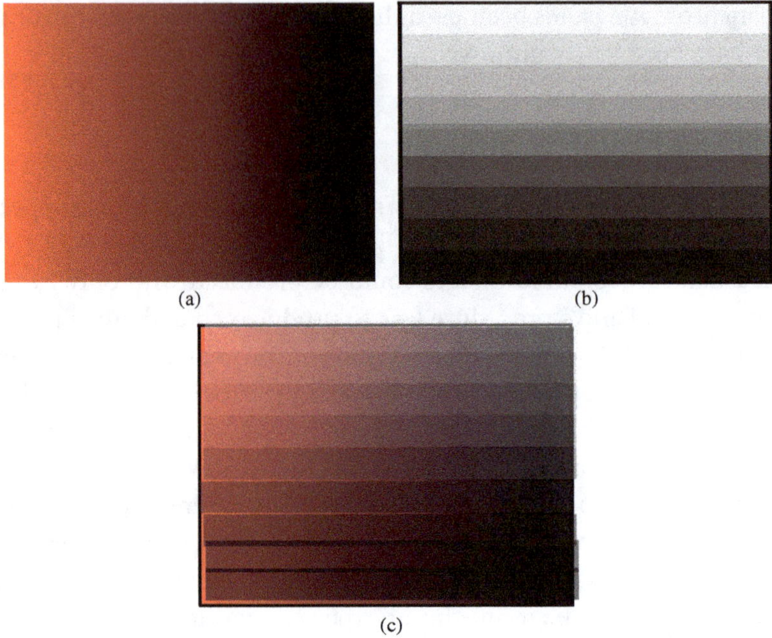

(a)

(b)

(c)

Figure 10.5   (a) A north–south red wedge. (b) An east–west white wedge. (c) The sum of the two intensities

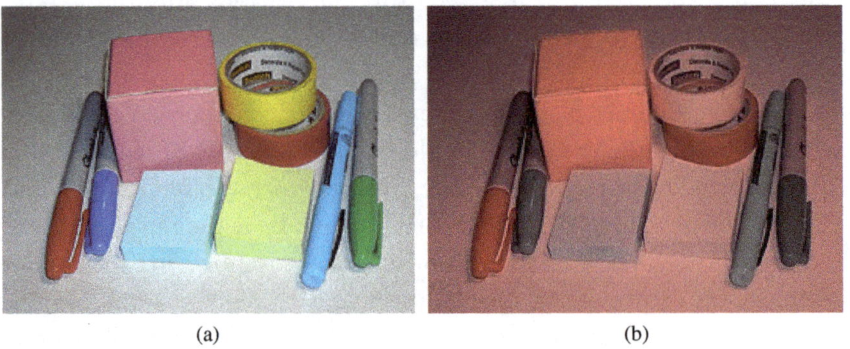

(a)

(b)

Figure 10.6   Land's experiment (a) The original scene. (b) The two-colour projection

smoothly and predictably, no unexpected colours are seen. In Figure 10.7(a) there is shown a random collection of white to black squares with various shades of grey — i.e. intensities of white. In Figure 10.7(b), there is another random collection of squares with reds of different transparencies; since

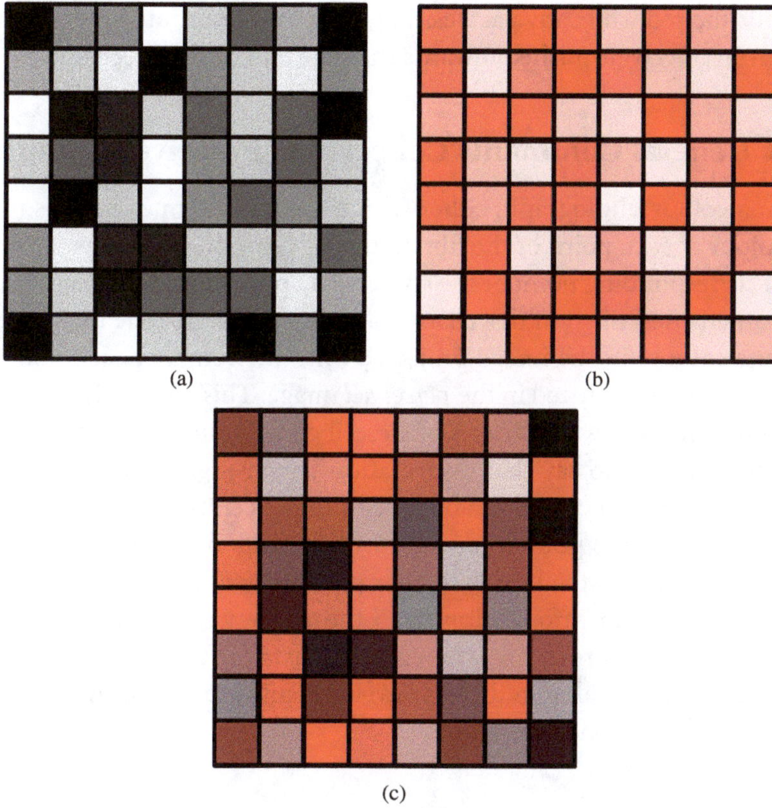

Figure 10.7   (a) Random grey squares. (b) Random pink squares. (c) The sum of (a) and (b)

there is a white background what is seen are reds of different saturations looking like various shades of pink. By superimposing Figure 10.7(b) on Figure 10.7(a) one obtains Figure 10.7(c). Now each square of Figure 10.7(c) can only be emitting a mixture of red and white light, yet other colours are faintly perceived, particularly magenta, yellow and some hints of blue. The effect is much more striking when carried out with bright lights

The Land effect is related to the phenomenon of colour constancy, described in Section 6.2. The overall general pink appearance of the image, produced by the red and white projection lights act like an external illumination of the scene being photographed. Now the principle of repulsion, described in Section 6.1, comes into play. Any part of the scene which is redder than the average pink will have its perceived colour pushed further towards the red while any part less red, i.e. a lower saturated red, will have its perceived colour pushed towards the blue end of the spectrum.

10.3 General Comments Concerning Perceived Colours

When a colour photograph, either with a digital or film camera, is taken, the colour at each point of the film faithfully reproduces what was present at the corresponding point of the scene being photographed. However, the phenomena described in this chapter and the preceding one make it clear that the colours in the image projected onto the retina at each point are not faithfully reproduced in the *perceived* image. This has partly to do with the neural networks which can be described as both diverging and converging, which is to say that information is converging from each small region of the retina onto a ganglion cell near its centre and information is diverging from each point of the retina onto a number of ganglion cells in its vicinity. There is then some further processing in the visual cortex that averages the colour information from the whole visual scene and carries out the repulsion process to give colour constancy that, as we have seen, has some survival value so that its development would be favoured by the Darwinian evolutionary principle.

Chapter 11
Early Colour Photography

The process of photography consists of creating an image of a scene in some way and then storing the image so that it can be viewed whenever required. The first stage, that of producing an image, goes back a surprizing long way but photography, as we know it today in its monochrome version, is just over 200 years old and colour photography about 100 years old. Here we describe the progress from the first ways of producing a monochrome image to the first early successful ways of producing and storing coloured images.

11.1 The Pinhole Camera and Camera Obscura

A pinhole camera, illustrated in Figure 11.1, consists of a light-tight box with a small pinhole at the centre of one of its sides, and a translucent screen on the opposite side. The idea goes back about 2400 years to the Chinese philosopher Mozi, who probably used thin rice paper, something like tracing paper, for the translucent screen. Light travels in a straight line from a point on the object, through the pinhole and eventually falls on the screen to produce a point of an inverted image. The finer the pinhole the sharper, but fainter, is the image so a compromise is required to achieve an image sharp enough to be distinct and bright enough to be seen.

A larger-scale version of a pinhole camera, where the box is either a dark room or a tent, is the *camera obscura* (Latin for 'dark room').

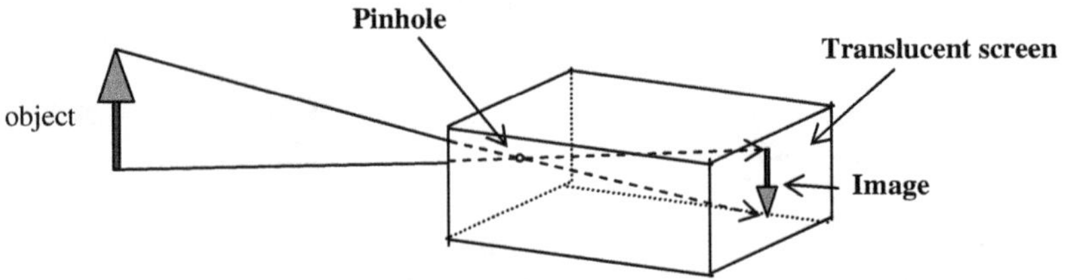

Figure 11.1   A simple pinhole camera

An eclipse of the Sun was viewed using a camera obscura by the Muslim scientist Ibn al-Haytham, known as Alhazan (965–*circa* 1040). The renaissance painter Leonardo da Vinci described the construction of a camera obscura, which was used by many artists of his time to trace out an image of a scene that was then used to guide their painting.

In the 16th century, the camera obscura was improved by substituting a lens for the pinhole, thus obtaining a brighter and sharper image. In addition, by using a mirror to intercept the rays from the lens, a non-inverted image could be projected onto a horizontal table.

Many country houses incorporated a camera obscura, used both as a means of education and for entertainment. The National Museum of Photography, Film and Television in Bradford, West Yorkshire in the UK has, as one of its exhibits, a camera obscura that can be used to view the surrounding cityscape and the activity within it.

11.2 Storing Images

The Catholic saint and Dominican friar, Albertus Magnus (1193–1290), who was also an early alchemist, discovered that silver nitrate, AgNO3, turned black when exposed to light and over the years it was found that other chemicals behaved similarly. The action of light on silver nitrate is to decompose it, giving metallic silver that, in the form of fine grains, appears to be black. In 1790 Thomas Wedgewood (1771–1805), the son of the famous English potter Josiah Wedgewood, made outline images of objects by exposing them to sunlight on paper impregnated with silver nitrate. Since the paper would turn uniformly black if kept in the light Thomas Wedgewood stored his images in a darkroom where they were viewed by dim candlelight. Thomas Wedgewood is sometimes give the accolade of being the 'Father of photography' but this honour was better earned by the next individual whose work we describe.

11.2.1   Joseph Nicéphore Niépce

As will become apparent, French scientists and inventors played a leading role in the development of photography and the first of these, Joseph Nicéphore Niépce (1765–1833; Figure 11.2), fully deserves the title of 'Father of photography', although the process he used to produce a permanent image, which could be seen in full daylight, bears little relationship to photography as we know it today. He began by coating a metal plate with a solution of bitumen — a black material derived from petroleum — in lavender oil. The plate was then exposed to an image produced by a camera obscura for about eight hours. Exposure to light bleached the bitumen and also hardened it so when the plate was subsequently washed in lavender oil the amount of bitumen removed was greatest where the plate had low exposure and least where the plate was most exposed and the bitumen was very hard. The remaining bitumen was a pale grey colour and the metal plate was relatively darker, the net effect being a positive image of

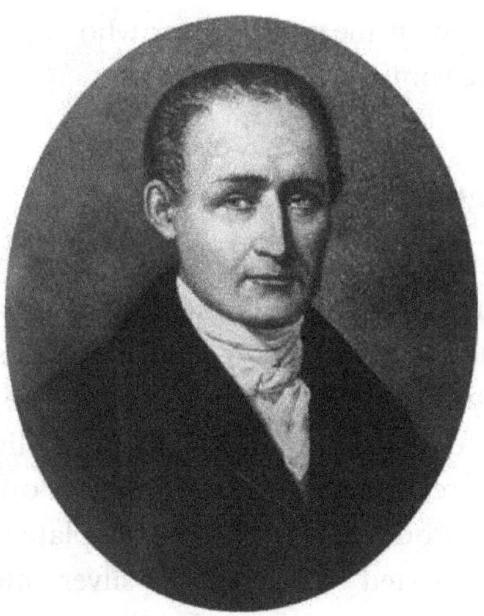

Figure 11.2   Joseph Nicéphore Niépce

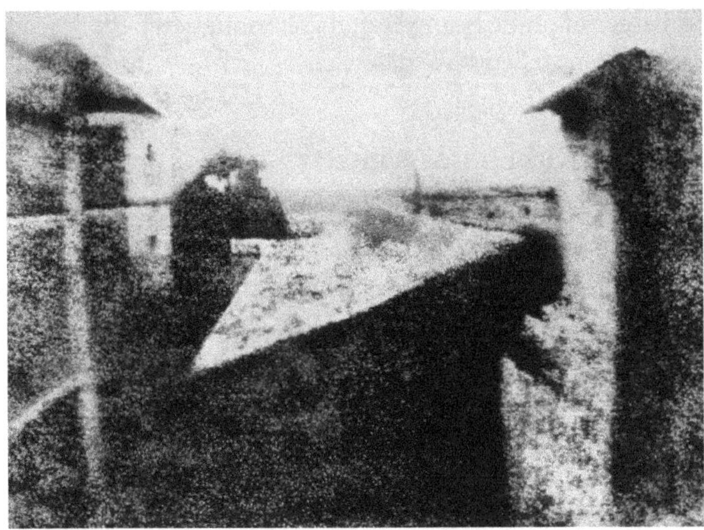

Figure 11.3   A heliograph image of a view from a window at Le Gras

the recoded scene. Niépce called this process *heliography* ('Sun writing') and an early example, produced in 1826, is shown in Figure 11.3.

Because of the long exposures required, Niépce tried to find a more practical technique, working in collaboration with Louis Daguerre (1787–1851; Figure 11.4), a well-known theatre designer who was also a chemist. After Niépce died, Daguerre continued the work alone.

11.2.2 Louis Daguerre

In 1837, Daguerre described and displayed a photographic process that gave a permanent image in a few minutes, giving what became known as *Daguerreotypes*. A silver-coated copper plate was exposed to iodine vapour that converted the silver to silver iodide. The image was then projected onto the plate for a few minutes; the action of the light decomposed the silver iodide and the greater the exposure at a point on the plate the greater the amount of silver produced there. Next the plate was exposed to mercury vapour that converted the deposited silver into silver amalgam, a shiny compound of silver and mercury. Finally, washing the plate with salt water removed everything except the shiny amalgam, the density of which

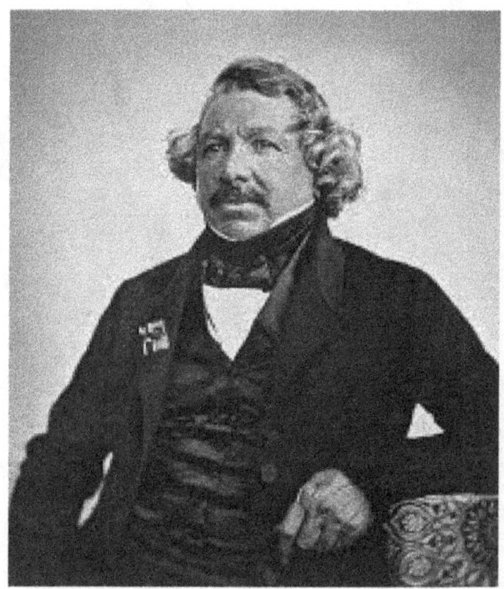

Figure 11.4   Louis Daguerre

was proportional to the original exposure at any point. By viewing the plate obliquely a positive image was seen with the plate brightest where the image had been brightest; direct viewing gave a negative image. The image was also inverted but this could be corrected by laterally inverting the image falling on the plate with a mirror. A Paris street scene, taken by Daguerre in 1839, is shown in Figure 11.5. Because of the long exposure no traffic can be seen but at the bottom left a man having his shoes polished can be seen; he stayed still for long enough to record an image. This unknown man and the shoe polisher have the honour of being the first people ever to be photographed.

11.2.3 William Henry Fox Talbot

The British inventor, William Henry Fox Talbot (1800–1877; Figure 11.6) had perfected a process for producing permanent images some years earlier than Daguerre, but he did not announce his discovery for producing what he called *calotypes* (Greek *kallos* means 'beautiful') until he patented the process in 1841. This process began with high quality smooth paper that had been soaked in silver nitrate solution and then partially dried; silver nitrate is photosensitive (it was used by Thomas Wedgewood) but

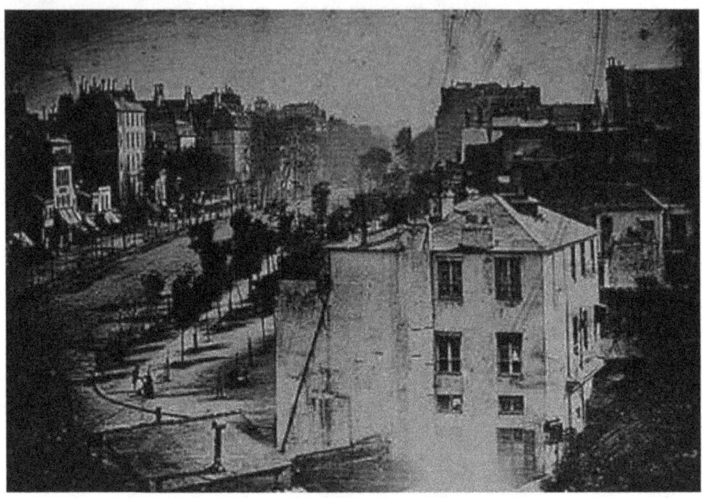

Figure 11.5 A Paris street scene taken by Daguerre.

much less so than silver halides — for example silver chloride, iodide or bromide. The paper was then immersed in a solution of potassium iodide that produced insoluble silver iodide in the paper, which was then rinsed and dried. This last process had to be carried out in weak candlelight because the paper became photosensitive; the prepared paper could then be stored in a light-tight container.

Just before a photograph was to be taken the paper was soaked in a solution of *gallo-nitrate of silver*, an equal mixture of silver nitrate and gallic acid ($C_6H_2(OH)_3COOH$), and then dried again. This increased the sensitivity of the paper, thus reducing the required exposure. The partially dry paper was then inserted in the camera and the image was focussed on the paper for a time anywhere between 2 seconds and a few minutes, depending on the brightness of the image. It was then immersed in a solution of gallo-nitrate and the latent image gradually emerged. When it was at the right intensity, the paper was transferred to a fixing agent, for example sodium thiosulphate ($Na_2S_2O_3$) known as *hypo* to modern photographers, which removed all the remaining photosensitive material from the paper.

The image at this stage was a negative. The paper for producing positive images was first soaked in common salt (sodium chloride), and then

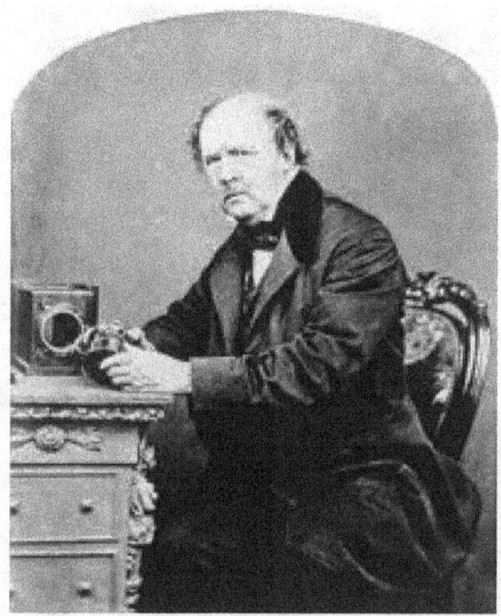

Figure 11.6   William Henry Fox Talbot

brushed on one side with silver nitrate solution to produce photosensitive silver chloride. The negative was placed in contact with this print paper and then exposed to bright sunlight for fifteen minutes or so, which produced an image on the print paper. This was finally fixed with hypo, rinsed in clean water and dried. An early calotype image is shown in Figure 11.7. The calotype process was far more practical than that of Daguerre since many positives could be produced from a single negative.

An individual linked to Fox Talbot's work in the development of photography was John Herschel (1792–1871), a mathematician, astronomer, chemist, botanist and inventor in the field of photography, who was a son of the famous astronomer William Herschel. He discovered that hypo could be used as a fixer and he also gave the name *photography* (derived from Greek and literally meaning '*light writing*') to this way of producing images using *negatives* and *positives*.

11.2.4 The wet collodion process and modern film

The Fox Talbot process was soon replaced by the *wet collodion* process invented in 1851 by the British sculptor, Frederick Scott Archer (1813–1857; Figure 11.8). A glass plate was uniformly coated with collodion — a

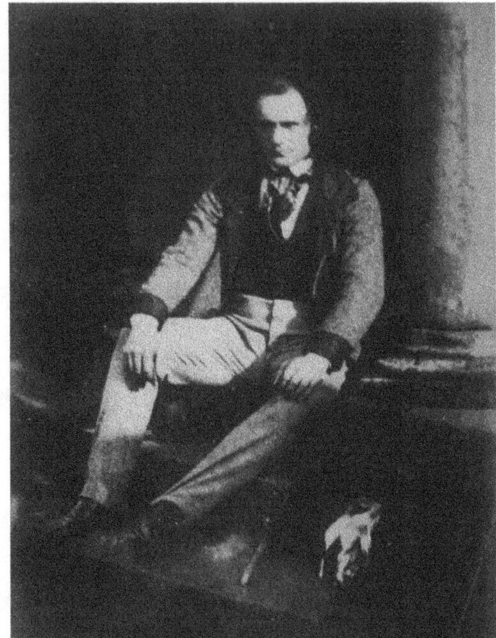

Figure 11.7   A calotype image of Thomas Duncan taken in 1844 (National Gallery of Scotland)

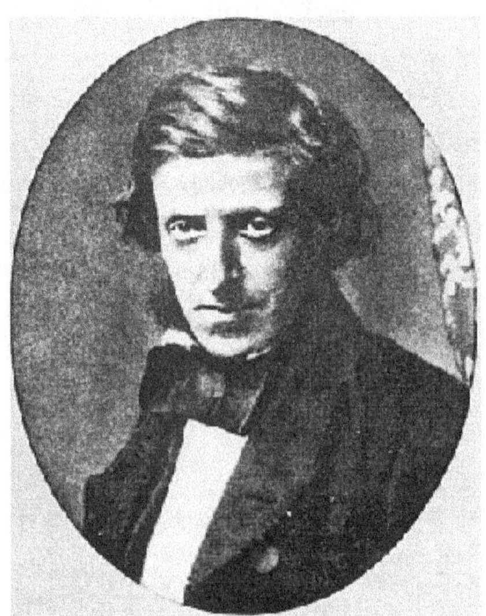

Figure 11.8 Frederick Scott Archer

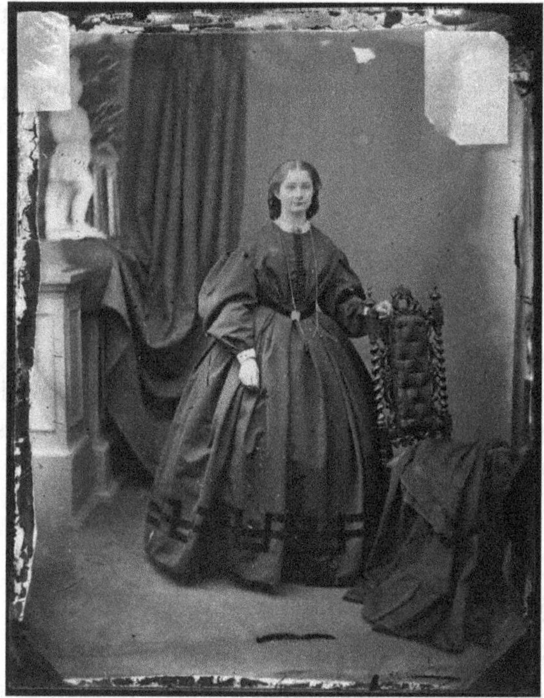

Figure 11.9   An early wet-collodion photograph

sticky solution of cellulose nitrate in ether and alcohol — impregnated with a soluble halide salt (e.g. sodium chloride, bromide or iodide). When the plate was immersed in a tank of silver nitrate in a darkroom it produced silver halide particles suspended in the collodion. This plate, in a wet condition, was loaded into a plate-holder and inserted into the camera. Exposures could vary from a couple of seconds to several minutes. The plates were then developed in a mixture of ferrous sulphate, acetic acid and alcohol and then fixed either in hypo or potassium cyanide.

The process gave negatives of high quality; Figure 11.9 shows a photograph produced in this way. Although it gave good results the process was difficult and complicated. In 1871 an English doctor, Richard Maddox (1816–1902) produced a dry plate in which the photosensitive chemicals were embedded in a layer of gelatine on thin glass plates. These could be stored in light-tight boxes and used when required. Shortly afterwards, in

1878, an American inventor, George Eastman (1854–1932), the founder of the Eastman Kodak Company, produced roll film made of celluloid coated with impregnated gelatine. This, together with the design and marketing of an easy-to-use camera, moved photography from being a specialist activity into the mass market.

11.3 Early Colour Photography

The production of the first projected coloured image by Maxwell was described in Section 10.1. However, that was projection, not photography, and scientists and inventers were soon chasing the holy grail of producing permanent coloured images by a photographic process. As with monochrome photography, it was French scientists and inventors who led the way in this endeavour.

11.3.1 Louis Ducos du Hauron

The French scientist, Louis Ducos du Hauron (1837–1920; Figure 11.10) produced the first true-colour photograph, which depended on the use of subtractive colour as explained in Section 4.4. He described his process in an influential book, *Les Couleurs en Photographie* and he certainly deserves the title of 'Father of colour photography'.

At first Ducos du Hauron only conceived his method as a theoretical exercise that could not be put into practice because the available photographic plates were mainly sensitive to blue light and completely insensitive to red light. This changed when, in 1873, a German chemist and photographer, Hermann Wilhelm Vogel (1834–1895) showed that adding corallin, a yellow dye derived from coal tar, to the collodion on a plate increased its sensitivity in the red-to-yellow region of the spectrum. Later he showed that other dyes could give other changes of colour sensitivity. With these innovations Ducos du Hauron could now put his theories into practice.

Ducos du Hauron made black-and-white glass negatives of a scene taken through orange, green and violet filters using plates dyed so as to be sensitive to those colours. He then prepared three sheets of paper coated with gelatine, each containing a different pigment — carmine (crimson),

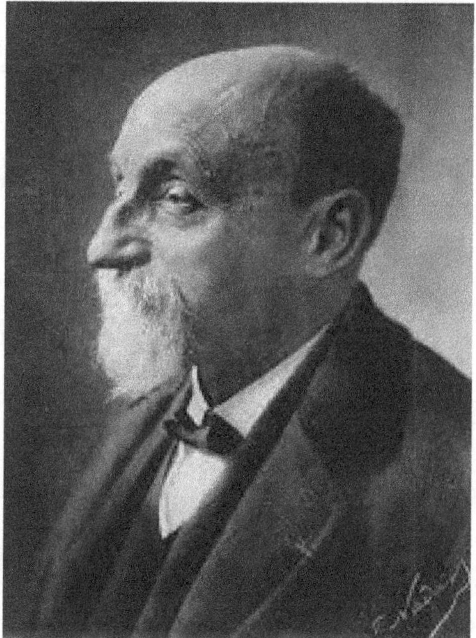

Figure 11.10   Louis Ducos du Hauron

Prussian blue and orpiment (yellow–orange) — which were made photo-sensitive by adding ammonium dichromate ($(NH_4)_2Cr_2O_7$) dissolved in alcohol. The paper sheets were then placed in contact with the negatives and exposed to light — red paper with the green-filtered plate, blue paper with the orange-filtered plate and yellow–orange paper with the violet-filtered plate.

We now consider the effect on the three paper-plate combinations. The green filter would be opaque to light at the red end of the spectrum so a red region of the scene would be clear on the negative. Thus the paper with the red pigment, in contact with the green-filtered negative, would be most exposed to the red parts of the scene. The effect of the dichromate on the gelatine is to harden it when it is exposed to light so the gelatine is hardened in the red parts of the scene. By washing the paper the unhardened gelatine is removed leaving red-coloured gelatine approximately in proportion to the transparency of the negative at each point. The gelatine from the sheet was then transferred to a separate glass plate by pressing the paper onto the

Table 11.1   The Ducos du Hauron process for producing a colour print. Each entry gives at the top the density of the negative and at the bottom the contribution to the print

| | Colour of Part of Scene | | | |
Filter and Gelatine Colour	Red	Yellow	Green	Blue
Orange filter	Black	Black	Moderate	Clear
Blue gelatine	None	None	None	Strong
Green filter	Clear	Moderate	Black	Moderate
Red gelatine	Strong	Some	None	Some
Violet filter	Clear	Clear	Moderate	Black
Yellow-orange gelatine	Strong	Strong	None	None
Net result on print	Red with orange tinge	Yellow with orange tinge	Green	Blue with purple tinge

plate. By a similar process final glass plates were also produced with blue gelatine and yellow-orange gelatine with densities corresponding to the blue and orange-yellow content of the original scene at each point. Finally each glass plate was pressed in turn in exact registry onto a piece of paper to give the final print. Table 11.1 shows the relationship between the colour in the original scene and what is seen on the final print.

The process was very demanding in time, and great care had to be taken, especially in the final stage to ensure that the colours were in exact registry. However, good results could be obtained and Figure 11.11 shows a print produced by Ducos du Hauron in 1877 of the city of Agen in the Aquitaine region of France.

11.3.2 The Lippmann process

The processes described for photography so far, either monochromatic or coloured, were totally dependent on the products of chemistry. A completely different process, dependent on the wave nature of light, was invented by the Luxembourg-born, but French, physicist, Gabriel Lippmann (1845–1921; Nobel Prize for Physics, 1908; Figure 11.12).

His process depended on the way that light, an electromagnetic wave motion, behaved when it was reflected from a mirror. In the language of

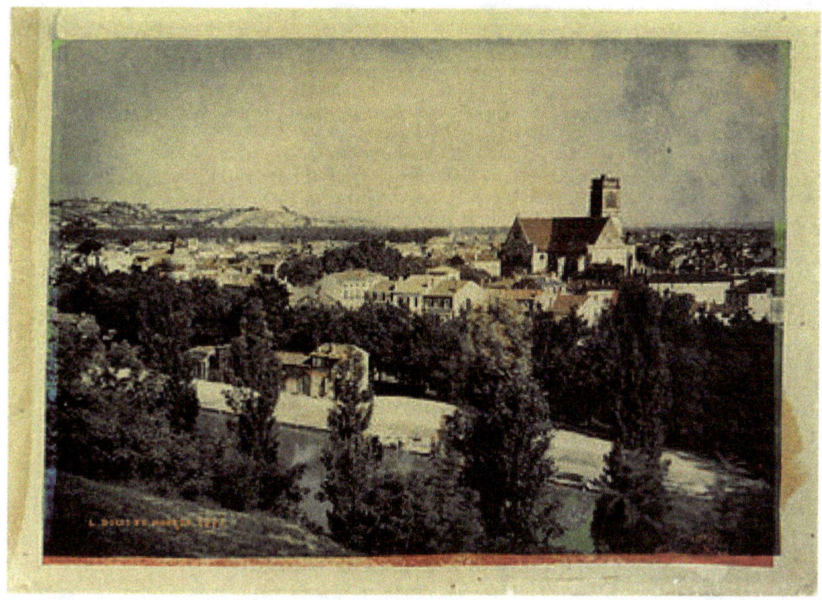

Figure 11.11   A photograph of Agen taken by Ducos du Hauron in 1877

physicists, at the mirror the phase of the wave changes by 180°. This meant that, whatever the electromagnetic disturbance is at the mirror surface from the oncoming wave, it is equal and opposite to that of the reflected wave, so they cancel out and there is no net effect at the mirror surface. The oncoming wave and the reflected wave interfere with each other so that at any point and at any time the resultant electromagnetic disturbance is the sum of the two disturbances. In this case the net effect is to set up what is called a *standing wave*, the form of which is shown in Figure 11.13. Every wave motion has an associated period, T, which is the time taken for it to go through one cycle so that the situation at the end of the cycle is similar to that at the beginning. Starting at a particular time the disturbance is indicated by curve 1. After a time $T/8$ it is curve 2 and then in successive periods of $T/8$ it becomes curves 3, 4, 5, 4, 3, 2, 1 and the cycle is complete. At a point marked *node* in the figure the electromagnetic disturbance is always zero as is the intensity of the light there. At a point marked *antinode* the electromagnetic disturbance, and the intensity of the light, is a maximum.

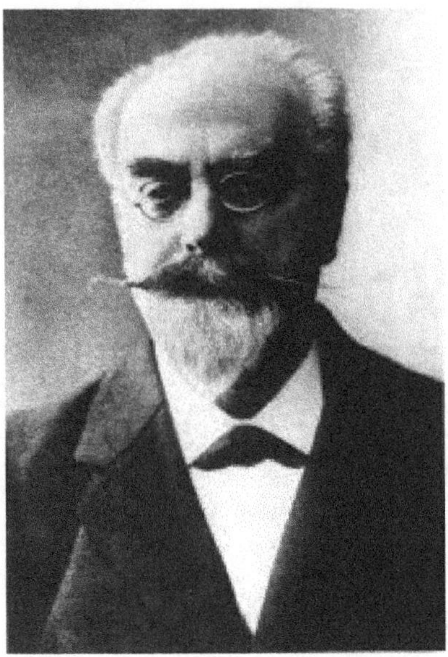

Figure 11.12   Gabriel Lippmann

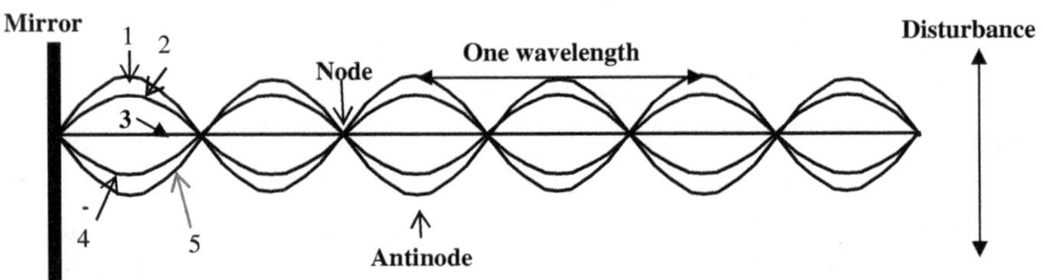

Figure 11.13   A standing wave showing successive electromagnetic disturbance

In the Lippmann process a glass plate is coated with a very thin emulsion, with a thickness of a few wavelengths, which contains very fine photosensitive grains. The plate is placed with the emulsion side on a mercury surface, which acts as a mirror. If light of a single wavelength fell on the plate then, within the emulsion, wherever there was a node there would be no blackening of the emulsion and where there was an antinode there would be maximum blackening of the emulsion. The general effect is shown in Figure 11.14.

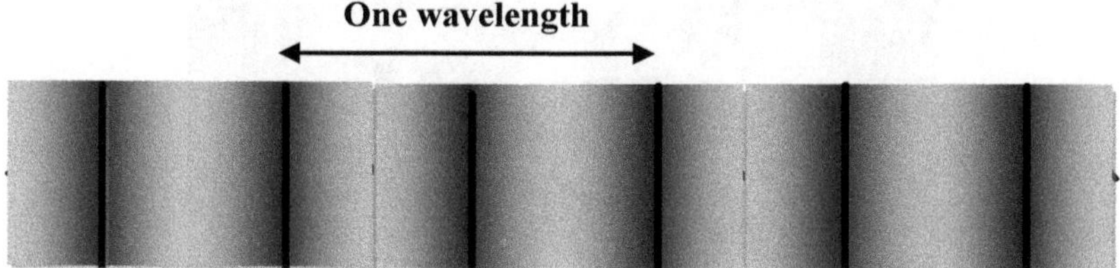

Figure 11.14   The nodes and antinodes of the standing wave and blackening within the emulsion

If a single wavelength were present in the original illumination and white light was projected onto the developed plate then the silver grains that happened to scatter the white light backwards would interfere with the oncoming light in such a way that the only colour seen would be that in the original illumination. The periodicity in the plate would give constructive interference between the light back-scattered from successive darkened regions for the wavelength in the original illumination, while for other wavelengths the net intensity would be zero. When many wavelengths, or indeed a complete spectrum of wavelengths, is present in the image then the blackening of the plate at any point is the sum of the blackening from the components of all the wavelengths and with white-light illumination the colour seen at the point is the colour at the corresponding point in the original scene with the original distribution of wavelengths. An example of an early Lippman colour picture is shown in Figure 11.15.

11.4 Comments on Early Colour Photography

Both the Ducos du Haumon and the Lippmann processes for producing coloured pictures satisfy the criterion that the images are permanent but what is obtained is just a single image and the only way to produce another similar image is to repeat the whole process again. They are also both very demanding on the skill of the photographer and neither of them could form the basis for large-scale routine colour photography. What is required is a process that is simple to perform and will give the ability to produce

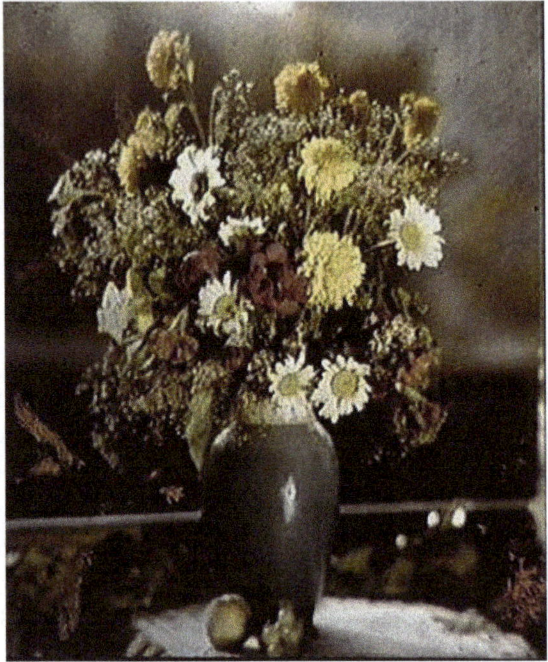

Figure 11.15   An early Lippmann colour photograph

multiple permanent images, much as is available using negatives with monochromatic photography. However, these early efforts were important in establishing that colour photography was feasible and they provided a foundation upon which others could build.

Chapter 12
Colour Photography

We have dealt with three ways of producing coloured images. The first, due to Maxwell, uses colour addition with three primary colours to produce a projected coloured image. The second is that of Ducos du Hauron that uses a subtractive colour process involving overlapping pigments behaving like three coloured filters. The third process, the one designed by Lippmann, uses the interference of light to produce a coloured image. To have colour photography, in the sense that John Herschel envisioned it, we need to have a process that provides a negative from which any number of coloured positives can be produced, giving a true rendering of the colour of the original scene.

12.1 The Autochrome Process

As we have already seen, French scientists and inventors were pre-eminent in the development of photography and, through the work of Ducos du Haumon and Lippmann, in the early development of colour photography. This leading French role also extended into motion film making, especially through the work of the Lumière brothers (Figure 12.1) — Auguste (1862–1954) and Louis (1864–1948). It was the Lumière brothers who invented the first commercial process for colour photography in 1907 — the *autochrome process*. It did not satisfy the condition that many positives

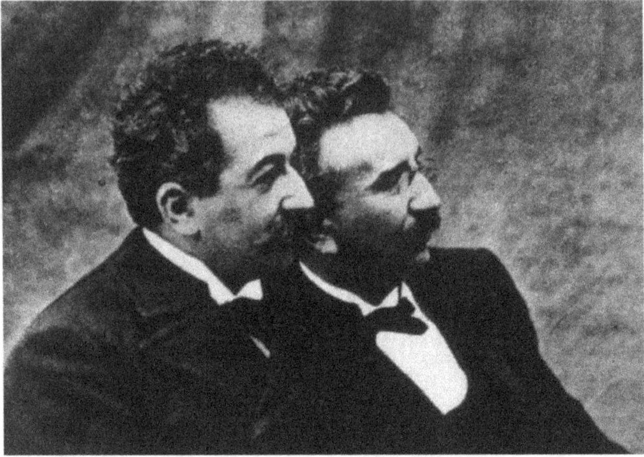

Figure 12.1   The Lumière brothers

could be produced from a negative but it was commercially viable and many photographers used it to produce single positive images of good quality.

The manufacture of the glass plates for the autochrome process, carried out in the Lumière brothers' factory in Lyon, was quite complicated. Transparent potato starch grains were produced and passed through a series of sieves until only those with diameters between 10 and 15 microns were isolated. These were divided into three batches that were then dyed red, green and blue although other combinations of three colours could be used. A mixture of the red, green and blue grains was thoroughly mixed so that there were no local concentrations of any one colour of grain. Next, a glass plate was coated with a thin layer of transparent sticky varnish and the mixture of grains was spread over the plate just one grain thick. The relative numbers of red, green and blue grains was such that the plate appeared grey by white transmitted light. Inevitably there were some gaps between the grains but these were reduced by passing a roller over the plate subjecting it to a pressure of five tonnes per square centimetre, which squashed the grains and reduced the gaps between them. Then a fine powder of carbon grains was spread over the plate and carbon grains stuck to the plate wherever the sticky varnish was not covered by starch grains; the remainder of the carbon was then shaken or blown off the plate. At this

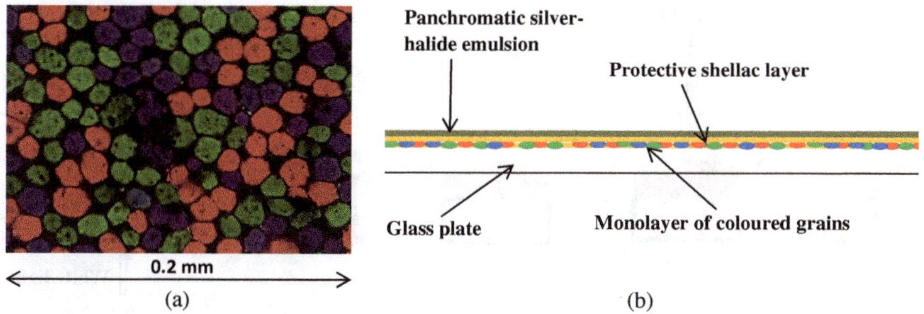

Figure 12.2 (a) The distribution of grains on the glass plate. (b) The layers on the autochrome plate

stage there is an intimate mixture of the three kinds of coloured starch grains spread over the plate, at a density of over 600,000 grains per square centimetre, with any gaps blacked out with carbon. The grains were then covered with a thin transparent layer of shellac to protect them from a wetting process that occurs in developing the image and, finally, a panchromatic silver halide emulsion, sensitive over the whole spectral range, was spread over the plate. A representation of the distribution of coloured grains is shown in Figure 12.2(a) and the cross section of the plate in Figure 12.2(b).

It is apparent that the production of the autochrome plates was complicated and technically demanding, but using them for photography was comparatively simple. Because of all the layers on the plate, exposure times were greater than for black-and-white photography but, otherwise the process of taking a photograph was the same.

The plate was placed in the camera so that the light passed through the coloured grains before reaching the photographic emulsion. When light falls on a red grain the transmitted intensity, and the amount of silver halide converted into silver, varies according to the red content of the light. The grain acts as a red filter preferentially letting through red light. The first stage of the developing process is to immerse the plate in a solution that dissolves away the silver but leaves the silver halide intact. The position now is that the amount of silver halide present at each red grain position in the plate is greater if the red content is less. Next the plate is exposed to light and all the remaining silver halide is converted to opaque silver. The plate is now a positive; for the position of a red grain, the greater

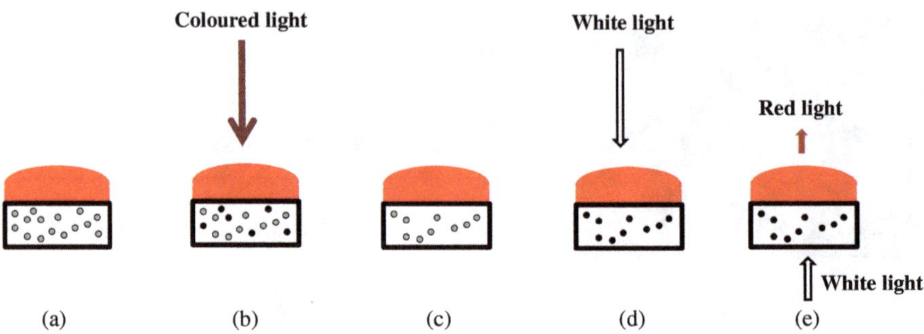

Figure 12.3   (a) A red grain over photographic emulsion. The grey dots are silver halide particles. (b) The image falls on the plate. The number of silver halide particles converting to silver is proportional to the red content of the exposure. (c) The silver particles are dissolved away. (d) Remaining silver halide particles are exposed to light and converted to silver. (e) When viewed by white light passing through emulsion the transmitted light is red with intensity proportional to the red content of the image

the amount of red light falling on the grain the more transparent is the emulsion layer. If the plate is viewed by transmission of white light through it then the amount of red light passing through the red grain will be proportional to the amount of red light in the image at that point. A similar process occurs for the green and blue grains. The grains are much too small to be visually resolved so what is seen in each resolvable region of the plate is the addition of red green and blue light that will reproduce the original colour in that region of the image. The process is shown schematically, and explained, for a red grain in Figure 12.3.

A particularly striking autochrome image with a wide range of colour, taken by a professional Belgian photographer shortly after 1910, is shown in Figure 12.4. However, although the autochrome process was very successful in achieving what it set out to do, it still had not achieved the ultimate goal — to produce a negative from which positive coloured prints could be obtained in any required number. To achieve this aim we must move from the old world to the new, to the United States of America.

12.2 The Kodachrome Process

The autochrome process depended on colour addition and was the invention of two individuals, the brothers Lumière, whose background

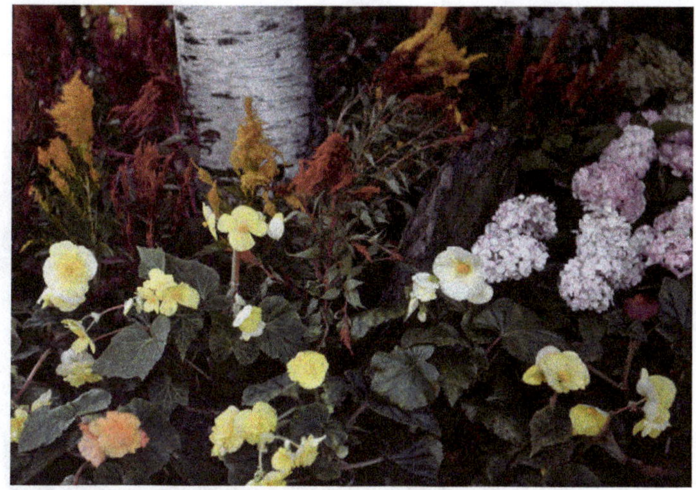

Figure 12.4   A floral autochrome image

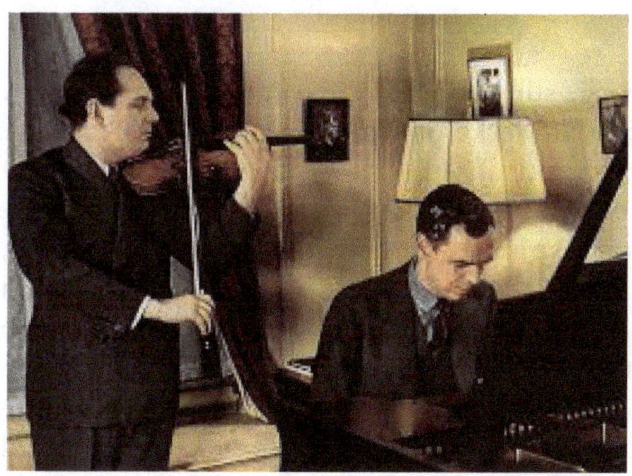

Figure 12.5   Leopold Godowsky and Leopold Mannes

and expertise was in the film industry. The next development depended on the phenomenon of colour subtraction and was the invention of a most unlikely pair of individuals — two American professional musicians (Figure 12.5). Leopold Mannes (1899–1964) was a pianist and composer and came from a family steeped in music. He studied physics

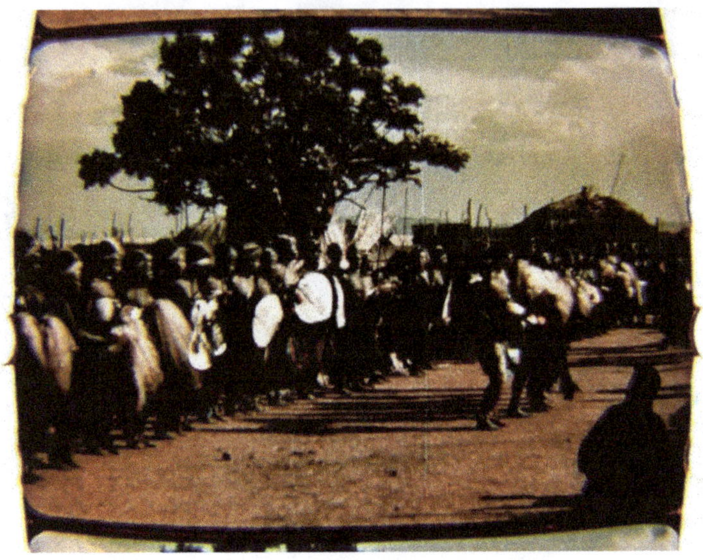

Figure 12.6   A still from a Prizma Color movie

at Harvard while still performing as a concert pianist, which gave him a necessary scientific background for his contribution to colour photography. The other member of the pair, Leopold Godowsky Jr. (1900–1983), was a soloist and first violinist with the Los Angeles and San Francisco Symphony orchestra and, like his friend, Leopold Mannes, also had a scientific background having studied physics and chemistry at the UCLA (University of California, Los Angeles). In 1918, the two friends went to see the film *Our Navy*, the first moving picture in Prizma Color (Figure 12.6). This system recorded black-and white images on alternating frames taken through cyan and red–orange filters. The film was then projected through a coloured disk containing cyan and red–orange filters synchronized with the corresponding frames. The visual system fused the colours by addition giving a range of colour, albeit not all spectral colours. Later a better Prizma Colour system was evolved, this time based on subtractive colour, but still with only two basic colours in different proportions. Mannes and Godowski were disappointed with what they had seen and embarked on a project to produce better colour film.

Mannes and Godowsky set up a laboratory to carry out their work and by 1924 they had patented some of their ideas. In 1930 they were invited by the film manufacturing company Eastman Kodak to move to Rochester, New York, to take advantage of the company's extensive laboratory facilities. By 1935 the work came to commercial fruition with the production of a subtractive colour film, *Kodachrome*, which could be used for home movies but was also available in cartridge form for producing slides for home projection.

The essence of the Kodachrome process is illustrated schematically in Figure 12.7 taking the example of a greenish-yellow light falling on the film. Three layers of photographic emulsion were deposited on the colour film, sensitized to absorb red, green and blue light respectively. When light of a particular colour hit the red-absorbing layer then the red component was absorbed and the amount of exposed silver halide silver was proportional to the red component. Similarly, in the next layer the amount of exposed silver halide produced was proportional to the green component of the light and in the final layer the amount produced was proportional to the blue component. The *total* amount of silver halide exposed in the three layers would be proportional to the intensity of the light falling on the film at that point.

We take greenish-yellow light having equal red and green components with a much smaller blue component (Figure 12.7(a)). Now the steps in producing greenish-yellow transmission of white light through the film are described in simplified form. The actual process involves more steps than are given here.

Step 1

In Figure 12.7(b) we show the amount of exposed silver halide (black dots) produced and the unexposed silver halide (white dots) in the three layers. Equal amounts of exposed silver halide are produced in the red and green-sensitive layers and comparatively little in the blue-sensitive layer.

Step 2

The film is placed in developer which converts the exposed silver halide particles to silver. The silver is then chemically removed.

Step 3

The remaining silver halide is exposed to light and the film is placed in a developer that converts it to silver. At the same time, due to the action of *colour couplers* in the developer, which become oxidized, the three layers are dyed — cyan in the red-absorbing layer, magenta in the green-absorbing layer and yellow in the blue-absorbing layer. The intensity of the dye in each layer is proportional to the amount of silver it contains. This is the situation in Figure 12.7(c).

Step 4

The silver is removed chemically from the three layers (Figure 12.7(d)). For the greenish-yellow light we are considering, the cyan and

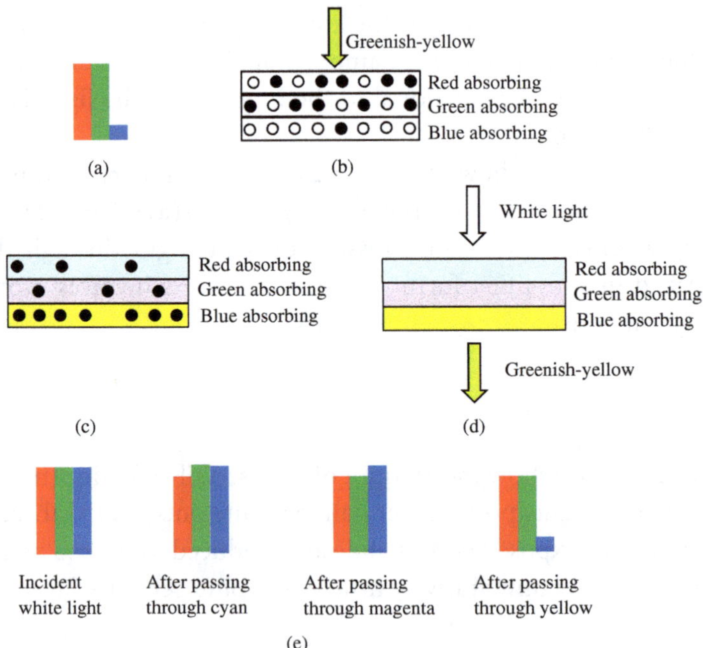

Figure 12.7   (a) The tricolour composition of greenish-yellow light. (b) Exposed silver halide grains in the three emulsion layers. (c) Originally unexposed silver halide converted to silver and emulsion layers are dyed. (d) All silver removed. (e) Incident white light is transmitted as greenish-yellow

magenta-dyed layers are of low intensity but the yellow dyed layer is of quite high intensity.

Figure 12.7(e) shows how white light passing through the three layers gives greenish-yellow transmission. When the light passes through the low-intensity cyan layer, red parts of the spectrum are slightly reduced and other parts of the spectrum unaffected. Similarly, when the light passes through the low-intensity magenta layer, green parts of the spectrum are slightly reduced and other parts of the spectrum unaffected. Finally, on passing through the intensely yellow layer, the red and green pass through but the blue regions of the spectrum are heavily absorbed. The net transmission corresponds to greenish-yellow light.

While taking colour photographs with Kodachrome film was as simple as taking a black-and-white photograph the development process was extremely complex and the exposed film had to be sent to a Kodak developing centre to obtain the final product. In 1936, the German company Agfa produced a colour film based on the same general principle but with the colour couplers incorporated within the original layers in the emulsion, which gave a much simpler developing process.

Although the process as described here is for coloured slides it is possible to obtain colour negatives from the slides that, used with specially coated paper, can produce colour prints. It will be seen from the Kodachrome print — Figure 12.8 — that the quality of the Kodachrome images was good as judged by the rendering of skin colour and that of grass. In 1942, Eastman Kodak introduced *Kodacolor*, a colour negative film produced specifically to give colour prints. However, by the end of the 20th century the use of film for photography was much reduced and Kodak ceased to provide a processing service to produce colour prints in 2009.

12.3 Digital Cameras

In 1969 the Canadian–American physicist William Boyle (1924–2011) and American physicist George E Smith (b.1930), working at the Bell Research Laboratory in America invented the *charge-coupled device* (CCD), for the invention of which they jointly received the Nobel Prize for Physics in 2009. A CCD is an array of light-sensitive elements fabricated on a silicon crystal. Each element is a *pixel* (picture element) of an image that is

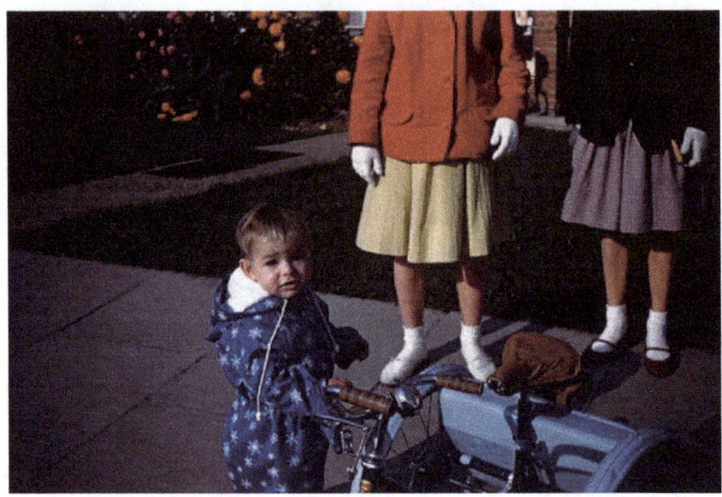

Figure 12.8   A Kodachrome print showing a wide range of colour

projected onto the surface of the CCD. The first CCDs were very crude devices; by 1974 an array of 100×100 pixels had been constructed but nowadays, with each pixel about 0.03 mm square the number of pixels in a single CCD in a good digital camera can be 10 million (10 megapixels) giving high-resolution images. Specialist cameras can have even higher resolutions. Ordinance Survey, the UK government mapping agency, modify existing maps using information from aerial survey photographs using 190 megapixel cameras, which can pick up the smallest detail of interest to cartographers.

When light falls on a light-sensitive element it generates an electric charge that is proportional to the intensity of the incident light. This charge is then transferred along a sequence of elements (giving rise to the term *charged-coupled*) and when it reaches the end the charge is converted into a voltage that is then transformed into digital form and stored in the digital camera memory. This digital information can then be downloaded to produce an image directly on a camera screen, downloaded into a computer where it can form an image on the computer VDU (visual display unit) or go directly to a printer to obtain a printed image. This satisfies the basic condition of a satisfactory camera — that many copies of the image, either in digital or printed form, can be produced once the picture has been recorded.

A great advantage of a CCD is that it utilizes more than 70 percent of the visible light that falls on it, a figure known as the *quantum efficiency*, compared to just two percent for film. This increased sensitivity makes it particularly useful for photography under dim light conditions, such as photographing wildlife at night with just moonlight as the illumination. However, one of the important uses of CCD imaging is in astronomy as it enables images to be formed of faint objects must faster than can be done with film. Again, for space telescopes, such as the HST (Hubble Space Telescope) the image is acquired in digital form, which is very convenient for radio transmission to ground stations. The Wide Field Camera on Hubble images onto a 4096 × 4096 CCD array. Although very sensitive to light, digital cameras cannot distinguish light of different wavelengths and, indeed they record well into both the ultraviolet and infrared regions of the electromagnetic spectrum (Figure 12.9).

To use a CCD array for colour photography it is necessary to use coloured filters. An array of red, green and blue filters is placed over the CCD elements and the signal from each element must be represented in the same colour at the corresponding pixel of the final image. The most commonly-used is the *Bayer filter* (Figure 12.10), designed in 1976 by Bruce E Bayer of the Eastman Kodak Company. To allow for the fact that

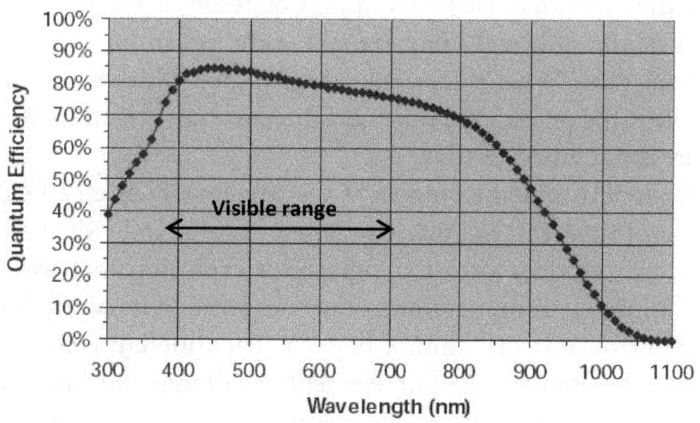

Figure 12.9   The quantum efficiency of a CCD detector

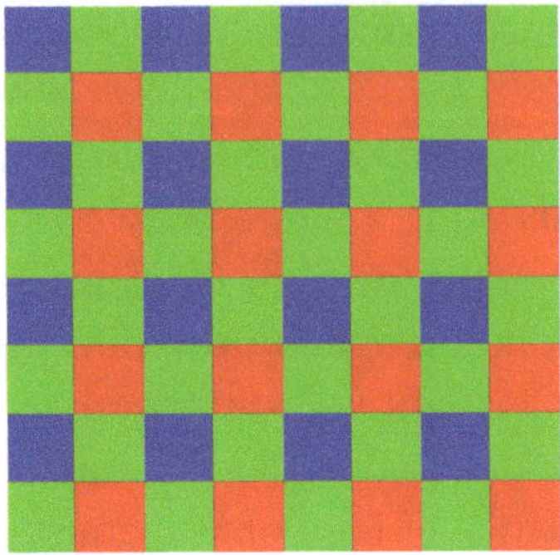

Figure 12.10   A section of a Bayer filter array

A reduced Bayer filter    **A comparison greenish grey**

Figure 12.11   An unresolved Bayer filter (at a distance) and a comparison Green-tinted grey

the eye is more sensitive to green than to red or blue, while a CCD is more uniformly sensitive over the visual range, the filter has two green elements for every red or blue one. The eye cannot resolve thee individual coloured elements in the final image so in different regions of the image the colour seen is by colour addition of the three primary colours at their respective intensities. Figure 12.11 gives a reduced version of Figure 12.10, at such a scale that the individual elements cannot be resolved for an observer at a suitable distance, although they are still there as can be confirmed with a magnifying glass. What is seen is a greenish grey, which would be green-tinted white if the pixels were much brighter; a comparison slightly green-tinted grey is put adjacent to it.

Finally, to illustrate the power of CCD imaging, Figure 12.12 shows an HST image of the Crab Nebula, assembled from 24 individual exposures. This object is the debris from a supernova explosion that was seen on Earth by Chinese astronomers, and others, in 1054. At its centre is the Crab pulsar, a neutron star that cannot be seen. The different colours indicate the dominant presence of certain elements — orange indicates hydrogen, blue is neutral oxygen, red is doubly-ionized oxygen and green is singly ionized sulphur.

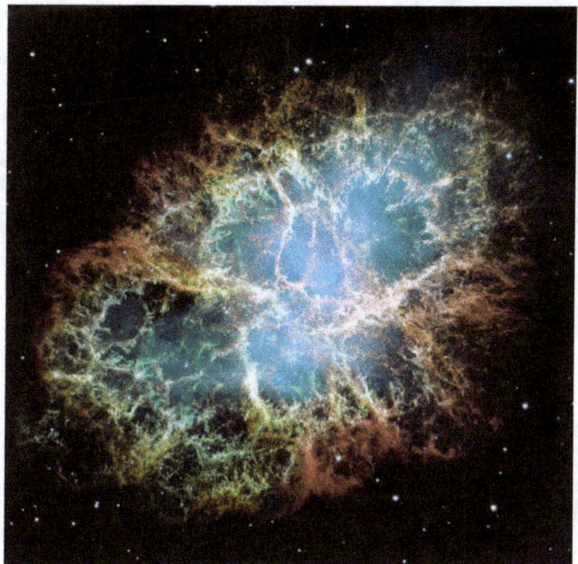

Figure 12.12   A Hubble image of the Crab Nebula

12.4 Photography as an Art Form

Painting as a form of art can slightly distort real life to emphasize some aspect of the scene that the artist wishes particularly to bring to the viewer's attention. There is a saying that 'the camera cannot lie' and in a sense that is true since the photographic image must faithfully represent the scene being photographed. Nevertheless, photographs can be doctored to create an image that looks authentic but does not represent the original scene. The dictator of the onetime Soviet Union, Joseph Stalin (1878–1953), ruthlessly eliminated anyone who crossed his path but they were not only physically dispatched but also photographically dispatched. Figure 12.13 shows a photograph after and before the airbrush removal of a Soviet commissar, Nikolai Ivanovich Yezhov, who fell out of favour with Stalin.

Discounting fakery, by a careful choice of subject, photography has been used effectively for artistic expression. A very eminent English photographer, Frank Meadow Sutcliffe (1853–1941), specialized in taking photographs in and around Whitby, a fishing port in North Yorkshire, and

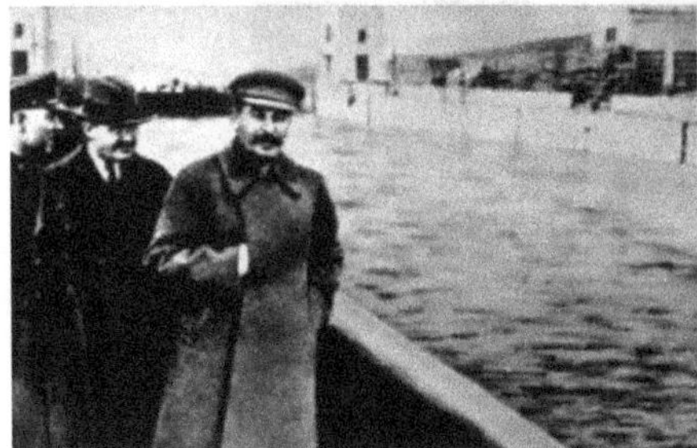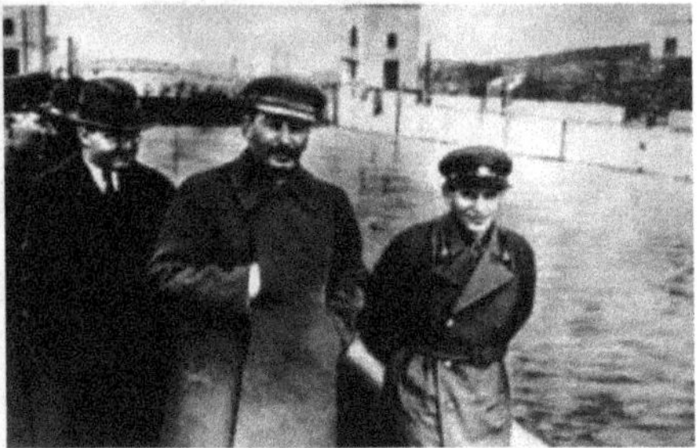

Figure 12.13   An example of removal of part of a scene by airbrushing

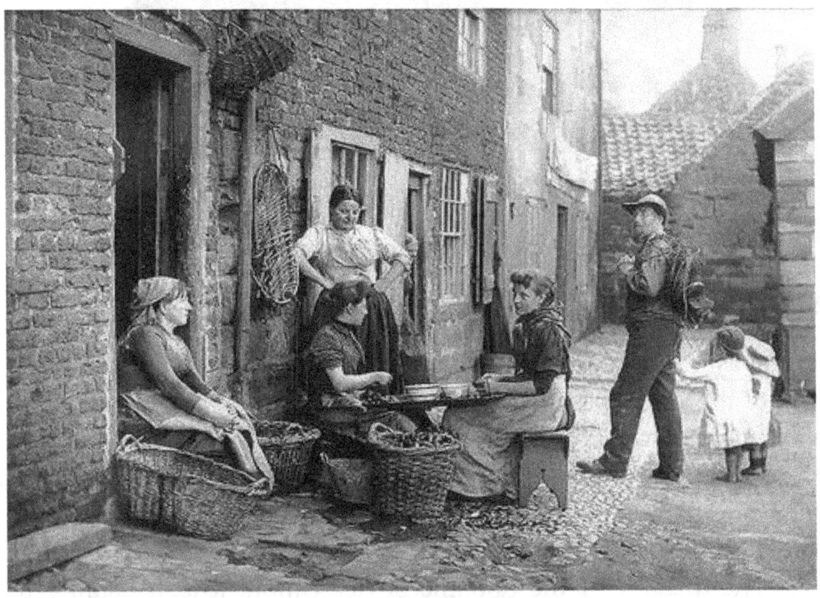

Figure 12.14 A street scene in Whitby in 1890 (Frank Meadow Sutcliffe)

his record of the local scenes, particularly of people and boats, gives a vivid impression of the life people led and the conditions in which they led those lives (Figure 12.14).

In the nature of his subject matter it is doubtful that colour would have added to the impact of Sutcliffe's photographs but there are many types of subject matter for which colour greatly enhances the artistic

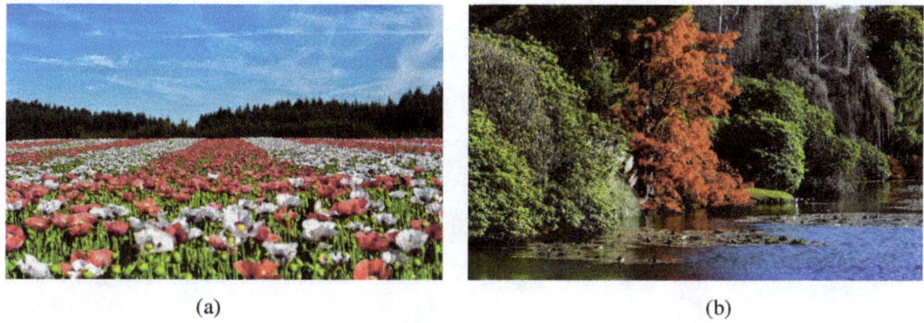

Figure 12.15   Photographs of (a) A poppy field. (b) A lakeside autumn scene (Karen Arnold)

qualities of photography. Figure 12.15(a) shows a field of red and white poppies and Figure 12.15(b) is a photograph of autumn colours by a lakeside. They are both beautiful pictures and, while they require less effort to produce than an equivalent painting, the skill of the photographer in composing such photographs should not be underestimated.

Chapter 13
Colour Cinematography

13.1 Persistence of Vision

When light falls on a rod or cone the chemical configuration of the visual pigment it contains is changed and a chain of events is initiated ending with an electrical impulse travelling along the optic nerve to the visual cortex. There are a series of chemical processes that take place, which operate over a finite period of time. This means that if the impulse on the receptor is bright but very brief the image will not be equally brief but will persist for a fraction of a second. This gives rise to the phenomenon of *persistence of vision*, which has duration of about 0.04 seconds. Thus if we look at a scene that is changing with time — a car moving along a road or the action of a ball game — what is seen at any instant is the average of what occurred in the previous 0.04 seconds. In that time a car travelling at 100 km hr^{-1} will move one metre but if the eyes move to follow the car then the car is seen without blurring but the background becomes slightly blurred. For the Forbes' disks, shown in Figure 10.2, the colour seen will be the addition of the colours of the disk if the rotation speed is about 25 revolutions per second, i.e. the disk makes a complete rotation in 0.04 seconds. If the speed of rotation is somewhat less then colour addition still occurs but there will be a distinct flicker in what is seen.

Now, if we imagine that a scene, moving or otherwise, is being seen through a rotating shutter that briefly blocks out the passage of light to the eye 25 times per second then the scene will be seen continuously since during the blocked out period the visual system is still seeing what happened previously. There would be no sense of flicker in what is seen although the intensity would be reduced; the *average* intensity would fall because of the times when no light reaches the eye. At a lower shutter speed, say one that blocks out the light 10 times per second with the blocked out times exceeding 0.04 seconds, we would see a distinct flicker and be aware of the on-off nature of either seeing or not seeing. However, even if what was being viewed was a moving scene, we would still know what we were looking at and receive an impression of jerky movement.

A useful application of persistence of vision is the *stroboscope*, a device that produces brief flashes of intense light at intervals that can be controlled. One example of its use would be to look at the working of rapidly moving machinery. Let us say that the motion of the machine is rotary and it is spinning at 100 revolutions per second. If the machine is illuminated by the stroboscope 100 times per second with light flashes of duration, say 5 microseconds, then at each flash the machine is in the same configuration and would appear to be stationary. There would be a slight blurring due to the duration of the flash, but since the machine would only rotate through 0.18° during the flash the blurring would be minimal. Without the stroboscope it would not be possible to see individual moving components of the machine but, with the stroboscopic view, one could see individual components and judge by their behaviour whether or not they were being unduly stressed. If the strobe rate were slightly reduced, say to 99.9 flashes per second, then at each flash the components of the machine would move slightly forward so giving the impression of slow motion, By slightly increasing the strobe speed, say to 100.1 flashes per second, then, again, there would be the impression of slow motion but this time in a reverse direction.

Although persistence of vision may be regarded as a flaw in the visual system, since it limits time resolution, in practice it is a very useful feature that can be exploited in various ways.

13.2 The Birth of Cinematography

The principle of cinematography is easily illustrated by anyone with a book containing several pages that can be desecrated by drawing pictures

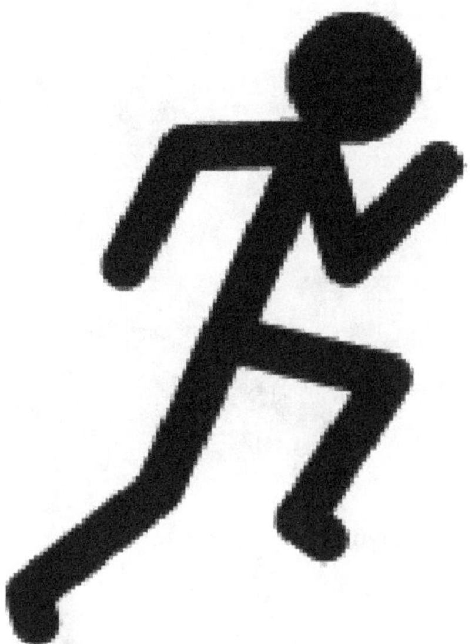

Figure 13.1 A running stick man

on it. If in one corner of each page a stick man (Figure 13.1) is drawn with the limbs slightly moved from one page to the next then by flicking the pages quickly an impression of movement is obtained. Because of persistence of vision it appears as though the motion is continuous. This illustrates the basic requirement for cinematography — to present to the eye a temporal sequence of views with a blank period between views. In the case of flicking the book the blank time is when the page corner is not face-on to the viewer. The blank period is bridged by persistence of vision and so is not detected.

13.2.1 The work of Louis Le Prince

The person with the best claim to be 'the father of modern cinematography' is the French scientist, painter, photographer and inventor, Louis Aimé Augustin Le Prince (1841–1890?; Figure 13.2). There is some doubt about the date he died since he disappeared in mysterious circumstances on a train journey from Dijon to Paris in 1890.

Le Prince went to Leeds in England in 1866 to join a brass foundry owned by an English friend, John Whitley; he married Elizabeth Whitley,

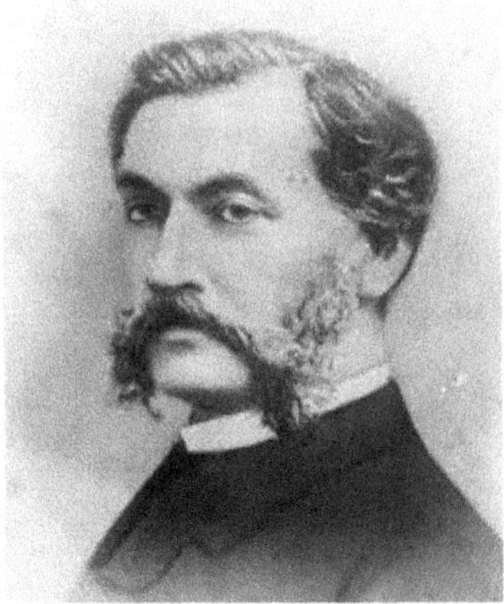

Figure 13.2   Louis Le Prince

his friend's sister, and settled down in Leeds. In 1881, he was sent to New York as a representative of the company and while there he became interested in the problem of how to produce moving pictures. He was given workshop facilities at the New York Institute for the Deaf, where his wife worked as an art teacher. In 1886, he invented and patented a device for producing a moving picture. This contained 16 lenses but since they were all photographing the image from different viewpoints the resultant projected moving image jumped about. He returned to Leeds in 1887, leaving his wife in New York, and a year later patented a movie camera using a single lens that made use of roll paper film produced by Eastman. The device repeatedly exposed a frame and then moved forward to the next frame while the film was shielded from the light. This gave a series of negatives on the paper film strip but then came the problem of producing positives that were transparent so that they could be projected. Le Prince did this by producing positives of each frame on glass slides. To project them he mounted the slides on three fibre belts, with a mechanism that moved them in sequence in such a way that there was always an image being projected, a system that, despite the low frame rate gave little flicker. The first film he produced, in 1888, showing perambulating figures, was taken outside the Whitley home, now a mansion and restaurant in Roundhay Park in Leeds. Figure 13.3 shows the sequence of frames giving this first proper moving picture. Later, he took pictures of the traffic and

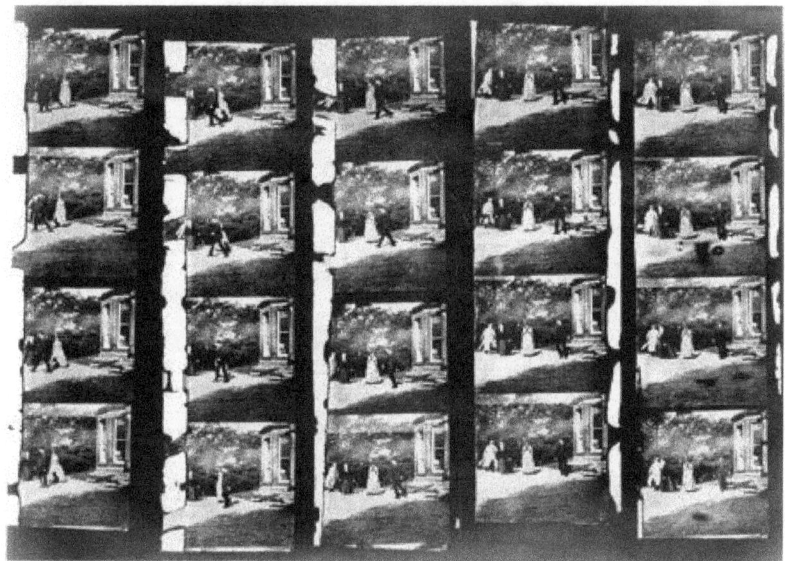

Figure 13.3   Frames from the first projected moving picture

pedestrians on Leeds Bridge in the centre of the city, an event commemo-rated by a plaque on the bridge. When these moving images were given a public showing in Leeds they were the first motion picture show to an audience in the modern sense.

Le Prince intended to return to New York to re-join his wife but first went to France to visit his brother in Dijon. It was on his return journey to Paris that he disappeared — a mystery never solved.

13.2.2 Other pioneers of cinematography

Following closely on Le Prince's heels, in the late 1880s and 1890s, there were many other individuals developing cinematography in a number of countries. A significant technological advance that happened in 1889, was the production of the first transparent celluloid roll film by the American inventor and entrepreneur, George Eastman (1854–1932; Figure 13.4), the founder of the Eastman Kodak company.

The pioneering work of Louis Le Prince seems to be largely unknown and it is the English portrait photographer, William Friese-Greene

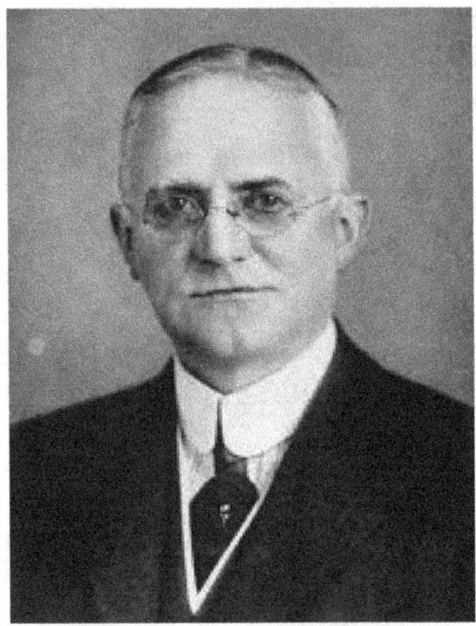

Figure 13.4   George Eastman

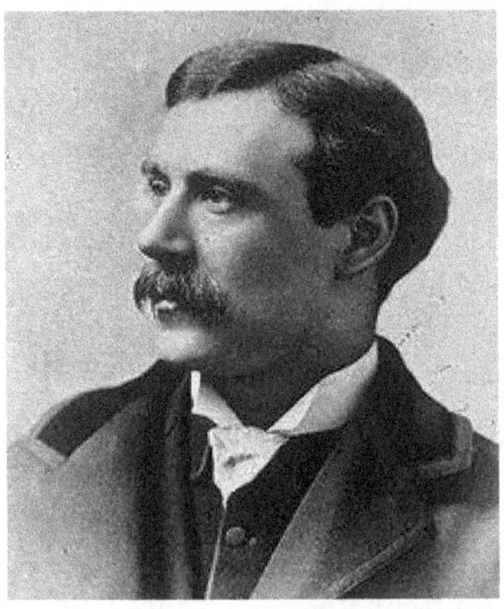

Figure 13.5   William Friese-Greene

(1855–1921; Figure 13.5), who is often quoted as the inventor of cinematography. He designed a camera capable of taking 10 frames per second using perforated celluloid film However, the low frame rate gave an annoying degree of flicker and jerkiness and his equipment was not very

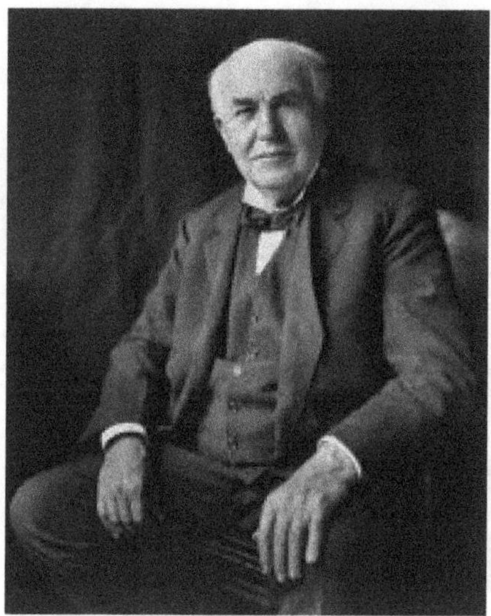

Figure 13.6   Thomas Edison

reliable so the public performance of his moving images to the public in 1890 was not a great success.

Concurrently with Friese-Greene's work, between 1889 and 1892, the prolific American inventor, Thomas Edison (1847–1931; Figure 13.6) and his assistant, William Dickson (1860–1935) were designing two devices, one for taking moving pictures — the *Kinetograph* — and the other for viewing them — the *Kinetoscope*. The Kinetograph produced a sequence of images on 35 mm perforated film at a rate of 48 frames per second (Figure 13.7(a)). The Kinetoscope (Figure 13.7(b)) did not project the image; the viewer looked through an eyepiece with a magnifying lens system to see the moving picture. Although the quality of the moving image was good the fact that only one viewer could see it limited its commercial value.

In 1892, a French inventor, Léon Bouly (1872–1932), designed the *Cinématographe*, a device that could perform all the tasks of taking films, developing them and finally projecting them. He was unable to pay the patent fees and in 1895 the Lumière brothers applied the name to a device of their own making. They made a series of short films, lasting from 38 to 49 seconds, which they presented to a public audience in 1895. The first short film was *La sortie de l'usines Lumière*, showed workers

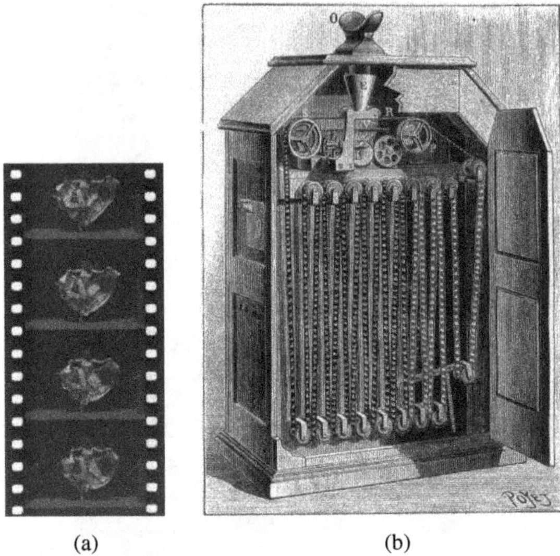

(a)   (b)

Figure 13.7   (a) A sequence of images produced on 35 mm perforated film by the Kinetograph. (b) The Dickson and Edison Kinetoscope, the forerunner of the modern cine projector

leaving the Lumière factory (Figure 13.8) and the last, *La mer*, showed people bathing in the sea. Through the Lumière brothers' work, Paris was for many years the world centre of the film industry. However, in 1914 the Great War (later called World War I) halted progress in Europe and thereafter Hollywood in the USA became the dominant centre for film production.

13.3 The Introduction of Colour

Early motion films were taken in black-and-white and an early way for introducing colour was to hand tint the film frame by frame. This was a labour-intensive process, did not give very good results and was only practical for very short films. Very often this form of colouring spoilt, rather than enhanced, the black-and-white film. Another scheme was to colour whole frames with a single colour that reflected the mood of what was being shown — red for a battle scene, green for open countryside, yellow for candlelight and blue for a seascape or night scene. The eminent

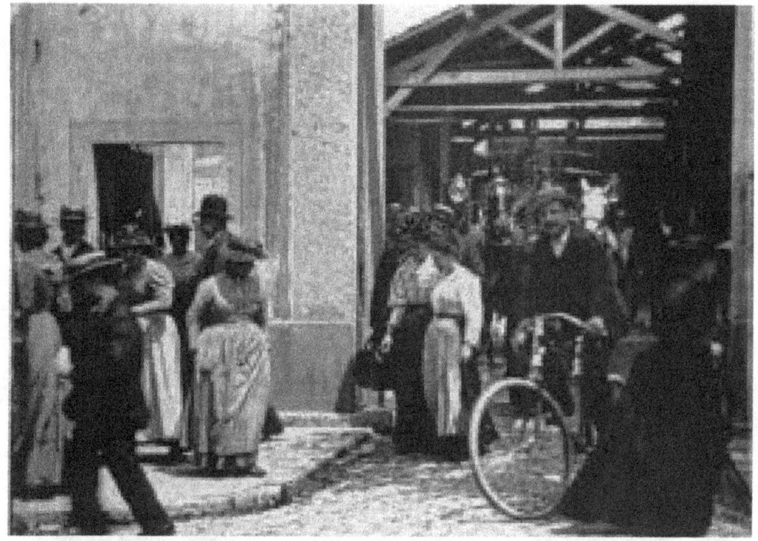

Figure 13.8   A still from the Lumière brothers' film *La sortie de l'usines Lumière*

Russian film-maker Sergei Eisenstein (1898–1948) produced films during the era of the Soviet Union, during which time films, as well as other art forms, were required, where possible, to extol the virtues of the communist state. In his famous film *Battleship Potemkin*, made in 1925, which told the story of a mutiny on a Russian battleship in 1905, at one stage the mutinying sailors run up a flag, which was hand-painted in red, the colour of the flag of the Soviet Union (Figure 13.9).

The introduction of colour for still photography, which began in the first decade of the 20th century, stimulated the search for commercially effective ways of introducing colour into cinematography.

13.3.1 Dufaycolour

An early form of colour motion films was *dufaycolour*, an Anglo-French enterprise devised by the French inventor Louis Dufay (1874–1936) in the period 1907–1910. It was similar to the autochrome process except that it did not use dyed starch grains but established a red, green and blue network (French word *reseau*) on the base of the film on which the

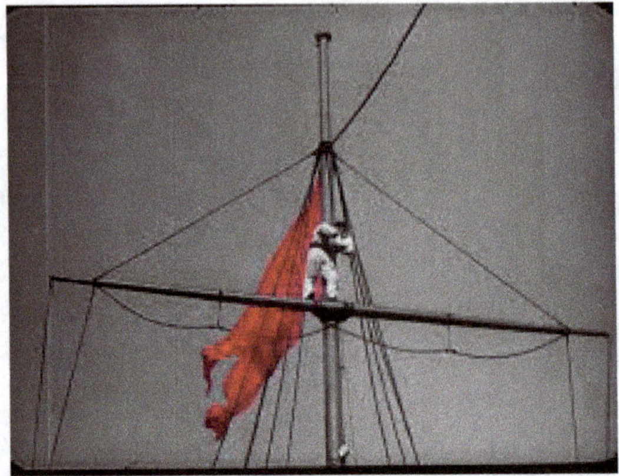

Figure 13.9   A scene from *The Battleship Potemkin* with hand-painted red flag

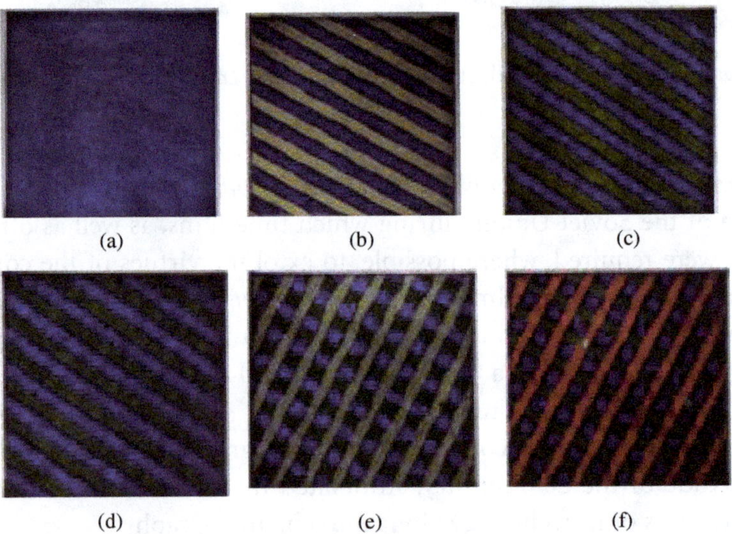

Figure 13.10   The steps in producing a Dufaycolour *reseau*

photosensitive emulsion was deposited. The final form of this network is illustrated in Figure 13.10. The method of setting it up is as follows:

(a)   The film is covered with a layer of blue dye.

(b)   A set of parallel lines is printed over the blue dye with a resistive ink that can neither be printed on nor bleached out. The thickness of these lines and the spacing between them is about 0.05 mm. The film is then placed in bleach that removes the blue dye where it is not protected by the resistive ink.

(c) The film is dyed green, which only attaches to the film in the bleached strips.

(d) The ink resist is removed chemically so that now the film is coloured alternately blue and green in strips with no resisting ink on the film. A set of resisting-ink strips is now printed on the film at right angles to the blue and green strips.

(e) The film is again bleached. The film is now clear of blue and green dye in the areas not protected by the resisting ink.

(f) The film is dyed red, which only attaches to the film in the bleached areas. The resisting ink is removed and the network is covered by a layer of high-sensitivity panchromatic photographic emulsion.

The picture was taken with the light passing through the *reseau* and, essentially the process was the same as autochrome but with the *reseau* playing the role of the dyed starch grains. Dufaycolour gave a high quality image with good colour rendering and was available for still photography as well as for moving pictures. It was used by amateur photographers until the mid-1950s but, although several short films used the process, only one full length film was made using the system — *Sons of the Sea*. Figure 13.11 shows a still from the film.

Despite being cheaper to produce than an American system, Technicolor, it was eventually supplanted by Technicolor, the colour rendering of which was much more saturated and spectacular — although many would argue much less natural than Dufaycolour with its softer tones.

13.3.2 Technicolor

The colour-film process known as *Technicolor* is usually associated with films produced in Hollywood in the period from the late 1930s to the late 1950s — a period which included such films as *The Wizard of Oz* (1937), *Gone with the Wind* (1939) and *The African Queen* (1951). However, the name Technicolor goes back much further than that. In 1912, the

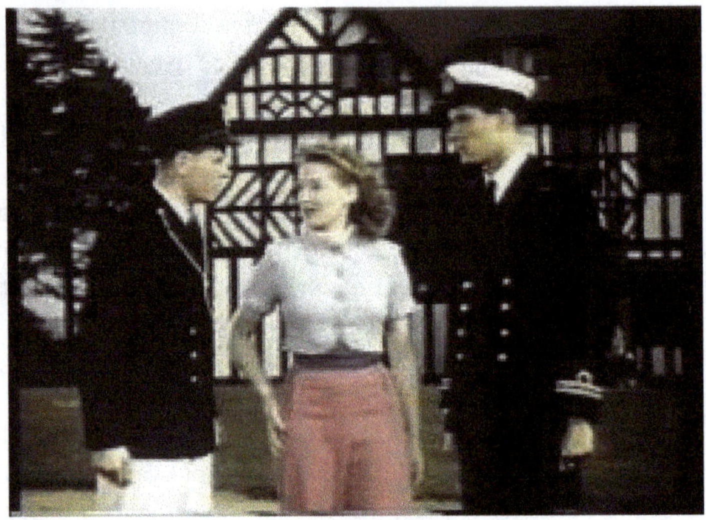

Figure 13.11   A still from *Sons of the Sea*

Technicolor Motion Picture Corporation was set up jointly by two American scientists and engineers — Herbert Kalmus (1881–1963), who was President of the company and Daniel Comstock (1883–1970).

The first process they devised, Technicolor Process-1, was essentially based on the principle of Maxwell's first projected colour picture (Section 10.1) but with only two projection colours, red and cyan. The picture was taken with a camera containing a beam-splitter that sent light respectively through red and cyan filters onto two consecutive frames of perforated film. The two pairs of positives were then projected through red and cyan filters, where the projector contained an adjustable prism that could deflect one of the projected images so that they coincided on the screen. Figure 13.12 shows a still from *The Gulf Between* (1917), the only film produced with Technicolor 1. Since there were two frames per visual image to produce the same number of visual images per unit time as a black-and-white film, and so avoid flicker and jerkiness, the camera and projector had to be run at twice the normal speed. The system gave colour fringing and fuzzy images since it was difficult to maintain registration of the red and cyan images. Even as this process was being developed and the motion picture was being produced a new and better system was being devised.

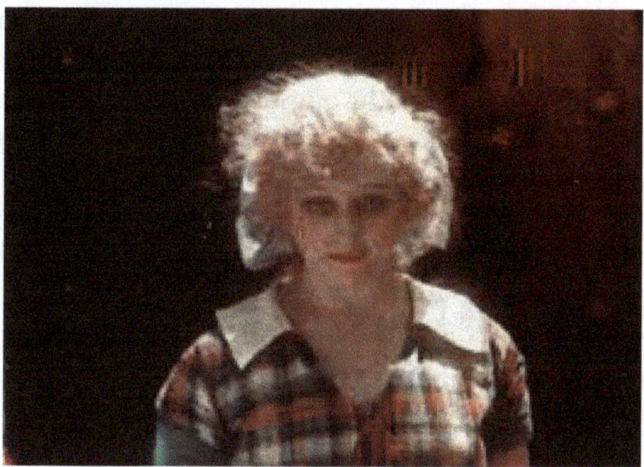

Figure 13.12   A still from *The Gulf Between*

Despite the fact that the best of engineering technology had gone into Technicolour Process-1, because of its drawbacks it was decided that an additive colour system that required multiple projection was impractical. The Dufaycolour system was also an additive colour system but since the film was broken up into small regions sensitive to different primary colours, then this inherently led to a loss of resolution.

Technicolor Process-2, developed in 1922 used subtractive colour but once again with only two dyes, red and cyan. The first step was similar to that of Process-1 with the red and cyan-filtered negatives on alternating frames of a single strip of film. Now positives were made on special *matrix film* where the gelatine hardened when exposed to light. Part of the red-filtered negative which corresponded to a red part of the scene would be very dark and hence the positive would be little exposed and the gelatine there would remain soft. Conversely, for a cyan part of the scene the negative would be clear and in the corresponding part of the gelatine would be hard. During the positive development process the soft gelatine is washed away; for the red-filtered scene the thickness of the gelatine is less the greater is the red component of the corresponding part of the scene. It also follows that for the cyan-filtered scene the thickness of the gelatine is greater the greater is the red component of the corresponding part of the scene.

Next the gelatine of the positives is dyed — cyan for the red-filtered positive and red for the cyan-filtered positive. When the original negatives were produced the red and cyan film strips were made the mirror images of each other. Now the two film strips are cemented together in perfect registry with the gelatine surfaces on the outside, since the gelatine could not be exposed to contact with cement. When white light passes through the thin cyan strip, green and blue pass freely but, since the strip is so thin red is only weakly absorbed. Then the light passes through the thick red strip, which absorbs almost all the green and blue but freely passes the red light. The transmission is thus red. The effect of the cemented film is that the components of red and cyan transmitted are proportional to the components of those colours at the corresponding point of the scene being imaged.

The individual strips were half the thickness of normal film so the final Process-2 product was of normal thickness; the gelatine layers were not very thick so there was only a small variation in the thickness of the cemented films. Figure 13.13 illustrates how this process works at all stages for a red part of the original scene but only showing the final cemented film for a green and yellow part of the scene.

A still from the first film produced in 1922 by Process-2, *The Toll of the Sea*, is shown in Figure 13.14. The colour combinations used made it impossible to reproduce deep blue and film-makers using this process avoided scenes where blue rendition was important. There were other

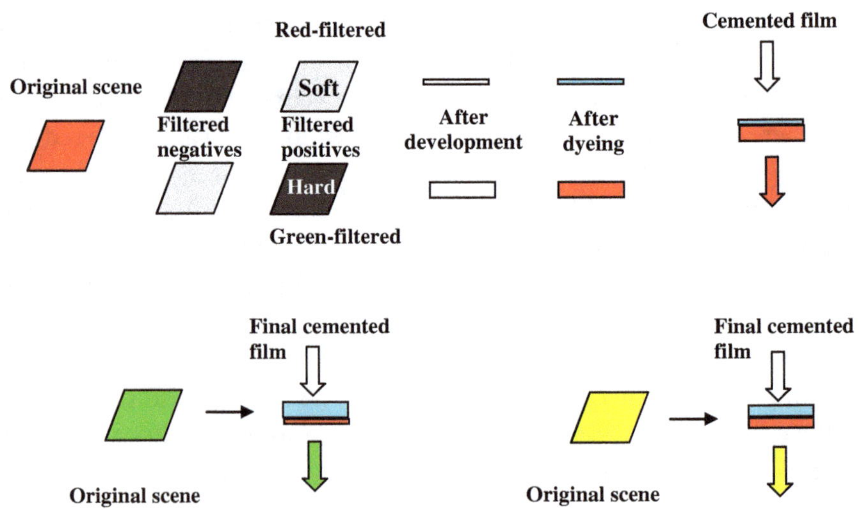

Figure 13.13   A representation of the Techicolor Process-2

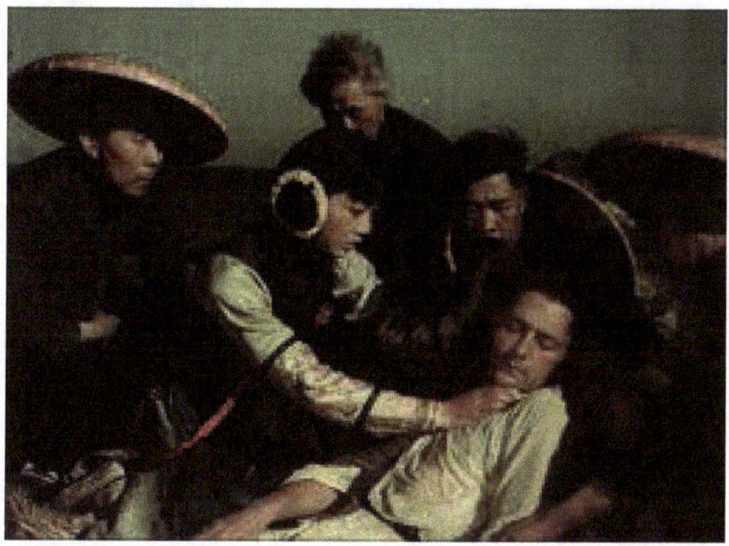

Figure 13.14   A scene from *The Toll of the Sea*

problems with Process-2. Sometimes the cement failed in places and the two parts of the film separated. Although the variation in the thickness of the final film was small it could lead to focussing problems. Finally since there were two exposed gelatine surfaces to become scratched, the film deteriorated more quickly than a normal film.

To overcome the problems of Process-2, occasioned by using two cemented film strips, in 1928 Technicolour produced Process-3, based on a similar principle to that used by Ducos du Hauron (Section 11.3.1), but still only using the two colours red and cyan. The steps in this process are virtually the same as Process-2 except that the dyed gelatine of varying thickness was transferred by contact — passing them through rollers under pressure — onto a blank filmstrip; the greater the thickness of the gelatine the more the amount of dye that was transferred.

Process-3 was free of the main problems of Process-2 since there was only a single filmstrip and a single gelatine layer. However, it shared with Process-2 the limitation of colour rendition due to using only red and cyan as the basic filter colours.

The final Technicolor development was Process-4, which was identical to Process-3 in involving dye-transfer but where there were three layers of

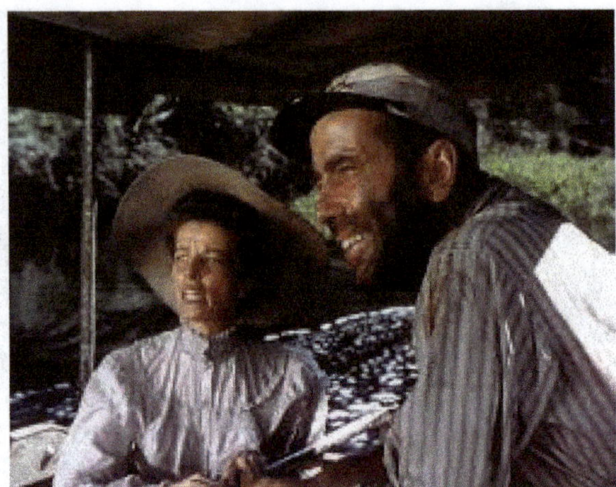

Figure 13.15   A still from the Technicolor Process-4 film *The African Queen*

dye transferred with colours cyan, magenta and yellow. Figure 13.15 shows a still from the classic film *The African Queen*, produced in Hollywood in 1951.

Technicolor Process-4 was used from 1932 to 1955 when it largely superseded by Eastmancolor film that was similar to the Kodachrome film used for making slides and described in Section 12.2. This was much easier to use since all the technology was incorporated in the film itself and it was not necessary to use colour filters and combine the contributions of differently-filtered images of a single scene. However, the quality of Eastmancolor was no better than that of Technicolor Process-4 and the Eastman films were more prone to fading with time.

Various other film-producing technologies were introduced and used from time-to-time — for example, Agfacolour from Germany — some of which were also used for amateur home movies. However, the advent of digital technology has now made such photographic processes largely redundant.

13.4 Digital Film Technology

Just as most still photography, for both the amateur and the professional, is now carried out using digital cameras, as described in Section 12.3, so digital technology has become the method of choice for producing motion films.

However, there is still a debate about the relative quality of motion pictures produced by film and digital technology. Film gives a smooth unbroken image of the scene being recorded with a continuous variation of intensity while, by its very nature, digital recording must break up the image into a number of pixels, and intensity and colour can only be recorded in a discrete digital form. If the number of pixels is too small then when projected onto a large screen the discrete pixelated nature of the image becomes apparent and the resolution of the image is poor. Currently the number of pixels in a frame image of the highest definition, described as 4K technology, is 4096×2160, the ratio of these two numbers giving the aspect ratio of a normal cinema screen. The technology of digital motion-film making is quite complex so here we will concentrate on what the technology does rather than the detail of how it works.

For each pixel forming the image it is necessary to define the colour and its intensity in digital form. The greatest colour definition is given by what is called *true colour* in which each of the red, green and blue signals is represented by 8 binary bits. With 8 bits all numbers from 0 to 255 can be represented in binary form. Thus zero is 00000000 and 255 is 11111111 $(1 + 2 + 4 + 8 + 16 + 32 + 64 + 128)$. If for each colour the component is zero then the colour is black; if each component is 255 then the colour is white. If each component is 127 then the red : green : blue ratio is unchanged but the intensity is lower so the result is dark white, or grey. Representations of various combinations of numbers are shown in Figure 13.16, from which the general nature of the system is illustrated.

The number of combinations of colour-plus-intensity is $256 \times 256 \times 256 = 16,772,216$. There are other lower-colour-resolution systems — for example, *high colour* that uses 5 bits for each of red and blue and 6 bits for green so that the number of combinations is reduced to $32 \times 32 \times 64 = 65,536$; in practice, for most people the difference between high colour

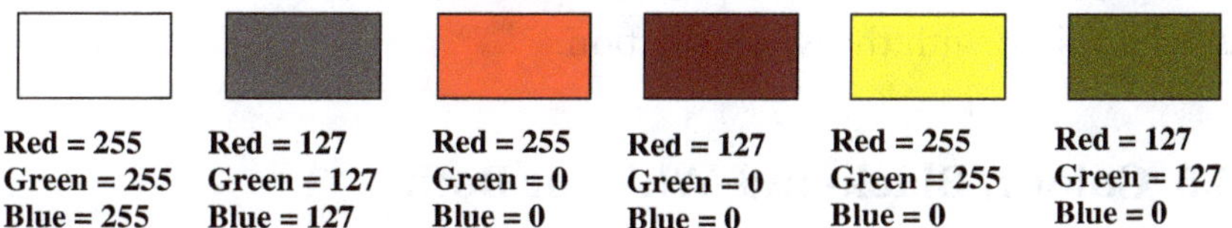

Figure 13.16   Various combinations of red, green and blue digital contributions giving — white, grey, red, dark red, yellow and dark yellow

and true colour is barely discernible but the difference in the load on the technical system is considerable.

The projection device for digital cinematography is known as DMD (Deformation Mirror Device). These devices are manufactured from silicon using the same kind of technology that is used for silicon chips. The silicon has an array of highly reflecting aluminium micro-mirrors on its surface, each about 10–16 microns across and corresponding to one pixel of the image. The micro-mirrors are mounted so that by application of an electric field on the mirror mountings the mirror can be in one of two positions, corresponding to a twist of order 12°. There is one DMD for each of three beams of light, one red, one green and one blue, produced by passing light from a powerful xenon lamp through filters. In one of the two possible positions, the *on position*, for each micro-mirror the beam from it illuminates the cinema screen in a position corresponding to one pixel; in the other position, the *off position*, it is deflected away from the screen, usually towards a heat-sink that absorbs the heat energy in the beam. Each mirror can vibrate between the on and off positions several thousand times per second and the intensity of the primary colour for that projected pixel will depend on the proportion of the time the mirror is in the on position; This is determined by the binary representation of the colour being projected. The differently coloured beams are combined and focussed by a lens system onto the cinema screen. A schematic representation of DMD is shown in Figure 13.17.

This description of the action of a DMD corresponds to the one designed by Texas Instruments, the original inventors of this type of technology. However, there are other variants produced by other manufacturers that differ somewhat in the way they operate. For example, a simpler *single-chip projector* uses one mirror per pixel. A rotating wheel with three colour segments — red, green and blue — illuminates the mirror and the rate of vibration of the mirror, reflecting the contribution of each colour, is synchronized with the wheel rotation.

13.5 Colour, Black-and-White or Both

With the availability of high-quality colour, either using film or digital methods, it might be thought that black-and-white cinematography

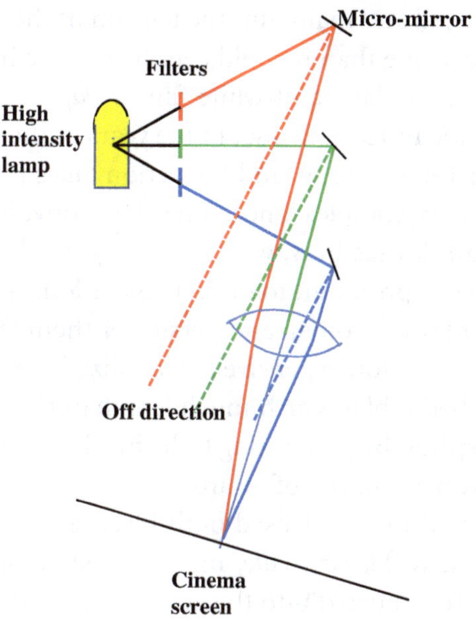

Figure 13.17   A schematic representation of the DMD process

would have ceased, but this is not so. An average of four to five films per year are produced in black-and-white, very often films of an artistic nature that win prizes at international film festivals. There are various reasons why black-and-white may be preferred, sometimes because the action of the film takes place in a period where black-and-white seems more natural, such as in the early part of the 20th century, or where the drama is better maintained by the starkness of black-and-white rather than the warm cosiness of colour.

An example of a film of high drama in black-and-white is the 1953 French/Italian film *Le Salaire de la Peur* (The Wages of Fear). The action of the film is based on two trucks, loaded with nitroglycerine, being driven on bumpy mountain dirt roads to an oil well in Mexico that is on fire; the explosive is required to put out the fire. The truck drivers employed by the oil company refuse to drive the trucks — nitroglycerine can be detonated by a sudden blow or jolt — so the company hires four down-and-out European men to do the job, one of whom is the French actor Yves Montand, who plays the lead in the film. The film is rated in the top ten of all films ever produced and maintains the tension of the action more effectively in black-and-white than it could ever have done in colour.

Another acclaimed black-and-white film is *Paper Moon*, an American comedy-drama made in 1973. It is set in the years of the Great Depression, which lasted from 1929 to 1939, and the action takes place in Kansas and Missouri. The plot is complex and somewhat convoluted but basically involves a con-man, Moses Pray, who is accompanied by an orphan girl, Addie Loggins, he has promised to deliver to her aunt in Missouri. Moses locates recently-widowed women and persuades them that their husbands bought, but did not pay for, expensive personalized bibles and the widows pay him for inscribed bibles worth much less than their cost. Addie helps Moses in this deception by pretending to be his daughter. The film and its principal actors won a number of awards.

A cleverly crafted film that used both black-and-white and colour is the American comedy *Pleasantville*, made in 1998. David and Jennifer, twin children, are transported into the action of a black-and-white television sitcom featuring the Parker family, who lead idyllic lives in an idyllic town. They become the Parker children and through their influence the town of Pleasantville is transformed from its idyllic state to the nitty-gritty of real existence. With each episode of transformation the environment and people affected change from black-and-white to full colour. The local black-and-white fire brigade, whose main function has been to rescue cats from trees, suddenly finds itself with a real fire and the now-colourful fire brigade is unable to handle hoses or find the fire hydrant. Jennifer dates one of the boys at her high school and they set off for a ride in his black-and-white open-topped sports car. Later in the film they return, with automobile and occupants in full colour; Jennifer has introduced her date to the real world! Towards the end of the film Pleasantville has become a normal colourful American town. Jennifer decides to stay in Pleasantville to complete her education but David goes back to the real world.

Chapter 14
Colour Television

The concept of television is much older than its implementation in a practical form. In 1873, the phenomenon of *photoconductivity* was discovered in the element selenium. When light falls upon a photoconductive material its electrical conductivity increases with the intensity of the light. This raised the possibility that an image, formed by variations of light intensity, could be converted into a variable electrical signal, based on the variation of the conductivity of photoconductive material, and transmitted over wires and then reformed into an image.

Here, we shall briefly describe the development of television from its crude beginnings to a more complicated and effective black-and-white form and then, finally, illustrate how colour has been incorporated.

14.1   Paul Nipkow and Mechanical Scanning

In 1884, the German inventor Paul Nipkow (1860–1940; Figure 14.1) was the first to design a system by which an image could be transformed into an electrical signal that could then be reformed into an image. The process was based on the *Nipkow disk*, a spinning disk containing square holes in a spiral arrangement as shown in Figure 14.2. If an image were projected on the disk, as shown in the figure, then the holes would scan across the image in a series of curved strips — 16 for the disk shown — that would completely cover the image. If a photocell, a device based on photoconductivity,

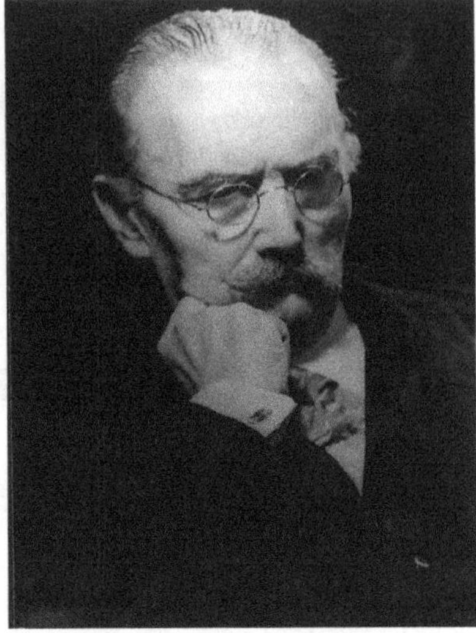

Figure 14.1   Paul Nipkow

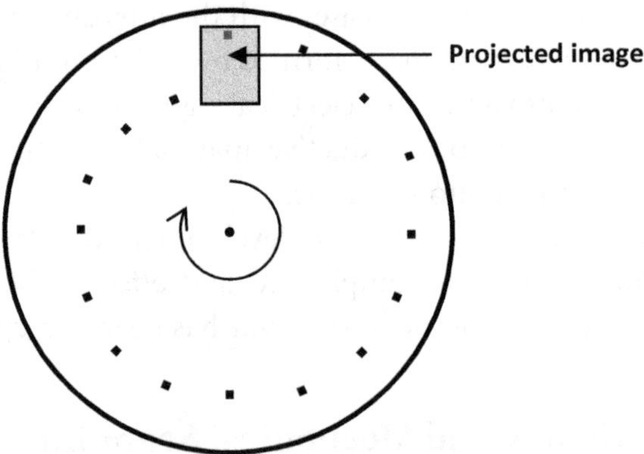

Figure 14.2   A Nipkow disk

placed behind the disk occupied the whole area of the image then at any instant it would generate a current that increased with the light intensity passing through a hole, although beyond some very high intensity the current would saturate and increase no further. The generated current could then, in principle, be transmitted along a wire to an electric lamp that projected light onto the whole back surface of a spinning Nipkow disk that was synchronized with the transmitting disk. A moving rectangular spot of light would then be seen that varied in intensity with that of the illuminated part of the photocell. If both disks spun very quickly then persistence of vision would give the appearance of a smooth transmitted image.

Although Nipkow's design was sound in principle and he patented the idea of the scanning disk in 1885, it is not known whether he ever made it work in practice. The currents generated by the photocell would have been small and it is doubtful that enough light could have been generated at the receiving end to give a visible image. It needed the invention of the valve amplifier in 1907, which could increase the current to a level that would enable this problem to be solved.

14.2 The First Working Television System

The invention of the valve amplifier enabled developments that led to a working system based on Nipkow's basic design. The first person to demonstrate a working television system was the Scottish inventor, John Logie Baird (1888–1946; Figure 14.3). He first publicly demonstrated moving pictures on March 25th 1925 at Selfridges department store in London.

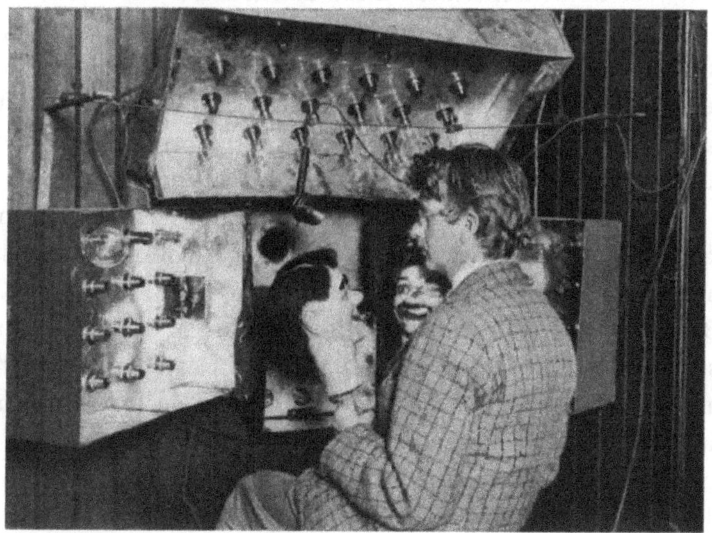

Figure 14.3   Baird with the ventriloquist dummy heads *James* and *Stooky Bill*

His equipment was a considerable advance on that described by Nipkow. Baird used a Nipkow disk but with each hole containing a lens so positioned that it focussed the light onto a photoelectric tube situated at a point on the extension of the axis of the disk. Despite this innovation and the use of strong lighting of the subject being imaged, the selenium photoelectric tubes he used had such poor sensitivity that the details of a human face could not be shown. Consequently he used two ventriloquist dummies for his demonstration, the painted faces of which gave far more contrast. On January 26, 1926, with an audience of 50 scientists at the Royal Institution in London, he demonstrated his 30-line system, in which the scanning took place fast enough to give a reasonably smooth moving picture. Then, in 1927 a transmission was made by telephone wire between London and Glasgow, a distance of 700 kilometres, and the system was clearly moving towards achieving commercial viability, on the basis of which Baird set up the Baird Television Development Company (BTDC).

Even while developments were at an initially crude stage, Baird was looking ahead and exploring many ways of improving the television experience. In 1928 he transmitted colour pictures by using synchronized scanning disks for transmission and reception that had three spirals of apertures, one for each of the primary colours — red, green and blue. Later that year he demonstrated three-dimensional television, based on simultaneously producing two images from different viewpoints, which then had to be viewed with a stereoscope.

The BTDC made the first transatlantic television transmission from London to Hartsdale, New York, in 1928 via the transatlantic telephone line and in 1929 the company made the first television programme for the British Broadcasting Company Ltd (BBC). From 1929 to 1932 the BBC broadcasted television programmes using the Baird 30-line process but by 1936 the number of lines had increased to 240. From 1936 the BBC alternated Baird 240-line transmissions with the EMI-Marconi 405-line electronic scanning system. However, by 1937 the Baird system was abandoned in favour of the much more advanced and flexible electronic scanning.

Baird accepted that mechanical systems were no longer viable and he continued to contribute to television development using electronic scanning. He demonstrated colour television in 1939, using a cathode-ray tube display in front of which was a spinning disk with filters in the three primary colours. In 1944, when television broadcasts were no longer being made because of the Second World War, he demonstrated a 600-line colour system but it was not until 1953 that the first regular colour television broadcasts were made in America by CBS (Columbia Broadcasting System) and the late 1960s before regular broadcasts were made in Europe.

14.3 Producing a Television Signal by Electronic Scanning

The development of electronics in the early 20th century was followed by many ideas for its practical application. In 1908 a Scottish electrical engineer, Alan Archibald Campbell-Swinton (1863–1930), suggested the use of a cathode-ray tube (CRT; Figure 14.8) both to produce a television signal and then to convert it back to an image. However, it was a theoretical concept and attempts to implement it as a working system all failed.

In 1928, the American inventor, Philo Taylor Farnsworth (1906–1971), used a device known as an *Image Dissector* to convert an image into an electric signal. The image was projected by an optical system onto a photocathode, a slab of photoelectric material such as an alkali metal that emits photoelectrons when light falls on it, contained within a high-vacuum tube. The photocathode was at a high negative potential relative to an anode, also within the high-vacuum tube. The rate at which photoelectrons are emitted at each point of the photocathode is proportional to the intensity of the image at that point. Because of the large electric field between the cathode and anode the photoelectrons are constrained to travel within a narrow cone from each point on the photocathode and are electrically focussed onto a point on the anode, which is in the form of a plate. The anode has a small aperture contained within it through which photoelectrons can pass and behind the aperture is an electron multiplier (Section 5.1) that amplifies the charge entering to give a much larger current as the output. With this arrangement the detector only picks up the photoelectrons from a small part of the image on the photocathode and the current produced is proportional to the brightness of the image in that region (Figure 14.4). By the use of electric and magnetic fields the electron image, i.e. the flow of electrons coming from the image on the photocathode, is deflected in raster fashion, as indicated in Figure 14.5. As the image moves so electrons coming from different parts of the image pass through

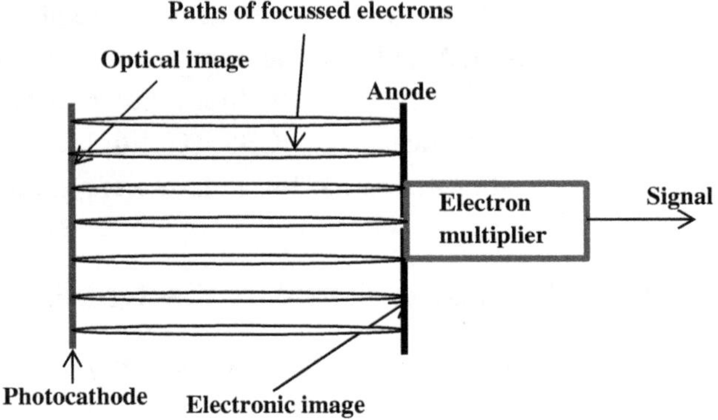

Figure 14.4   A schematic Image Dissector

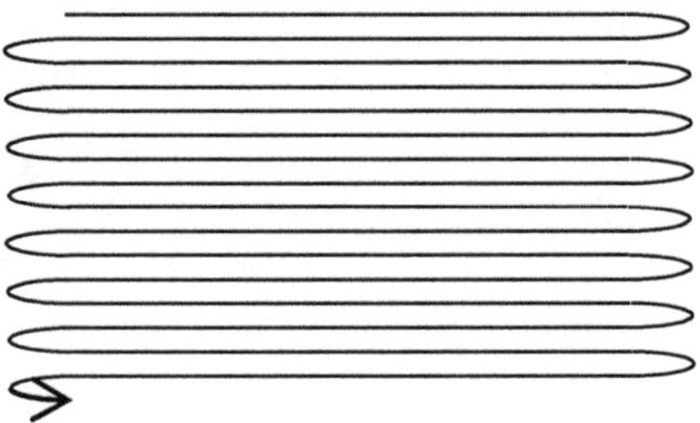

Figure 14.5   A raster scan

the aperture and are detected and the variation in the current coming from the detector contains the information to regenerate the image.

Most of the photoelectrons being produced at any instant are not being detected and so do not contribute to the signal. Consequently the Image Dissector has low sensitivity and a number of ways were tried to produce an electronic imaging system with greater sensitivity. One such electronic imager was the *Iconoscope*, designed in 1925 by the Russian, later American, engineer, Vladimir Zworykin (1888–1982). The main feature of this device was a *charge storage plate*, shown schematically in Figure 14.6. On a conducting base plate there is deposited a layer of insulating material, such as aluminium oxide, on top of which are evaporated tiny isolated patches of a photoelectric material, e.g. potassium hydride, forming a grid corresponding to image pixels. When an image falls on the plate each

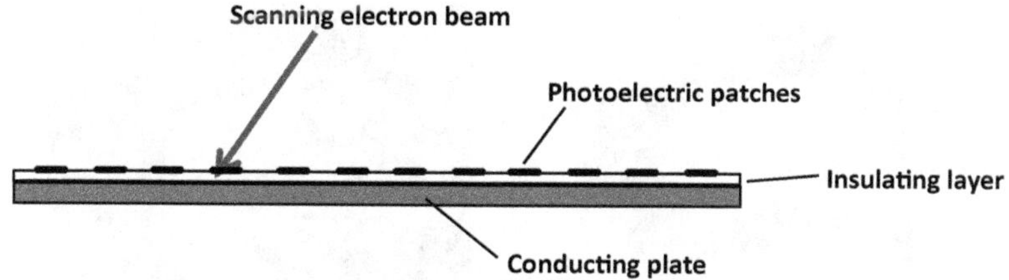

Figure 14.6   A schematic representation of an Iconoscope

patch emits electrons at a rate proportional to the intensity of light falling on it and, since it is losing negative charge, the patch acquires a positive charge proportional to the total amount of light it received. Each patch, separated from the conducting plate by an insulator acts like a tiny capacitor, a device that stores electric charge. The plate is scanned in raster fashion by a fine electron beam that, as it hits a patch, discharges it and produces an electrical output proportional to the intensity of light in the original image.

Although this device is much more efficient than the Image Dissector it gave a very noisy image. The reason is that when the scanning electron beam hit a photoelectric patch it released further electrons that were attracted to neighbouring positively-charged patches and so reduced the positive charge on them before they were swept by the scanning beam. This noise problem was overcome, leading to the *super-Emitron*, produced by the British company EMI, and the *Supericonoscope*, produced by Telefunken in Germany.

14.4 Viewing Television with Cathode-Ray Tubes

Having converted an image into an electronic signal, which can be broadcast in the same way as a radio signal, the next problem is to recast this into an image at the receiving end. The first way of doing so was by using a cathode-ray tube (CRT), which was invented by the German physicist, Karl Ferdinand Braun (1850–1918; Figure 14.7(a)), joint winner with the Italian inventor and electrical engineer, Guglielmo Marconi (1874–1957; IFigure 14.7(b)), of the 1909 Nobel Prize for Physics for their work in wireless telegraphy.

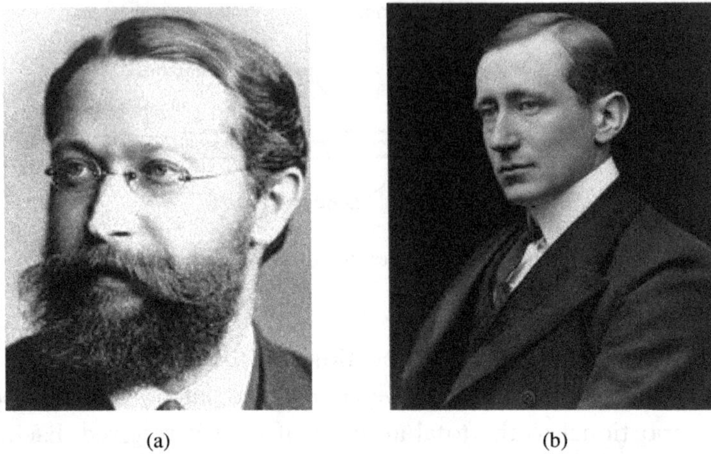

Figure 14.7   Pioneers of wireless telegraphy. (a) Karl Ferdinand Braun. (b) Guglielmo Marconi

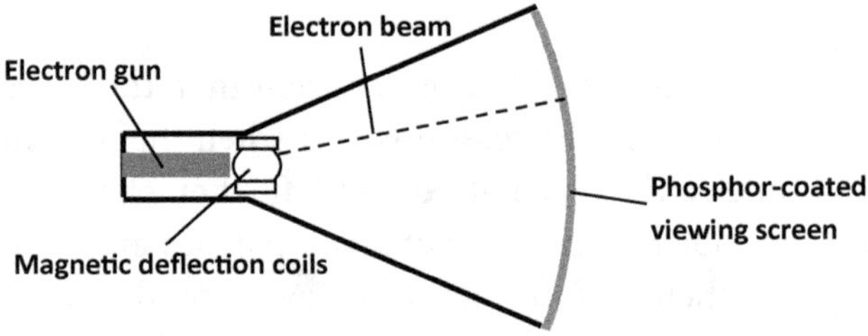

Figure 14.8   A schematic CRT

Originally designed just as a scientific instrument, the CRT turned out to be useful in a wide range of applications, such as imaging radar targets and viewing television images. The basic form of a television CRT, all contained in a glass envelope, is shown in Figure 14.8. The *electron gun* is a device in which a cathode, heated by an electric current, emits electrons by thermionic emission. Close to the cathode is a *control grid*, consisting of a cylinder or helix of fine wire, the potential of which, relative to the cathode, controls the flow of electrons away from the cathode. As the relative potential is changed from a negative to positive values so the flow of electrons away from the cathode increases. The control-grid potential is an amplified version of the television signal and the net effect is that the flow of electrons is proportional to the signal and hence proportional to the intensity at the corresponding point of the image. The electrons that pass through the control grid are accelerated in a high electric field and then focussed onto an anode. The anode contains a small aperture which allows through a fine beam of electrons with a fairly small range of energies.

A television CRT contains two sets of magnetic coils that deflect the beam passing through the anode in orthogonal directions (i.e. at a right angle to each other). The currents through these coils are arranged so that the electron beam executes a raster motion that exactly matches that of the imaging device, as shown in Figure 14.5. The viewing screen of the CRT is coated with a layer of a phosphor, a material that emits light of a particular wavelength when excited by an electron beam. Thus the variation in the intensity of the original image is reproduced on the viewing screen.

The definition of the image is defined by the number of raster lines. The most frequently used system, PAL (Phase Alternating Line) has 625 lines and generates 25 frames per second, which fits in with a 50 Hz[1] mains electricity supply in the using countries. In North America, South America and parts of Asia the NTSC (National Television System Committee) system is used with 525 scan lines and 30 frames per second, consistent with a 60 Hz electricity supply. Finally, France, Eastern Europe and parts of the Middle East use the SECAM (Séquentiel Couleur Avec Mémoire) system based on 625 lines and 25 frames per second but differing from PAL in the way that it handles colour. These systems all used interlaced rasters, as shown in Figure 14.9, alternately producing each half of a single frame, which gives a better image appearance and smoother motion, so the systems just mentioned make 50 or 60 raster scans per second.

14.5 Colour Television with CRT Displays

The idea of introducing colour came quite early in the development of television, as evidenced by Baird's demonstration in 1944 (Section 14.2). The first commercial colour television, as distinct from private demonstrations or broadcast trials, was made by the American CBS network in 1953, but the high price of colour television sets restricted the number of

---

[1] I Hz (hertz) is one cycle per second so 50 Hz is 50 cycles per second.

Figure 14.9   Interlaced scans as used in television imaging

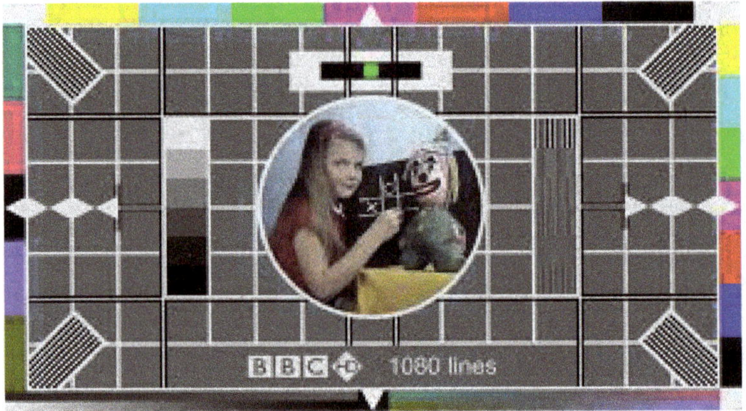

Figure 14.10   The BBC test card

viewers. It was not until the late 1960s that other parts of the world were regularly broadcasting in colour. Since then colour television has rapidly expanded everywhere and is the default system with black-and-white reception almost, if not quite, extinct. Figure 14.10 shows a test card transmitted by the BBC for several years from 1968 that had the function of assisting television engineers to adjust pictures for optimum performance when installing television sets.

Colour television is based on the same colour-addition principle as the Dufaycolour motion film system, described in Section 13.3.1. A very fine network of light-emitting red, green and blue patches, so fine that the individual patches cannot visually be resolved, leads to the colour

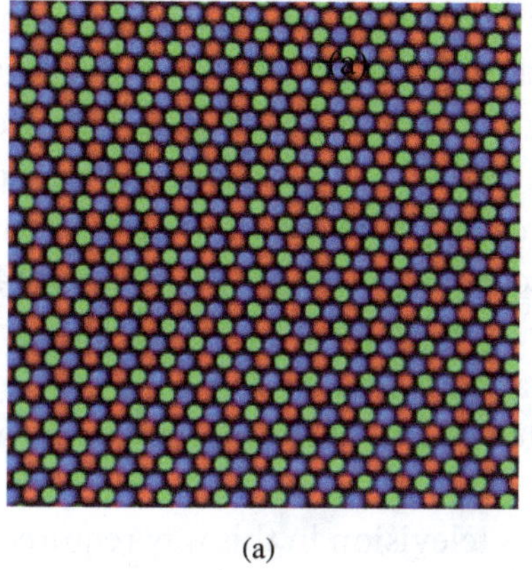

(a)

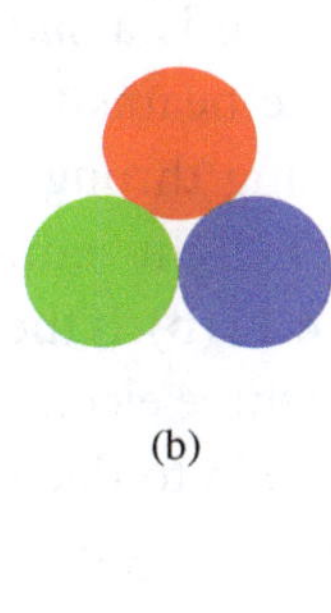

(b)

Figure 14.11   (a) The pattern of phosphors on a colour CRT screen. (b) A basic unit of the pattern

perceived at any point on the screen as the result of the addition of the red, green and blue intensities in its region. A CRT colour television screen, examined with a magnifying glass, is seen to be covered with a network of red, green and blue phosphors in the pattern shown in Figure 14.11(a). This pattern can be regarded as a close-packed arrangement of the basic triangular unit shown in Figure 14.11(b). If all three colours are emitting equally and strongly in a region of the screen then what is seen is white; If they are emitting equally but at a lower intensity then grey is seen. If all are not emitting then the perceived colour is black; the actual colour is that of the unilluminated screen but it is perceived as black. The colour produced on the screen obeys the rules we have met previously with mixtures of primary colours — for example, equal red and green with no blue gives yellow. With different combinations of intensity of emission of the three types of phosphor all possible colour effects with a range of intensities can be produced.

If the theory of producing colours on the CRT screen is straightforward, the same cannot be said for the technology that enables it to occur. The transmitted signal consists of three separate components, coming from the scene imaged through three filters — one red, one green and one blue. The television-set receiver separates out these three components, each being sent to a different electron gun within the CRT which modulates the signal according to the intensity of the relevant primary colour component as the raster scan takes place. Between the guns and the CRT screen there is a *shadow mask,* a thin metal screen perforated with fine holes. The beams from the three guns, coming from different directions and passing through one of the holes will only strike the corresponding patch of light emitting phosphor of one of the units shown in Figure 14.11(b). If the basic screen-colour unit is as shown in Figure 14.11(b) then the three electron guns are arranged to form a triangle. However, it is also possible to decompose the arrangement shown in Figure 14.11(a) as collinear red, green and blue patches and then the guns can also be collinear.

The technology that gives colour television in this way required precision of the very highest order but, these days, television technology has moved on. By the nature of a CRT the screen could not be precisely flat, although it was close enough to flat to be comfortable to view. In addition CRT television sets are bulky and heavy. However, nowadays it is usual to have *flat-screen television* where not only is the screen flat but the television set itself is quite thin. We will now describe the basis of this technology.

14.6 Liquid-Crystal Displays

Liquid-crystal displays (LCDs) are commonplace in modern life — in computer screens, digital watches, telephones, calculators and instrument panels in cars and aircraft. They are now also one of the ways of producing flat-screen television.

In a normal liquid the individual molecules move freely with limited mutual constraint which gives the liquid its ability to flow. The lack of mutual constraint also means that the constituent molecules are randomly oriented with respect to each other. If a normal liquid solidifies then the molecules take up a rigid ordered configuration. This transition from liquid to solid, forming a crystal, is illustrated in two dimensions in Figure 14.12.

A liquid crystal has a mixture of the characteristics of a liquid and a crystal. It is a liquid in that the molecules move freely but the molecules take up ordered orientations. There are several forms of liquid crystal but here we just consider display devices based on *nematic liquid crystals.*

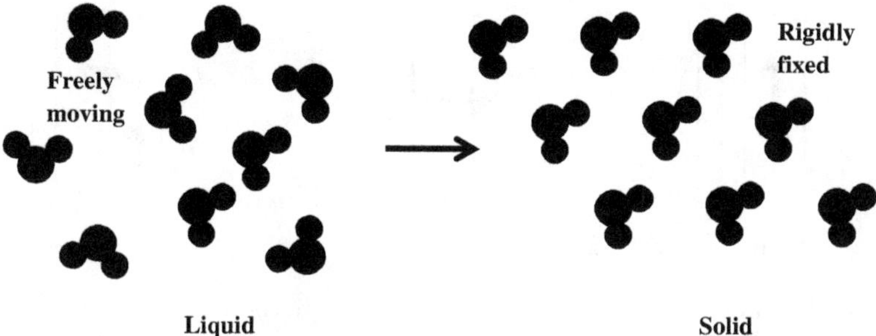

Figure 14.12   An illustration in two dimensions of the liquid and solid states

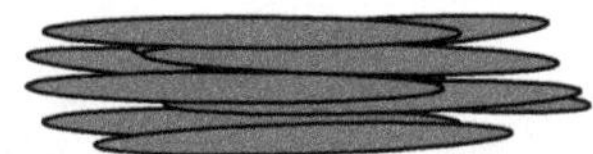

Figure 14.13 The arrangement of neighbouring molecules in a nematic liquid crystal

These consist of long stringy molecules and the word nematic is derived from the Greek prefix *nemato*, meaning threadlike. In a nematic liquid crystal the molecules tend to line up with their lengths more-or-less parallel, as shown in Figure 14.13, although their orientation with respect to twist around the long axis is random.

To understand how a LCD works we first need to know something about the nature of light, an electromagnetic radiation. An electromagnetic wave, as its name suggests, involves the interplay of electric and magnetic fields. It is a transverse wave, meaning that the variation of the electric field is perpendicular to the direction of motion of the wave. A beam of light from a normal incandescent lamp will not consist of a single infinitely long wave but will consist of a vast number of short wavelets, all with their electric-field vectors pointing in different directions perpendicular to the direction of the beam. Such a beam of light is said to be *unpolarised*. A *polarised* beam of light is when all the wavelets have their electric-field vectors pointing in the same direction. Such a beam can be produced by passing the light through a *polariser*, a material that will only allow the passage of light with its electric vector in one particular direction. If a wavelet happens to have its electric vector in the allowed direction then it passes through the polariser unchanged (Figure 14.14(a)).

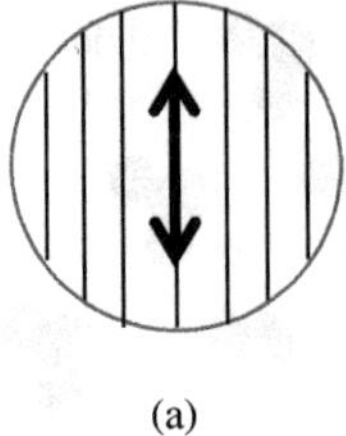 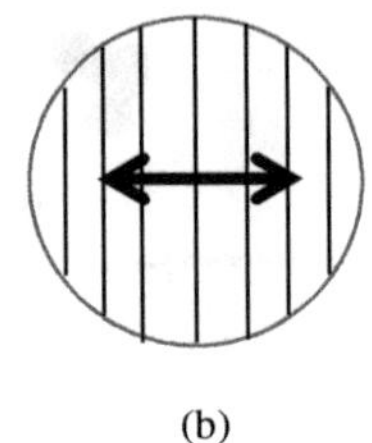 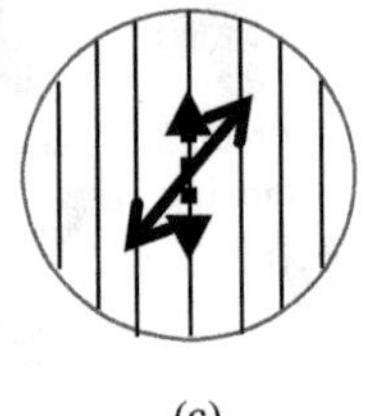

(a) (b) (c)

Figure 14.14   The effect of a polariser with acceptance direction indicated by parallel lines on waves with electric field vectors in directions of bold double-arrowed lines. (a) Wave passes through without modification. (b) Wave completely blocked. (c) Wave passes through with reduced amplitude of the electric field in the acceptance direction, as indicated by dotted bold double-arrowed line

If the electric-field vector is perpendicular to the allowed direction then the wavelet is completely blocked and nothing passes through the polarizer (Figure 14.14(b)). In an intermediate situation the wavelet passes through the polariser with a diminished intensity; the amplitude of the electric-field vector of the transmitted wavelet is the component of the amplitude in the permitted direction of the polariser (Figure 14.14(c)). This means that the whole beam is reduced in intensity since most of the wavelets will be reduced in intensity to some extent.

The lenses of polaroid sunglasses are polarisers. When sunlight is reflected from a road or pool of water it is largely polarized in a horizontal direction. With the acceptance direction of the spectacles vertical most of the glare from the reflected light is removed, enabling other parts of the field of view to be more easily seen.

Figure 14.15 shows a LCD unit. The nematic material is sandwiched between two glass plates coated with a transparent conducting material, normally a metallic oxide, which act as electrodes. These coats are then overlaid with a thin layer of polymer and each of the polymer layers is rubbed in one direction with a fine cloth, which creates very fine microscopic parallel grooves. The nematic material in contact with the plate is constrained to align the molecules with the grooves. The grooves in the two plates are perpendicular to each other, with the grooves in the top plate being in the x-direction and in the bottom plate in the y-direction. The tendency of the molecules to align with their neighbours, plus the constraint to be aligned with the grooves at the plate surfaces, causes the

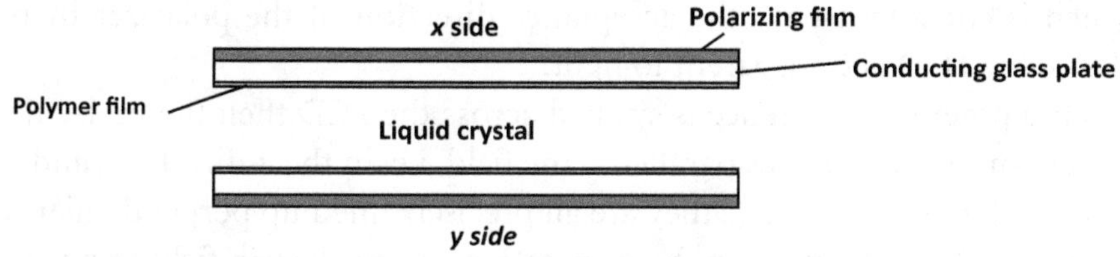

Figure 14.15   The structure of an LCD

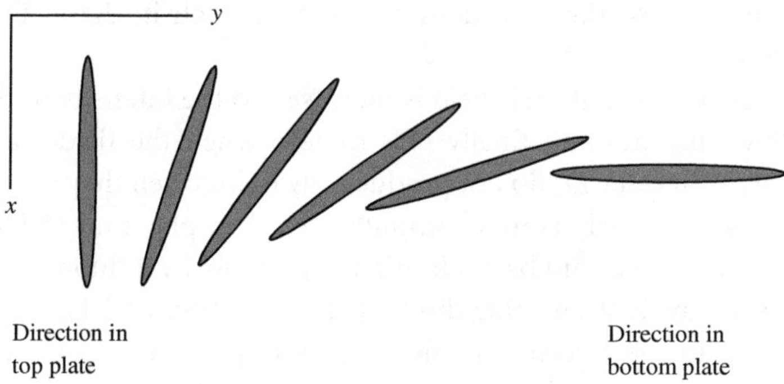

Figure 14.16   The twist in the direction of the molecules between top plate and bottom plate

molecules to twist gradually in going from one plate to the other. This is shown schematically in Figure 14.16. A nematic liquid crystal acts as a polarizer and will allow the passage of a light wave with the electric vector parallel to the molecules. The effect of the gradual twist in the molecules in going from the top plate to the bottom is that the electric-field vector of the light passing through the LCD is twisted from being in the x-direction to the y-direction with no change of intensity, except a minor change due to absorption in the nematic material.

On the outside of the glass plates are polarizing films, with acceptance in the x-direction on the top plate and in the y-direction on the bottom plate. This means that the light entering in the top plate has its electric-field vector in the x-direction, which is consistent with the direction of the molecules there and, on passing through the nematic material, the electric vector is the twisted to be in y-direction when it reaches the bottom plate, which is consistent with the acceptance direction of the polarizer there. Hence the LCD is transparent to light.

If a potential difference is applied across the LCD then the molecules tend to orient themselves parallel to the field, i.e. in the z-direction, and at a particular critical voltage they are all precisely lined up perpendicular to the plates. Now the twist in the orientation of the electric-field vector no longer occurs and light leaving the top plate with that vector in the x-direction arrives at the bottom plate with the vector in the same direction. However, that is perpendicular to the acceptance direction of the bottom polarizer so the light does not pass through it; the LCD is now opaque to light.

In practice, as the electric field is increased so the intensity of the light gradually diminishes and finally falls to zero when the field reaches its critical value. Since LCDs do not produce any light, when they are used for dynamic displays, such as in a computer visual display unit (VDU) or a television screen, they are back illuminated, usually by a fluorescent lamp or sometimes by light-emitting diodes (LEDs; Section 14.8.1).

An LCD image screen is made up of a large number of tiny LCDs arranged on a rectangular grid, each corresponding to a pixel of the image to be formed. The image comes to the screen, after electronic processing, as a stream of voltages to be applied to the pixels in sequence; the voltage applied to a pixel will determine its transparency and hence the intensity of the light coming through it. Since a screen may contain several million pixels it is clearly impracticable to have that number of individual circuits. To solve this problem the rectangular grid structure of the display is utilized. All the LCDs in a single row are linked together as are all the LCDs in a single column. When a signal voltage is received only one row is connected to it and only one column is connected to that row and to a voltage sink. Thus only one pixel has the voltage applied across it and it acquires the required transparency. There are various ways of scanning through the image but the basic technology for doing so is as just described.

Colour is introduced to the LCD screen by the usual colour-addition process. Sets of three LCDs, which we can call *sub-pixels*, form a single pixel of the image. There is a colour screen covering the area of the image screen dyed in the three primary colours as shown in Figure 14.17, with

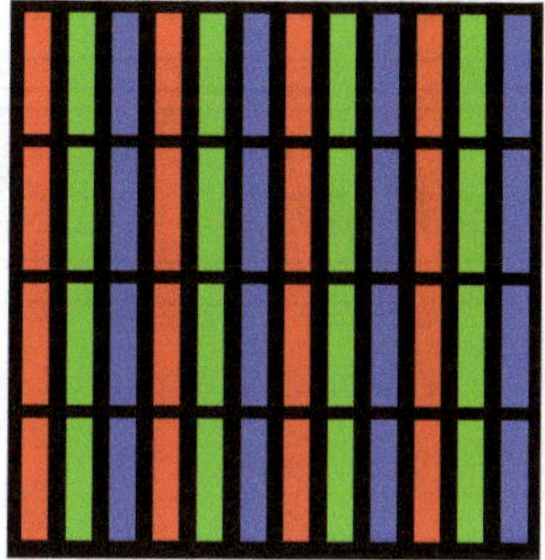

Figure 14.17   The structure of a colour LCD screen. Neighbouring red, green and blue elements form the sub-pixels of an image pixel

each strip corresponding to a sub-pixel. A set of three neighbouring sub-pixels correspond to an image pixel and the local relative intensity of the three primary colours gives the colour at that image point.

14.7 Plasma Displays

A plasma is often described as a 'fourth state of matter', in addition to a solid, liquid and gas. It is an ionised gas in which atoms have lost electrons so that it consists of an intimate mixture of negatively charged electrons and positively charged ions (atoms with one or more electrons missing).

The basic mechanism for a plasma display is that which operates for a household fluorescent lamp. The lamp contains mercury vapour and an inert gas, such as argon, at a pressure of a few thousandth of an atmosphere. A cathode within the lamp is coated with a material that emits electrons when heated by an electrical current that is produced by an electric potential applied across the lamp. The electrons coming from the cathode are accelerated in an electric field and ionize the inert gas atoms by collision, so producing a plasma. The greater the amount of plasma produced the higher is the conductivity and the greater is the current. To prevent this positive feedback giving burnout there is a safely device, a *ballast,* in the circuit that limits the current. The mercury atoms in the tube are excited by the energetic electrons, meaning that some of their electrons are pushed into states of higher energy. When

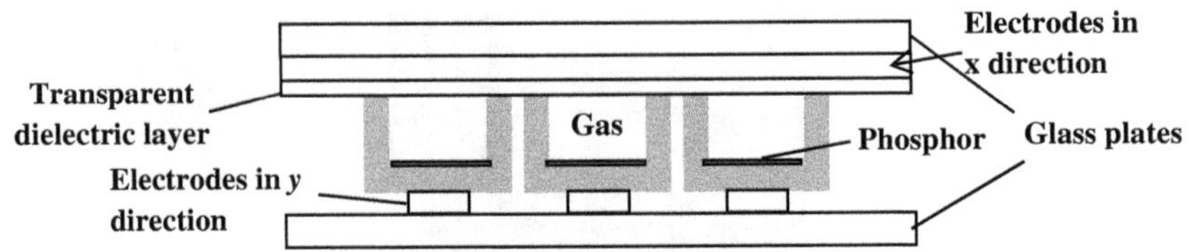

Figure 14.18   A schematic view of part of a plasma screen

they fall back to their original energy state they emit ultraviolet radiation. The glass walls of the lamp are coated with a phosphor that absorbs the ultraviolet radiation and emits visible light at one or more specific wavelengths.

A plasma screen, which is a marvel of modern technology, is essentially a matrix of tiny fluorescent lamps. The essential components of a plasma screen are illustrated in Figure 14.18. Each 'lamp' is a tiny cell, filled mainly with neon and xenon with a very small amount of mercury.

Just as for an LCD, the cells are connected separately in rows and columns by transparent electrodes. Above these there is a transparent electrically insulating layer of a dielectric material and the whole is sandwiched between glass plates. At the base of each cell is a phosphor giving red, green or blue light, so each cell acts as a sub-pixel with three sub-pixels making one pixel of the image. The individual sub-pixels are activated by the incoming signal voltages in the same way as for a LCD.

Since plasma screens emit light they are brighter than LCD screens and they also give better viewing at large angles. They can be used in very large screens for public display as well as on a smaller scale for domestic television. They use more power than a LCD television set, typically 250 watts compared with 75 watts for an LCD, and their typical lifetime, before their brightness diminishes to an unacceptable level, is about 100,000 hours.

14.8 OLED (Organic Light-Emitting Diode) Technology

We have already mentioned the light-emitting diode (LED) as a means of backlighting an LCD display. However, it has also been developed as a self-illuminating unit for various forms of display, including television.

14.8.1 **The basic technology of an LED**

A diode is a device that allows the passage of light in one direction far more easily than in the other. The first diodes were in the form of thermionic valves but modern devices are based on solid-state technology, in particular the use of semiconductors. Highly conducting materials, such as most metals, have electrons loosely bound to their parent atoms so that when an electric field is established in the metal, the electrons easily escape and move through the metal so producing a flow of electric charge, which is a current. At the other extreme the atomic electrons in insulators are tightly bound and cannot be wrenched loose, even in a very high field. Semiconductors are intermediate in their electrical properties, conducting electricity, but not as well as metals.

A typical semiconductor is silicon. It has a *valency* of four; we can think of it as having four tentacles coming out of the atom, each associated with an atomic electron and wanting to attach itself to another electron to create a stable configuration. In pure silicon the atoms form a tetrahedral structure (Figure 14.19) where each atom shares electrons with four neighbours — a pair of shared electrons contributing to the stability of two atoms.

If an electric field is applied to silicon then some electrons leave their bonded positions and become conducting electrons. Each electron that is free to move through the crystal leaves behind an empty space in the crystal structure. This space is called a *hole*, a region that would like to attract an electron to plug the gap, and it behaves as though it is a particle with a positive charge. When an electrical potential difference is applied across the crystal then holes migrate across the crystal, from one silicon-silicon bond to the next, in the opposite direction to the movement of the electrons. Negative charges moving in one direction and positive charges moving in the opposite direction both contribute to current in the same direction.

The properties of a semiconductor can be changed by a process known as *doping*, which consists of adding a small amount of impurity. For example, the element phosphorus has valency five so if it occupies the site of a silicon atom it has a spare electron with no other atom to share it with. This situation is shown in Figure 14.20. This forms what is known as a *n-type semiconductor*. The spare electron is available to act as a negative charge carrier to give the material conducting properties.

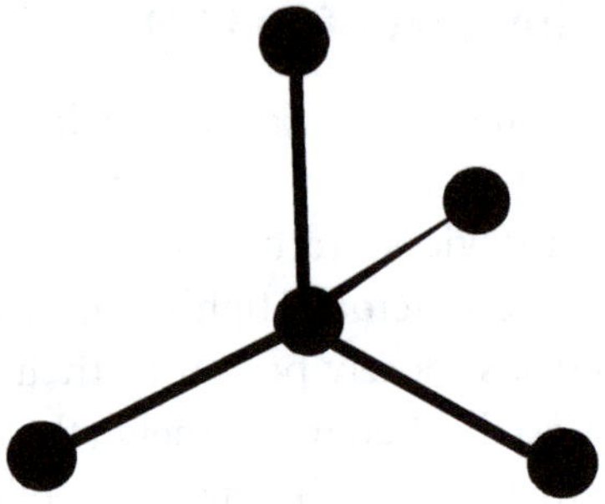

Figure 14.19   The bonding of an atom within a silicon crystal

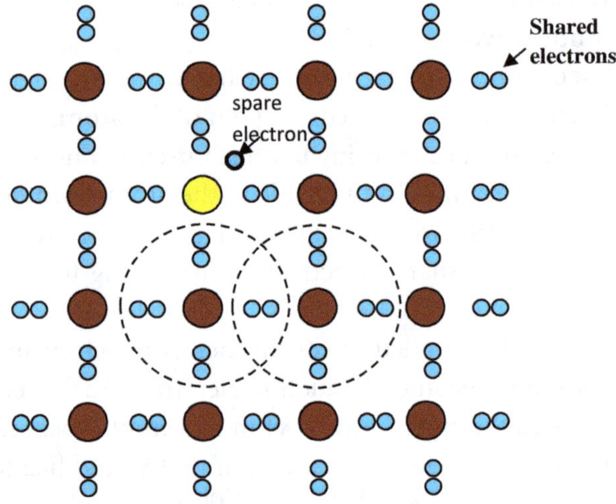

Figure 14.20   A phosphorus atom (yellow) within a silicon crystal giving an *n*-type semiconductor

By adding a valency-3 impurity, such as boron or gallium, to silicon a *p*-type semiconductor is produced (Figure 14.21). Here there is a hole formed, which will act like a positive charge and move through the material under the influence of an electric field.

Combining *n*-type and *p*-type semiconductors in various ways can produce many kinds of useful device but here we are just interested in producing a diode, which is done by joining together pieces of *n*-type and *p*-type semiconductors. If a battery is connected across the device as shown in Figure 14.22(a) then no current will flow. The negatively charged

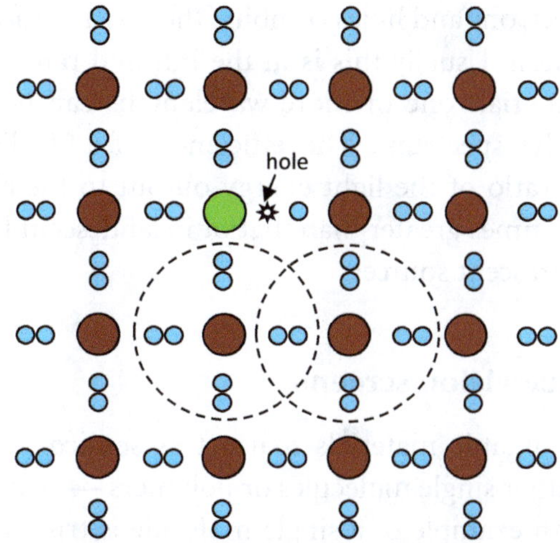

Figure 14.21   A gallium atom (green) is deficient in an electron to share with a silicon atom so giving a *p*-type semiconductor

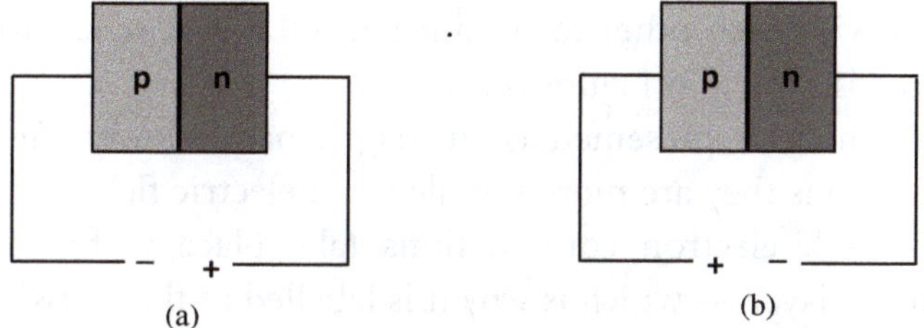

Figure 14.22   Semiconductor diode in (a) non-conducting configuration and (b) conducting configuration

electrons are attracted towards the positive side of the battery and the holes are attracted towards the negative side of the battery. Since no charge crosses the junction between the semiconductors no current flows through it. However, if the battery is reversed (Figure 14.22(b)) then a current will flow. Electrons and holes flow towards the junction where the electrons fill the holes. However, the electronic structures of the two types of semiconductor are not changed by the passage of a current; new holes and free electrons are constantly being created within the materials to maintain the current flow.

When the electrons and holes combine there is a release of energy that appears as a photon. Usually this is in the infrared range of wavelengths but for some materials one or more wavelengths can be emitted in the visible part of the spectrum. The efficiency of LED lighting devices, expressed as the ratio of the light energy output to the electrical energy input is about six times greater than that of incandescent bulbs and about twice that of fluorescent sources.

14.8.2 OLED television screens

There are some organic materials that act as semiconductors. The two main types are either single molecules or polymers — strings of connected identical units. An example of a single molecule is tris-(8-hydroxyquino-line)aluminium, known as ALq_3 (Figure 14.23).

Adding various dopants to an organic semiconductor, in the form of organic molecules containing heavy atoms, such as iridium or platinum, can create either *n*-type or *p*-type semiconductors that can be used in conjunction with each other to produce an OLED. A schematic view of such a device is shown in Figure 14.24.

Since the holes, represented as plus-signs, have a lower effective mass than the electrons they are more mobile in an electric field and hence the majority of hole-electron combinations take place within the *n*-type semiconductor layer — which is why it is labelled as the *emission layer*.

OLEDs can emit a wide range of colours, depending on the materials used and, in particular, strong red, green and blue emissions can be

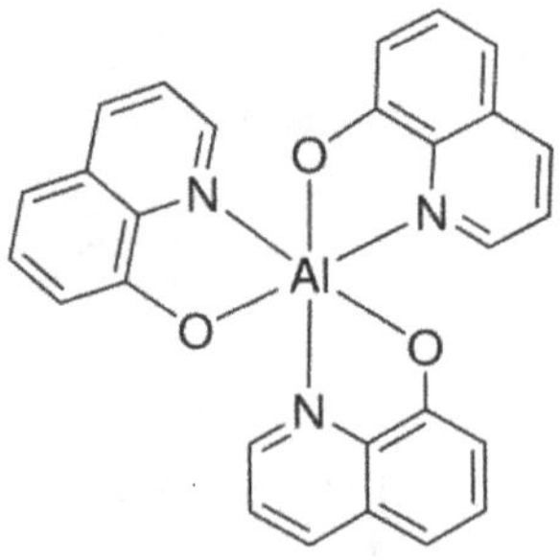

Figure 14.23   The structure of Alq_3. The unmarked apices are carbon atoms

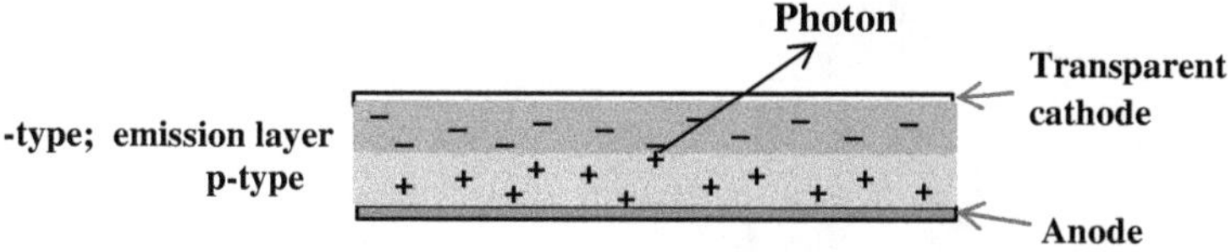

Figure 14.24   A schematic OLED

produced, the requirement for producing a complete range of colours and intensities. Television screens can be fabricated either by vacuum deposition of the various doped layers using a *shadow mask* (Section 14.5) that only allows the vapour to fall on selected areas of the substrate or by techniques that are similar to inkjet printing to form a matrix of intermixed red, green and blue emitters. However, there are some problems with this technology; blue emitters are less intense than red and green and a larger area of blue is used on the screen to produce a good white. In addition, the efficiency of the blue emitters fades more quickly than those of red and green emitters so it is necessary to balance the colours from time-to-time.

The cost of OLED in 2015 was considerably higher than that of the competing technologies — LCD and plasma — but is likely to fall considerably when the technology has greater acceptance and there are economies of scale. It has considerable advantages in that it gives a brighter image, greater contrast and a higher viewing angle than either of the other technologies. A television display can be just a few millimetres thick and the substrate can be plastic so the display can be flexible, although that property has no obvious application in television.

Chapter 15

Coloured Light Displays

Light displays are used for many purposes but mainly either for illuminated signs over shops, hotels and public buildings or for entertainment. There are a number of ways of producing the lighting display and here we discuss the more important techniques for doing so.

15.1 Fluorescent and Neon Lighting

One type of illumination that can be used for shop signs, and similar uses, is the fluorescent lamp described in Section 14.7. These tubes can be bent to create alphanumeric characters or images and, depending on the phosphor coating the tube, they offer a wide variety of colours. Another, and related, source of light is the *neon tube*, although this generic term is used for sources not dependent on neon. They are simply gas-discharge tubes containing a gas, usually at a low pressure but sometimes at around atmospheric pressure. A coated cathode provides initial electrons that, when accelerated in the electric field ionize the gas it contains so producing further electrons. A high voltage is required to initiate the current flow but once the ionization reaches a certain level and the resistance of the tube falls, the discharge can be maintained with a much lower voltage. Collisions between electrons and atoms and ions within the tube excite some of the electrons the atoms and ions contain into higher energy levels, and when they fall back to their original states the energy released appears as a photon, which can correspond to a wavelength in the visible range. The colour can also be dependent on the gas pressure.

Figure 15.1 shows a coloured-light advertising display in Piccadilly, London. The signs are bold, large, easily read and most of them change with time. Although their principle purpose is advertising, they also act as a light display that adds attractiveness to the otherwise sombre street scene.

By contrast, Figure 15.2 shows a night street scene in central Tokyo with an abundance of shop-sign and other lighting — indeed, in such abundance that individual signs become difficult to discern and appear just as elements in the total image. However, while the impact of each advertising sign is lessened by being such a small part of the whole, it cannot be denied that it makes this part of Tokyo seem a very dynamic and exciting place.

15.2 Son et Lumière

Son et Lumière (sound and light) is a show combining sound, narrative and a light display serving both an educational and entertainment purpose. Normally it is centred on some building, or natural feature, of historical interest and would consist of a narration describing the structure, or some event associated with the structure, while lights, often variable and coloured, would illuminate the structure, perhaps highlighting some part of it pertinent to the part of the story being told. Music or sound effects can be introduced at appropriate times.

The first *son-et-lumière* show was in 1952 at the Château de Chambord, a large French Renaissance château in the Loire valley. The success of this show stimulated similar productions, principally in other sites in France but also all over the world. Figure 15.3(a) shows part of a *son-et-lumiere* show at Amiens Cathedral. In 1980, a *son-et-lumière* show was put on at the Great Pyramid in Giza, Egypt. Figure 15.3(b) shows striking illuminations of the Great Pyramid and also the nearby Sphinx.

15.3 Floodlighting and Various Light Shows

Other light displays can be used either for aesthetic reasons, such as when prominent and important buildings are floodlit, or for entertainment.

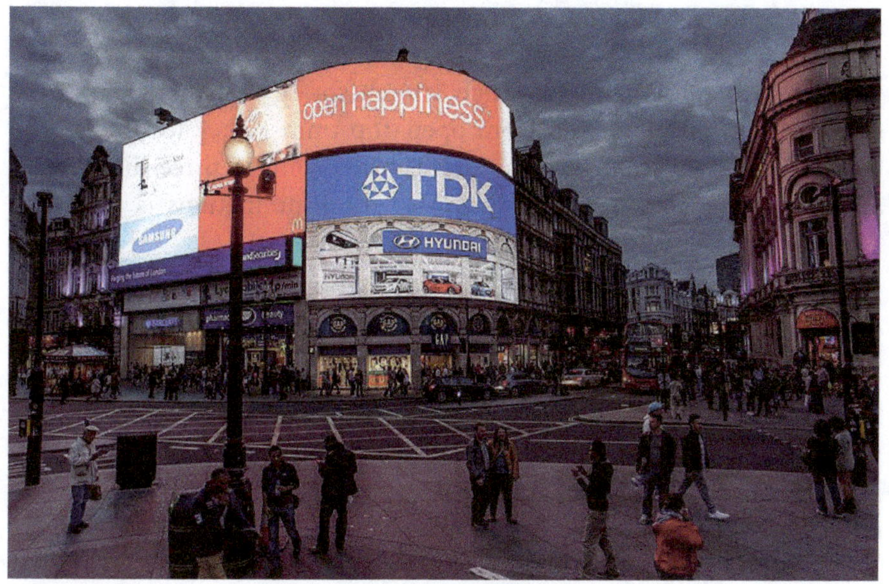

Figure 15.1   Piccadilly Circus, London

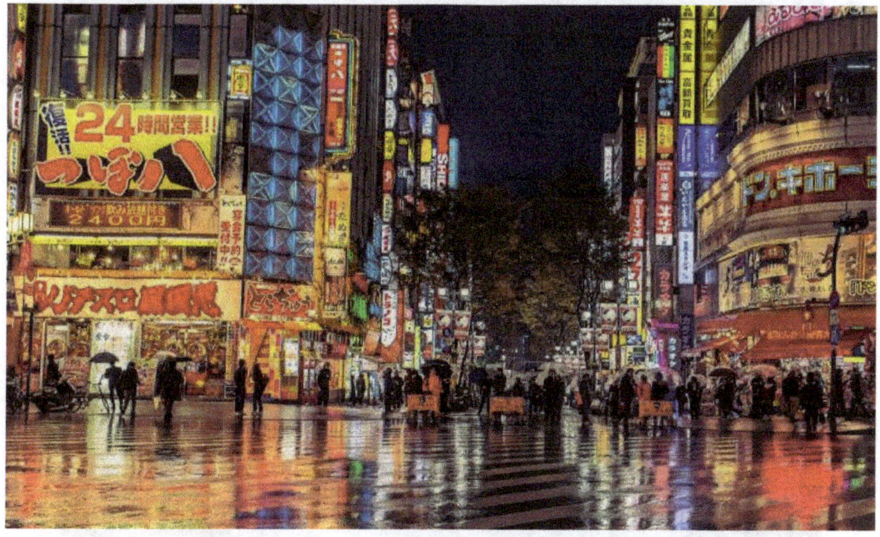

Figure 15.2   A Tokyo street scene

Every year, for about a month in the autumn period, the seaside town of Blackpool, in the north–west of England, puts on a lightshow known as the *Blackpool Illuminations*, which stretch for several miles along the seafront and can be viewed from open–top trams. They feature several hundred different scenic designs and features, some in three-dimensions and some animated. A small section of the Illuminations is shown in Figure 15.4.

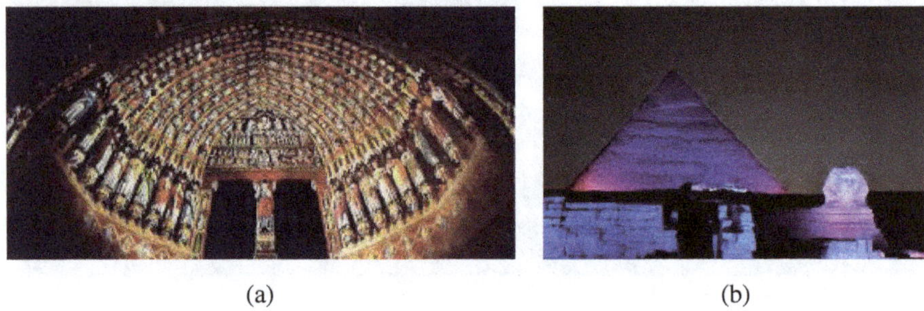

(a)   (b)

Figure 15.3   Parts of *son-et-lumière* productions at (a) Amiens Cathedral and (b) Giza, Egypt

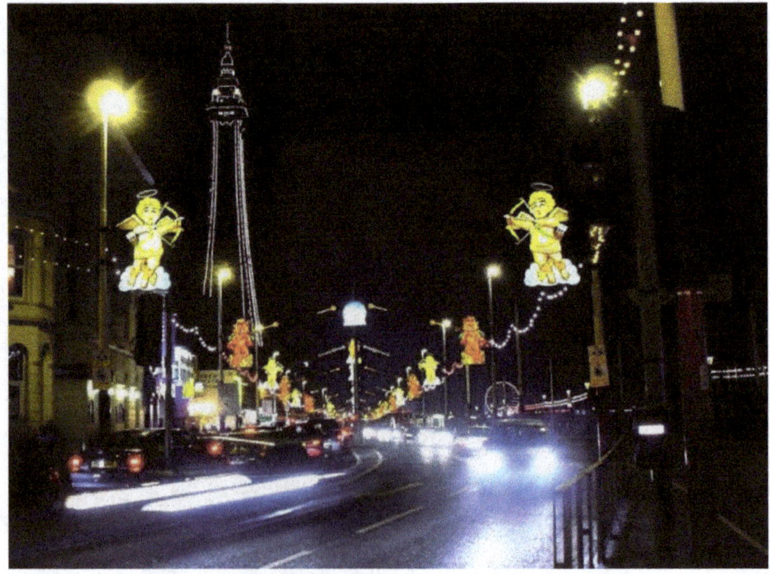

Figure 15.4   Part of the Blackpool Illuminations

Firework displays are another very popular form of entertainment. Most major cities all over the world put on lavish displays to greet the New Year and Chinese cities also celebrate the Chinese New Year in this way. The invention of fireworks was made by the Chinese, who had previously invented gunpowder. By adding various metallic salts to gunpowder, when it is ignited a large variety of colours can be produced — for example, strontium for red, calcium for orange, sodium for yellow, barium for green and copper for blue. Theme parks in Florida usually end the day with spectacular displays and there is a special night in England — Guy Fawkes Night, November 5th, — when firework displays occur all over the country. Guy Fawkes was a member of a plot to blow up the English Parliament and to restore a Catholic monarch to England. A large quantity of gunpowder was smuggled into cellars below the Parliament building but the plot was foiled on November 5th 1605 when Fawkes was discovered guarding the explosives. A scene from a firework display, with three colours, is shown in Figure 15.5.

Another popular form of lighting display involves *lasers*. Laser light sources occur in everyday life in various devices, for example, in the reading heads of CD or DVD players. They were the invention of two American scientists, Arthur Schawlow (1921–1999) and Charles Townes (1915–2015; Nobel Prize for Physics, 1964). A substance, which can be a solid, liquid, gas or vapour, is excited electrically so that the electrons of a particular type of atom are raised to a higher energy level. The substance is contained within a pair of parallel plane mirrors that can reflect light to-and-fro. Initially electrons spontaneously fall to a lower energy level, emitting photons of specific wavelengths. When one of these strikes an excited atom it stimulates the emission of a photon moving in the same direction with precisely the same energy and phase, i.e. it has a wave motion with synchronous crests and troughs as that of the colliding photon. If a photon travelling perpendicular to the mirrors stimulates an atom to emit a photon in phase with itself then there are two atoms moving in phase moving between the mirrors. Eventually the only mode of photon production is of stimulated photons moving along the axis of the device precisely perpendicular to the mirrors. If one of the mirrors is partially transmitting then from that mirror a very narrow parallel beam of radiation is emitted with very high intensity. The emitted beam has the characteristic that it consists of very long continuous wave trains with all photons precisely in phase — a beam of *coherent radiation.*

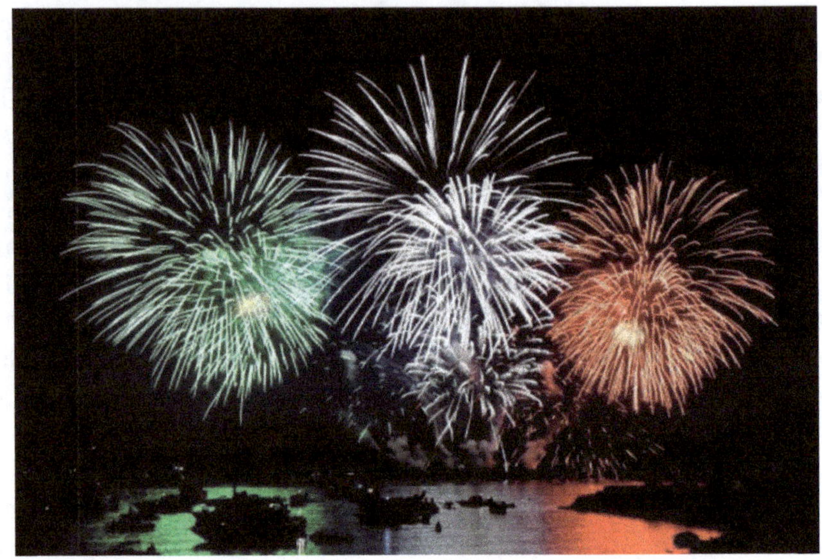

Figure 15.5　Part of a firework display

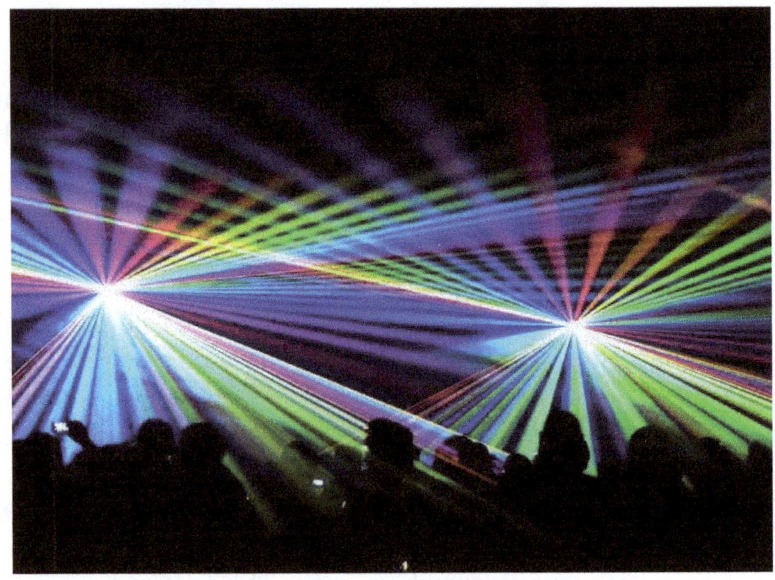

Figure 15.6　A still from a laser-light display

Depending on the laser material, the colour of the emitted beam of light can be within the visible range and laser displays are a popular accompaniment to many concerts of popular music. A still from one display is shown in Figure 15.6. Because it is so concentrated and intense, laser light can be harmful to the eyes, so laser displays are subject to very tight regulations to prevent harm to the audience.

Chapter 16
Practical Uses of Colour

16.1 Colour as a Safety Tool

There are many situations where making the right decision, or being guided to make the right decision, can be a matter of life and death. If the instructions cannot be given verbally then, in principle and sometimes in practice, they can be printed, preferably using words that are widely understood, like 'STOP'. The Cyrillic equivalent 'СТОП', used in Russia and some other countries, or the Turkish equivalent 'DUR', will only be understood by those who use, or have learnt, the language. However, colour can be regarded as a universal language and as long as everyone, regardless of the spoken language, uses the same meaning for a particular colour then safety can be maintained across state and language boundaries. We now consider various ways in which colour is used to promote safety.

16.1.1 Traffic lights

When the age of the motor car arrived, replacing much slower horse-drawn traffic, the speeds of vehicles made them dangerous in collisions, either with pedestrians or with other cars, and it became necessary to ensure the orderly passage of vehicles, particularly at road intersections. One answer to the problem was the introduction of roundabouts in the early 20th century, but for safety even these depended on everyone observing certain rules such as, in the UK, that traffic on the roundabout has priority over that wishing to enter it. Roundabouts are particularly effective at junctions of a number of roads, say five or six. However, there are situations in congested cities where the roundabout solution is impracticable and, even before roundabouts were introduced, the early solution was to have a traffic policeman, sometimes, but not always, situated in a box or on a stand, in the middle of the intersection, controlling the flow of traffic so that there were never intersecting streams.

This labour-intensive method of controlling traffic was revolutionized by the introduction of traffic lights in the late 19th century. The standard traffic light is a set of three lights — one red, one amber and one green, usually set vertically but sometimes horizontally. The red light indicates stop, the amber light is a warning that either the red or green light is about to be activated (its use varies from country to country and from state to state in the USA) and green gives permission to proceed. The convention for red and green is universal, which means that motorists going from one country to another can do so reasonably safely as far as traffic intersections are concerned. The sequence of lights as used in the UK is shown in Figure 16.1. Another advantage of the use of coloured lights over other kinds of colourless indication is that they are visible over large distances and so give the driver plenty of warning. Even a non-luminous patch of colour is more effective than a black-and-white sign, be it words or some symbol. Figure 16.2 shows a red patch, the word 'STOP' of about the same size and a cross. Seen at a distance the red spot will be clearly seen as red long after the word and sign become unresolved.

At junctions where traffic lights are being used it is particularly important that pedestrians are instructed about when it is safe to cross the road. Even at simple intersections of two roads, traffic may be turning left or right and it is common for all traffic to be stopped for an interval while pedestrians make their crossings. Pedestrian road-crossing lights use the red and green convention but sometimes reinforce the message with pictures of stationary or walking pedestrians. Figure 16.3 shows a Danish pedestrian road-crossing light; even for the most colour-blind individual the message given is clear.

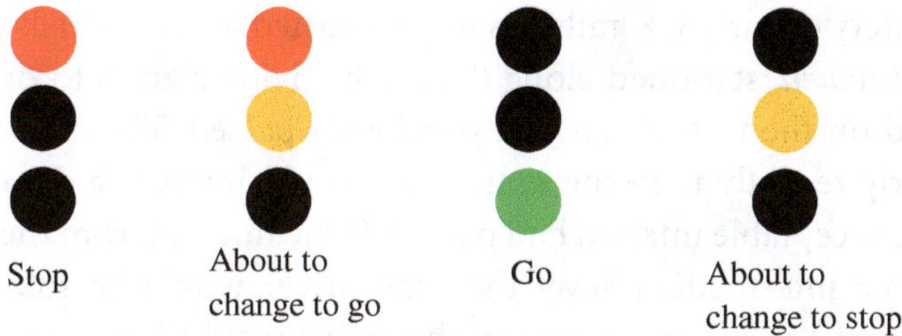

Figure 16.1   A UK sequence of traffic lights

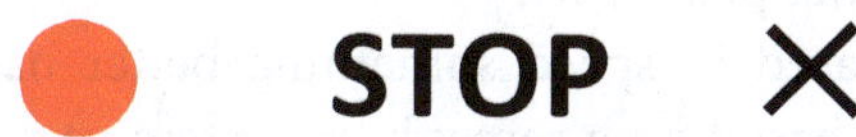

Figure 16.2   Three ways of indicating stop. The red spot is recognized at a greater distance than the other two

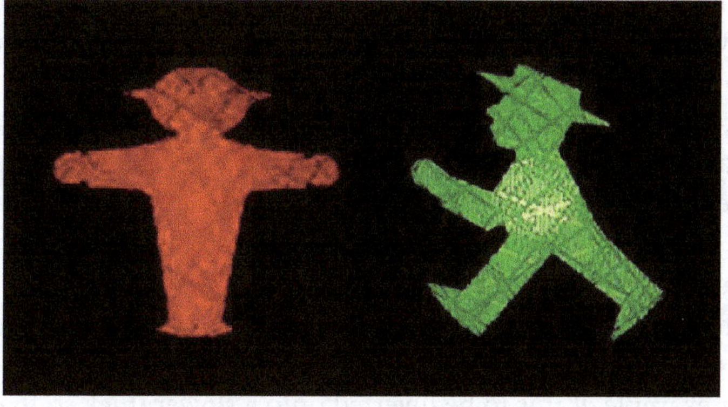

Figure 16.3   A Danish pedestrian road-crossing light

16.1.2 Railway signals

Railways have the particular problem that many trains are usually running on a single track and that for efficient use of the track the time intervals between trains should be as short as safety will allow. The most common type of railway accident is a shunt when one train runs into one before it and, when this happens, it indicates that a complex safety system, mainly based on the use of coloured lights, has failed.

The safety of early UK railways was entrusted to individuals, given the title of *policemen*, stationed along the track, giving signals to drivers that were based on the traffic that had previously passed. Thus if a train had passed fairly recently then the policeman would instruct a driver to stop until some acceptable interval had passed. If the interval from the last train was at some intermediate level then the driver would be told to travel slowly so that the interval between the trains would lengthen. However, since there was no contact between the policemen it was not a very safe system. If a train broke down between two policemen then a shunting accident was a distinct possibility.

As trains increased in speed something better had to be used and mechanical signals, based on a semaphore system came into use, eventually under the control of a signalman in a signal box who not only operated signals but also controlled points that diverted trains from one track to another. Two types of signal are generally used. The first is a *stop signal* shown in Figure 16.4(a) in its two configurations — 'stop' and 'clear'. The second type is the *distant signal* (Figure 16.4(b), usually placed well ahead of a stop signal and giving two messages — 'clear', meaning that the train can proceed without abating its speed, and 'caution' warning that a stop signal was ahead so that the train should reduce speed so as to be able to stop if necessary. So that the signals could be seen at night there are lights attached to the post that supports the semaphore arms that show red or green for a stop signal and green or yellow for a distant signal.

There are now signals that are just coloured lights and there are a number of signalling conventions depending on what the train is going to do — for example, if it is to be diverted onto a slower track so that it must slow down. For high-speed trains, travelling at 250 kilometres per hour or more, a four-aspect light system is normally used. This consists of four lights — one red, two yellow and one green. The lights shown and the message they convey is shown in Figure 16.5.

Tungsten filament lamps in railway signalling are now being replaced by light-emitting diodes that have now been developed to the point where they are intense enough for that purpose and have the advantage of long lifetimes, of order 100,000 hours, so lamp failure occurs less frequently. However, they have the disadvantage that their performance is temperature dependent.

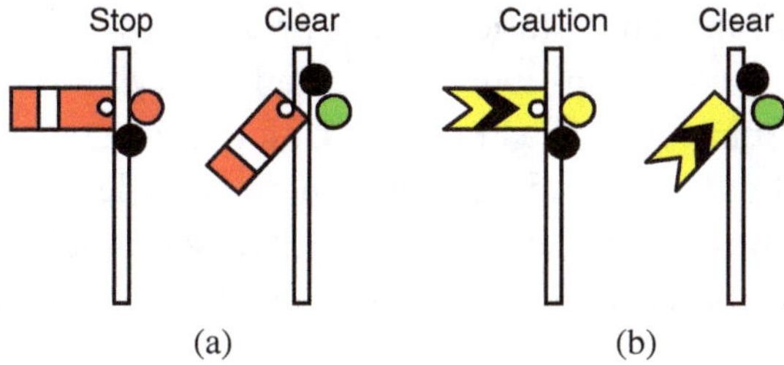

Figure 16.4   (a) Stop signal. (b) Distant signal

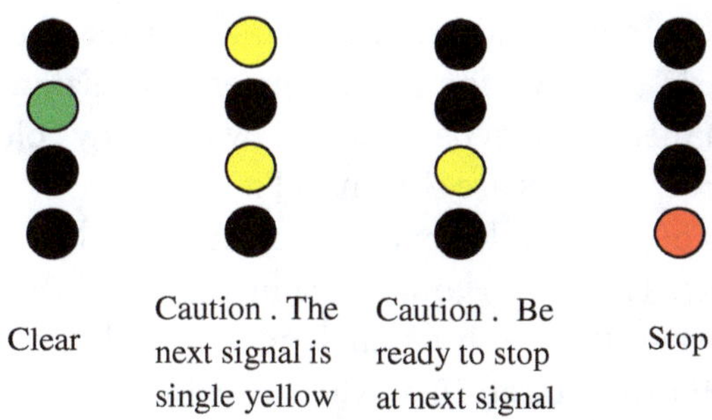

Figure 16.5   A four-aspect set of colour signals

16.1.3 Identifying gas in cylinders

There are many types of gas with a wide variety of uses that are provided under pressure in cylinders. Examples include acetylene and oxygen, used together for oxy-acetylene welding, and helium, used for filling party balloons and also *blimps*, large freight-and-passenger-carrying helium-filled airships. It is important that the correct gas is used in any application; filling a party balloon with carbon dioxide would do no more harm than having the balloons falling to the floor, but filling them with butane, a highly inflammable gas would be very dangerous. Simply writing on the cylinder the name of the gas is possible, but a German cylinder with the inscription *wasserstoff* might not be recognized as containing hydrogen in the UK. An alternative would be to use the universally accepted chemical notation, e.g. CO_2 for carbon dioxide, but not everyone would know that C_4H_{10} was butane or that C_2HF_5 is *pentofluoroethane* a hydrofluorocarbon used as a refrigerant. The solution to this problem would be to establish a universally-accepted colour-code marked on the cylinders but, unfortunately, this is not in place. The European Union has established a code that is used throughout its jurisdiction but there is no legal enforcement of colour coding in the United States. For that reason users must use all the information on the cylinder, words or symbols, and not depend on the colour alone.

The European Union colour coding can represent either or both of the identity of the gas and/or its characteristic properties. The colour that identifies the gas is situated around the shoulder of the cylinder and if, in addition, it is required to indicate the characteristics of the gas — flammable (red), toxic (yellow), inert (light green), oxidizing (light blue) or medical (white) then this can be indicated by the body colour. Some illustrative gas-cylinder colours are shown in Figure 16.6.

The colours of gas cylinders played a central role in a 1946 British film *Green for Danger*. The action took place in a hospital during the World-War-II period when the south of England was under attack from flying bombs — unmanned aircraft that, when they ran out of fuel, plunged to earth and exploded. A postman who was injured by one of these bombs was in the operating theatre and the operation goes badly wrong. His breathing became laboured and as the anaesthetist administered more oxygen to correct his breathing the situation became worse and the patient died. The cause of his death is eventually found to be that a cylinder of carbon dioxide, in those days painted green, had been overpainted black, the colour for oxygen at that time. Hence when oxygen was called for, the patient received ever increasing amounts of carbon dioxide and asphyxiated.

16.1.4 Colours of hospital pipelines

Gases for medical and other purposes are often transmitted by pipelines in hospitals and, for safety reasons, the pipes must be clearly marked as to their contents, the direction of flow and, sometimes, the pressure within the pipe. An example is the American National Standards Institute (ANSI) system for colouring pipes according to their content and also for giving written descriptions. Some examples are shown in Figure 16.7. There are

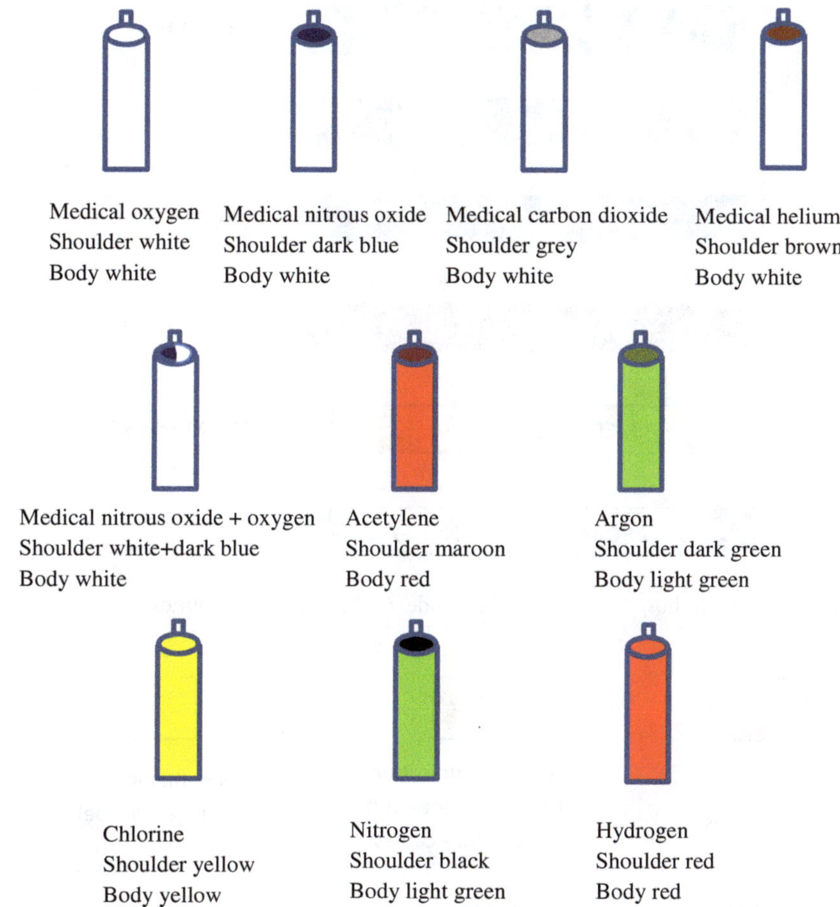

Figure 16.6   Shoulder and body colours for various gas cylinders

other rules concerning the spacing of the written descriptions — no more than 20 feet apart — and they must also be given at pipe junctions or where the pipes change direction.

16.1.5 Underground utility colour codes

The sight of a road being dug up, either to repair or to install some public utility, is quite common. To provide electricity, gas, water, communications of various kinds and sewerage to homes requires that under most roads in

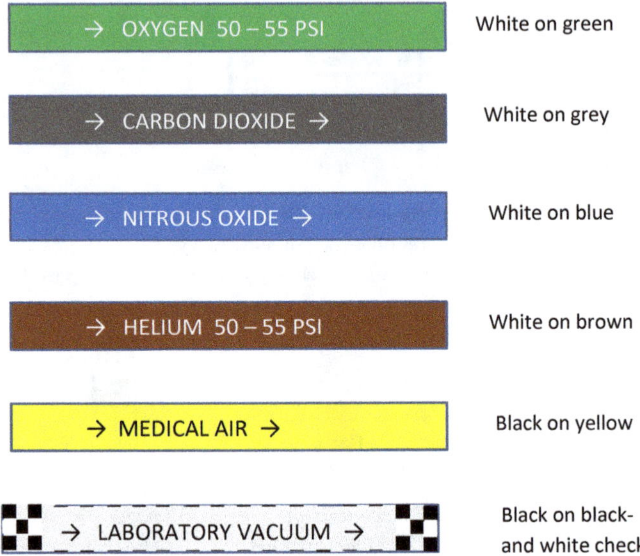

Figure 16.7   Some hospital pipeline colour codes (PSI is pressure in pounds per square inch)

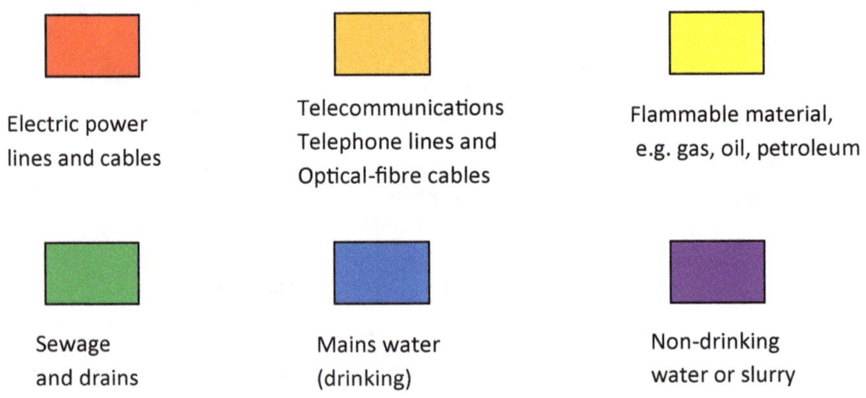

Figure 16.8   The principal utilities and their colour codes

built-up areas there are many pipes of various kinds. Maps are kept showing the disposition of these service ducts and it is also possible to locate the ducts by physical means, which will depend on the nature of their material. Metal pipes and cables can be detected by electromagnetic measurement and plastic or concrete pipes by ground-penetrating radar.

Although the nature of the ducts is often evident to the excavators from their structure and composition — e.g. metal, plastic or concrete — they are also coloured so that those working to correct some fault can readily recognize what they are carrying, which can be a matter of safety as well as convenience. The colour codes used in the USA and UK are shown in Figure 16.8.

16.2 General Use of Colour

There are circumstances where colour can be used as a substitute for alphanumeric information when space is restricted or to clarify the structure of a complicated diagram or chart. Here we give some examples.

16.2.1 Resistors

Resistors are components of electrical circuits and they are typically small barrel-shaped objects about one-to-two centimetres in length with a wire protruding from each end for connecting by soldering to neighbouring components. Resistance is measured in units of *ohms* (symbol Ω); if a resistor has a voltage V volts across it and a current I amps within it, then it has a resistance of V/I Ω. The values of resistances in circuits can vary from a small fraction of an ohm up to of order 10^9 Ω and a problem is how to indicate the value of the resistance and the tolerance — what percentage variation there could be in the indicated resistance — in a very confined space. The answer has been to use colour coding in which digits and tolerances are associated with particular colours. While this gives a convenient and easily visualized value for most individuals constructing circuits, it has severe limitations for those suffering from any form of colour blindness. Again, if a resistor overheats or becomes covered in dirt of some sort it may be difficult to distinguish some pairs of colours, e.g. red and brown or grey and silver. However, this latter problem does not arise at the stage where pristine resistors are being used to build a circuit.

For most everyday circuitry the number of significant figures to which the resistance should be specified is two, i.e. a resistance of 68 Ω, 68 $\times$ 10 Ω and 68 $\times$ 100 Ω are all specified to two significant figures. Although apparently the same values as the last two given, 680 Ω and 680 $\times$ 10 Ω are specified to three significant figures, indicating a higher degree of precision. A non-integral number expressed to two significant figures relating to some measured or estimated quantity has a built-in uncertainty since the value 68 is the nearest two-significant-figure value of any number between 67.5 and 68.5. However, we might over-ride that uncertainty by specifying that the value given has a tolerance of 5%, meaning that its true value could be anywhere between 64.6 (68 × 0.95) and 71.4 (68 × 1.05).

A 4-band indication of resistance gives two significant figures. Taking the example above we could have the first significant figure 6 and the second 8. The next band is a multiplier that goes in powers of 10 so, if it is 1 then 68 is multiplied by 10^1 (= 10) to give 680. The last colour band, slightly separated from the other three can give the tolerance, or uncertainty, in the value −1%, 2%, 5%, 10%, etc. The colour coding for these bands is shown in Figure 16.9. Figure 16.10 shows a barrel resistor with a nominal resistance of 680 Ω with a tolerance of 5%.

When greater precision is required a 5-band indication of resistance can be given. Figure 16.11 shows a barrel resistor with resistance 6.81 × 10^4 Ω and tolerance ± 1%.

16.2.2 The London Underground map

Many large cities worldwide have underground train transport systems, which have the advantage of moving large numbers of people quickly, without the delays of over-ground transport and without adding to the pressures of over-ground transport. Some cities, such as New York and London, have very extensive systems with many lines intersecting at transfer stations, with some stations being common to three or more lines.

A London map showing underground lines, which were run by different companies, for `1908 is shown in Figure 16.12. Colour has been used to distinguish the different lines and the lines indicated are marked along the actual sinuous paths that they follow. The system is comparatively simple, with eight lines, and easily comprehensible. However, the system steadily grew until the very large number of lines, snaking their way across the capital, made the map look very untidy although, by the aid of line colour-coding, it was still possible to plan a route with appropriate interchanges.

Color	Significant figures	Multiplier	Tolerance
Black	0	$\times 10^0$	–
Brown	1	$\times 10^1$	±1%
Red	2	$\times 10^2$	±2%
Orange	3	$\times 10^3$	–
Yellow	4	$\times 10^4$	(±5%)
Green	5	$\times 10^5$	±0.5%
Blue	6	$\times 10^6$	±0.25%
Violet	7	$\times 10^7$	±0.1%
Gray	8	$\times 10^8$	±0.05% (±10%)
White	9	$\times 10^9$	–
Gold	–	$\times 10^{-1}$	±5%
Silver	–	$\times 10^{-2}$	±10%
None	–	–	±20%

Figure 16.9   Colour coding for barrel resistors

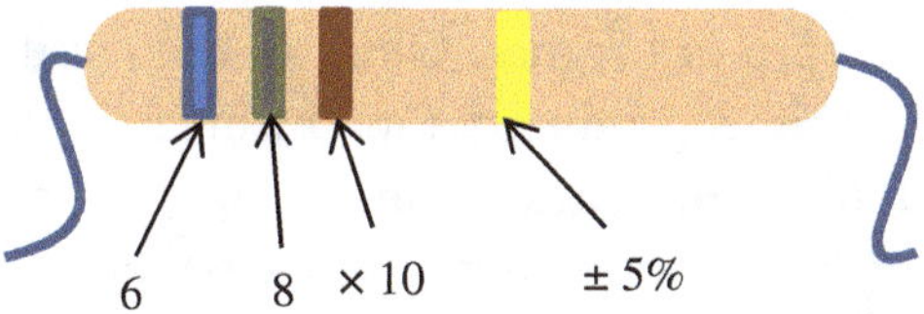

Figure 16.10   A barrel resistor with resistance 680 Ω and tolerance ±5%

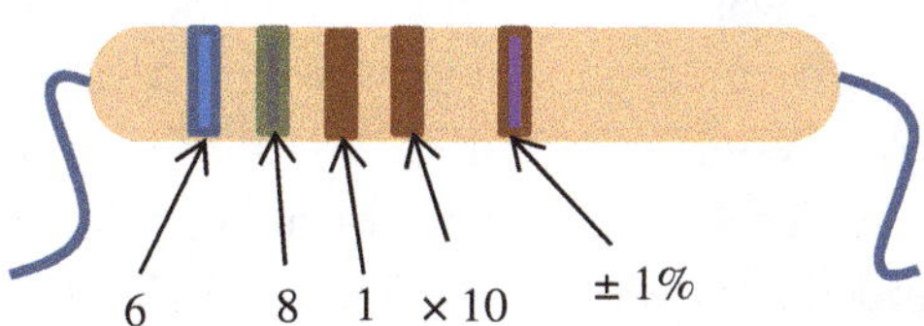

Figure 16.11   A 5-band indication of resistance 6.81×10^4 Ω and tolerance 1%

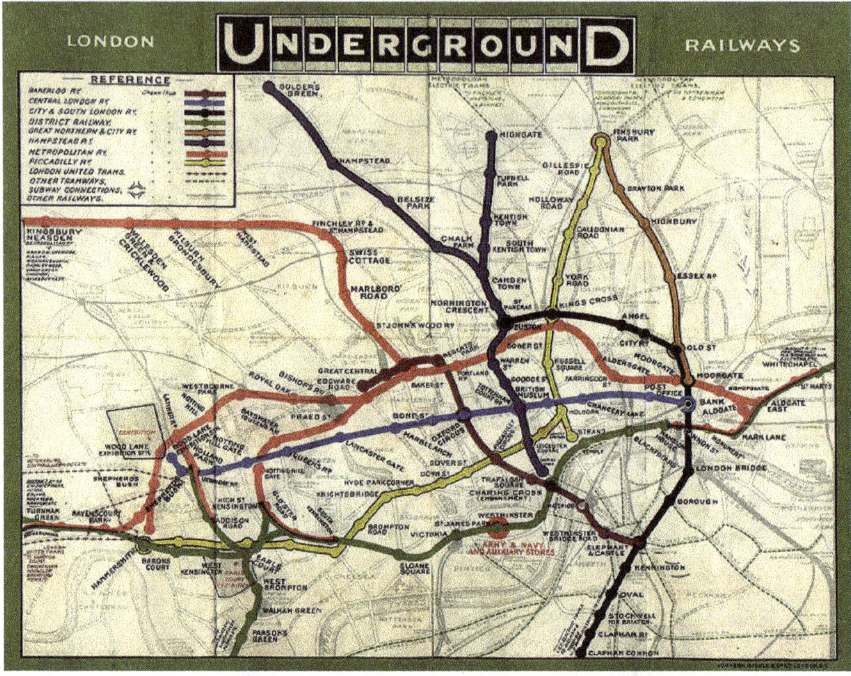

Figure 16.12   A 1908 map showing the underground rail lines in London

In 1931 Henry (Harry) Beck (1902–1978), an engineering draftsman at the London Underground Signals Office of the London Underground, working in his spare time, produced a map which abandoned the idea of geographical accuracy and, instead, concentrated on clarity. The central region of London, where stations were close together, was at a greater scale so that individual stations could more easily be seen and labelled. The sinuous nature of the lines was eliminated by straight sections with 45° bends where it was necessary. The resultant map, first issued on an experimental basis in 1933, was widely popular and Beck's concept is now the basis of all London Underground maps, which also shows connections with other transport systems, including main-line rail stations and some surface transport systems. The geographical map for 1933 is shown in Figure 16.13(a) and Beck's version in Figure 16.13(b). The Beck concept for producing maps of underground systems is now used in many other cities all over the world.

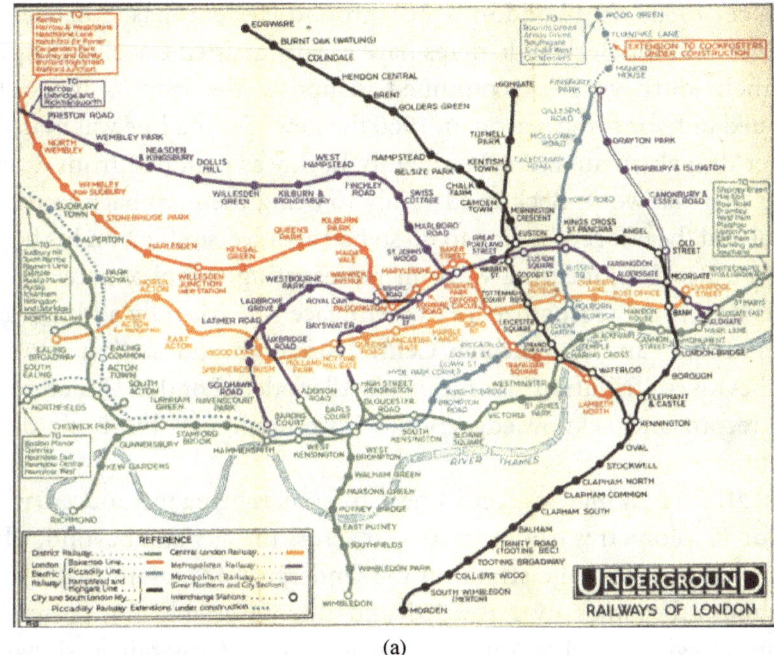

(a)

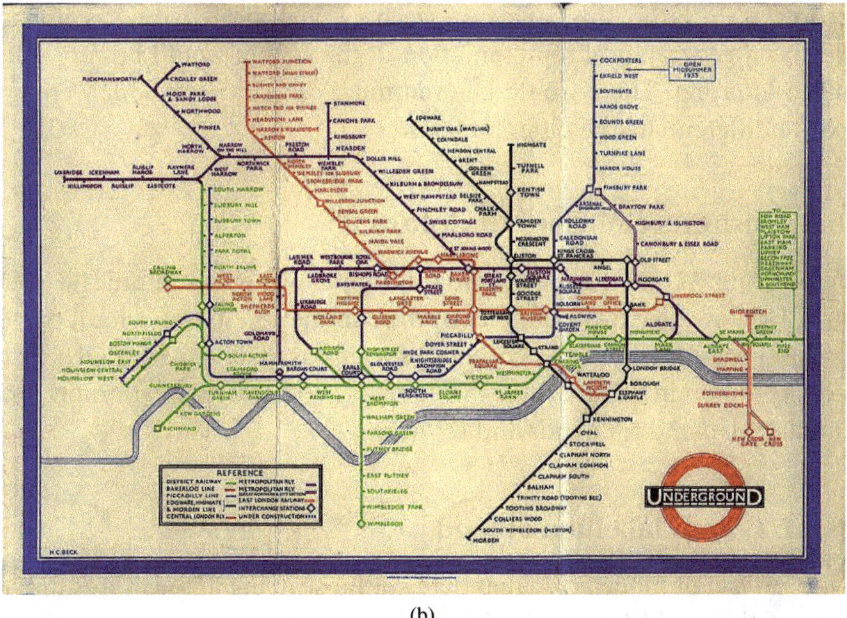

(b)

Figure 16.13   (a) A geographical London Underground map for 1933. (b) The Beck version

Since 1933, the London Underground system has considerably expanded and the Beck-style maps have greatly assisted travellers in planning their journeys. Beck continued to update the map as the system expanded but, for some reason, in 1960 the new Victoria line was added by another draughtsman and subsequently Beck was excluded from extending his original work. Beck tried vainly to bring the map back under his control and the effort of trying to do so had an adverse effect on his health. However, Beck's pioneering work in representing complex network systems is now highly recognized. His birthplace is marked by a blue plaque (Figure 16.14) and at Finchley Central underground station a plaque describes his contribution in some detail. All modern London Underground maps record and acknowledge Beck's introduction of the basic design concept.

In 2018, a new high-capacity line, Crossrail, is being introduced, which runs for 42 kilometres from east to west across the city and beyond, which is designed to relieve the strain on the Underground system that, during rush hours, becomes overcrowded and uncomfortable for passengers. A map showing the London underground plus Crossrail is shown in Figure 16.15. From this, one can see how complicated the system has become; a geographical representation of the system would be very difficult to interpret. There would be even more difficulty if colour were not used to differentiate the different lines.

16.3 Commercial Uses of Colour

It is well known that the use of colour is a good way to communicate effectively. Here we give two examples of the commercial use of colour, one to give information about the content of foods available in packaged form and the other in advertising, the industry that seeks to promote and stimulate demand for goods and services.

16.3.1 Colour labelling of food

It is a sad fact of modern life that many of those living in the more affluent parts of the world have unhealthy diets. People tend to eat food that is tasty without regard to what it contains and some of these eating patterns

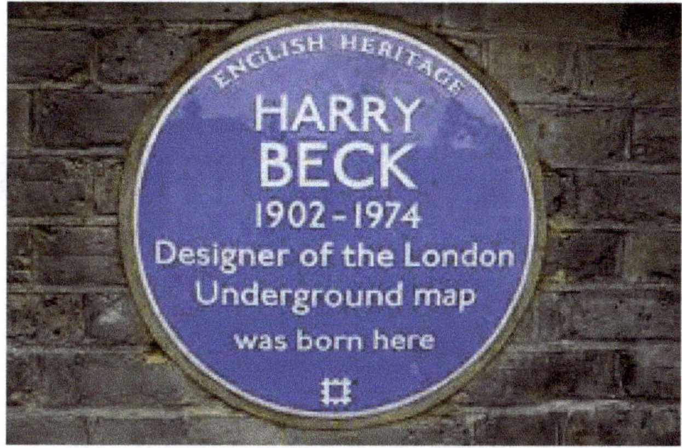

Figure 16.14   The plaque at Harry Beck's birthplace

seem to originate from mankind's early existence. The example we take here relates to the consumption of sugar. Going back to early mankind, the only source of sweetness was honey, which was limited in supply and often difficult to procure. About 8,000 years ago sugarcane was cultivated in New Guinea but the first production of sugar crystals was achieved in India in the fourth century. The availability of sugar spread, first into China and the Middle East and then into Europe. However, the supply was limited and the price extremely high so it was more of a novelty product than a regular part of everyday diet. Eventually sugar was produced more plentifully from sugar cane, grown in the West Indies using slave labour, and it became a more regular component of food consumption. The combination of an inbuilt craving for sweet foods, and the availability of plentiful and cheap quantities of sugar has led to an overconsumption of products sweetened with sugar, to the detriment of the health of those that overindulge.

There are four main food components, the overconsumption of which can be detrimental to human health. These are: total fat, saturated fat, sugar and salt. Many developed countries are experiencing a dramatic increase in obesity caused by a combination of increasing prosperity, and hence the ability to buy unhealthy processed foods, and the cheapness of those foods. It is ironic that in the Second World War, when many foods were stringently rationed in the United Kingdom, the health of the nation

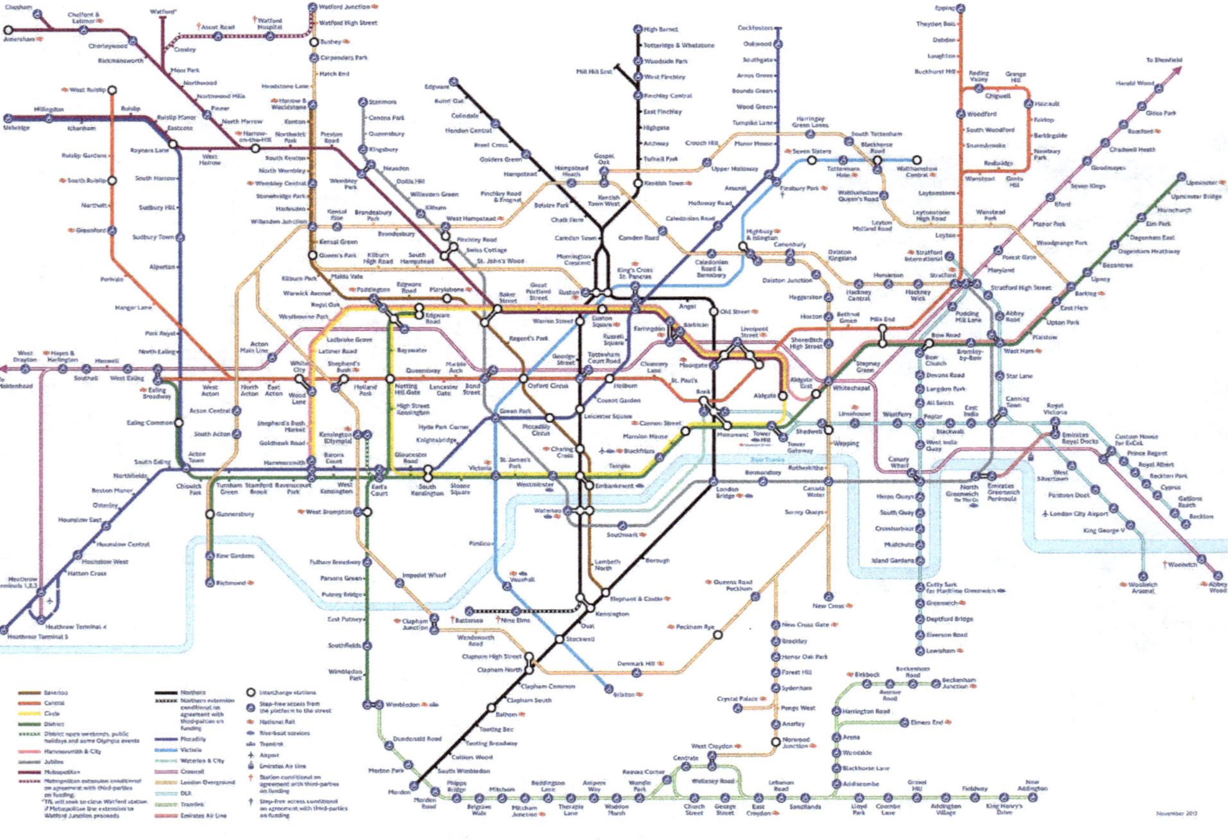

Figure 16.15   A modern London Underground map including Crossrail

actually improved. Life expectancy increased, infantile mortality decreased and by the end of the war fifteen year old boys were five centimetres taller than their pre-war counterparts. While salt was plentiful, fats and sugar were in short supply.

Many individuals would wish to avoid foods that were bad for their health but they lack knowledge of the levels of the substances that cause harm in excessive quantities. Manufacturers of processed food are bound by law to give an ingredients list of the various kinds of components in their products — not only the potentially harmful substances already mentioned but such components as fibre, protein and carbohydrate, which include various kinds of sugar. Nevertheless, how many would know, for example, whether 6 grams of saturated fat per 100 grams of product is a high level, reasonable level or low level? To meet this problem manufacturers are encouraged to use a traffic-light colour-coding system to indicate whether the level of each particular health-related substance is high (red circle), low (green circle) or within acceptable limits (amber circle). The guideline limits, which are not universally accepted, are:

Total fat	High	More than 17.5 grams per 100 grams
	Low	Less than 3 grams per 100 grams
Saturated fat	High	More than 5 grams per 100 grams
	Low	Less than1.5 grams per 100 grams
Salt	High	More than 1.5 grams per 100 grams
	Low	Less than 0.3 grams per 100 grams
Sugar	High	More than 22.5 grams per 100 grams
	Low	Less than 5 grams per 100 grams

A typical traffic-light indication is shown in Figure 16.16. The salt content is indicated as high but if the overall diet includes other products with low salt then this would be an acceptable component of a shopping basket. The intention is not that people should avoid all foods with red

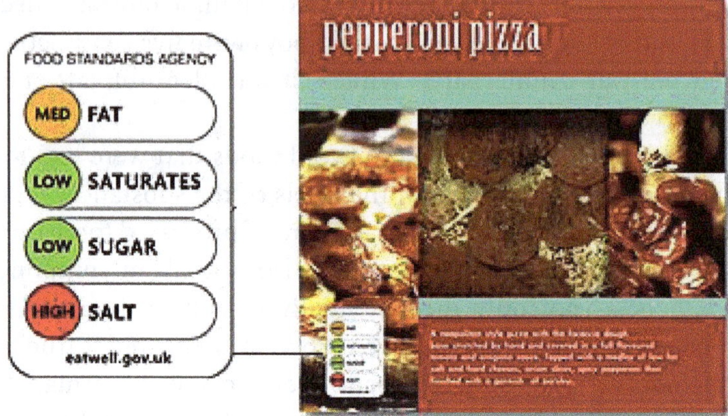

Figure 16.16   A food product with traffic-light indicators for potentially harmful components

circles but rather that they should be able to assess the characteristics of their total shopping basket. A preponderance of red circles would indicate an unhealthy overall choice of products. A few reds amongst a much larger number of amber and greens would give reassurance that the associated diet would be a healthy one.

16.3.2 Colour and advertising

Advertising agencies are employed by companies to produce material that will promote the sale of their products. Presentations can vary from combinations of pictures and words in newspapers and magazines to short presentations on commercial television or in cinemas. The type of presentation can also vary. There are factual presentations that give the characteristics of the product, laying stress on features that distinguish it from competing products. Other presentations attempt rather to give an impression of quality or effectiveness by showing the product in unusual situations — for example, a car travelling through a burning forest, which will have little relevance to the weekly trip to the local supermarket but gives the product an attractive aura. Finally there are those using cartoon characters that try to impart humour or fantasy into the presentation.

The choice of words can be important. Dorothy L Sayers in her book *Murder Must Advertise* points out the difference between saying 'made *with* strawberries', which just means that some strawberries are present but in the presence of other ingredients, and 'made *from* strawberries', which implies that it is the sole, or at least the dominant, component. These days there are rules with which advertisers must comply so claims for a product must be based on fact.

An important component of advertising is the use of colour, but it is surprising how sometimes colour is used in a way that seems to defeat the object of the exercise. Advertisements in magazines and newspapers usually consist of a mixture of pictures and words. Presumably the words are meant to be read but often the printing is very small, and difficult to read for those with less than 20/20 vision, and even those with perfect vision will be defeated by, and give up on, the task of reading pale pink or pale green print on a white background or black print on a dark green background.

The impression that an advertisement wishes to give depends on the type of product and the target readership. For example, advertising a particular brand of pizza would appeal to a different readership than that for an expensive diamond-studded watch. There are psychological aspects of colour that advertisers seek to exploit and different combinations of colour can create the desired set of reactions that will give the reader a favourable impression of the product. The impressions given to a reader can be influenced by colour and one suggested relationship between colour and impression is:

Red	Exciting,
Orange	Happy, sociable, affordable
Yellow	Happy, playful
Green	Peaceful, relaxed, eco-friendly
Blue	Serious, conservative, trustworthy
Magenta	Creative, high quality, luxurious
Silver and black	High quality, luxurious, sophisticated
Gold	High quality, luxurious

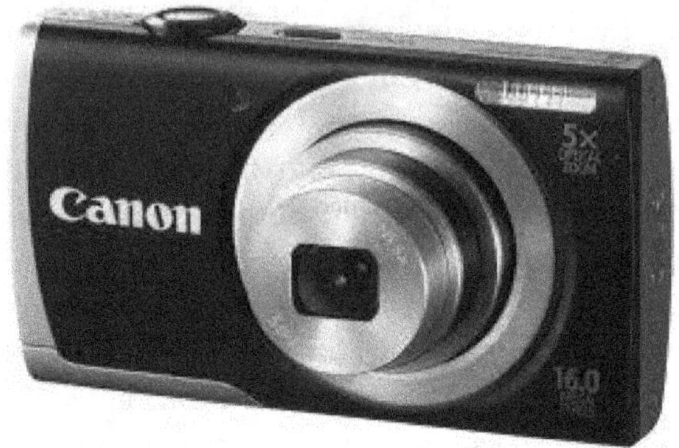

Figure 16.17   An advertising picture for an expensive camera

Figure 16.17 shows an advertisement image for a very expensive camera. The camera is shown in its true colour but the black and silver give an impression of high quality.

There are, of course, other considerations that may override the relationships given above. If the advertisement involves a heating system, then warm colours, such as red, orange and yellow, would be used and cool colours, such as blue would be avoided. It is ironic that, in an astronomical context, red stars are much cooler than blue stars!

Relationships between colour and the impressions they give are culture-dependent so advertising the same product in different countries may involve a complete change in wording and visual content, including colour. As an example, Red, yellow and green are considered as 'lucky colours' in Chinese culture; green is associated with money, an association completely different from that in the above list, which relates to western cultures.

Index

X

X-chromosome, 57

Y

Y-chromosome, 57
yellow ochre, 78, 82–83
Yezhov, Nikolai Ivanovich, 155

Young, Thomas, 28
Young's slits, 28
Young–Helmholtz theory, 50

Z

zinc white, 89
Zworykin, Vladimir, 184

CPSIA information can be obtained
at www.ICGtesting.com
Printed in the USA
LVHW050324120723
752151LV00003BA/168